My Life in E-flat

My Life in E-flat

Chan Parker

University of South Carolina Press

© 1993 Chan Parker et Librairie Plon

Published in Columbia, South Carolina, by the
University of South Carolina Press

Manufactured in the United States of America

03 02 01 00 99   5 4 3 2 1

Library of Congress Cataloging-in-Publication Data

Parker, Chan.
[Ma vie en mi bemol. English]
My life in E-flat / Chan Parker.
    p.   cm.

ISBN 1-57003-245-9 (pbk.)
    1. Parker, Chan.   2. Dancers—United States—Biography.   3. Parker, Charlie,
1920–1955.   I. Title.   II. Title: My life in E-flat
GV1785.P27713 A3   1999
792.8'092—ddc21
[B]   98-19682

CONTENTS

ILLUSTRATIONS

PROLOGUE

There is a house which recurs in my dreams. I am always in a car driving along familiar streets, up the long hill searching for that house on Park Hill Road where I lived as a child. My mother, widowed with two young children, sold real estate during the depression. No one was buying, so we moved into that lovely Victorian white elephant in Westchester, rent free. I don't know how she managed to heat its fifteen rooms, but it was a fairy-tale house to a young girl. Shingled, with turrets, gables, bay windows, gardens, two salons, fireplaces, a dumbwaiter, a central hall between innumerable bedrooms, a game room in the basement, with a full-size professional pool table, and best of all, for me, a finished attic which became my ballroom. Oh, the grand parties I planned; all the snobbiest girls and the most handsome boys would come. In the end, it was the pool room that attracted the boys and where I experienced my first closed-mouth kisses.

In my dreams I sometimes catch a glimpse of that house, but I've never been able to enter it. Surely, it no longer exists. Does Park Hill Road? Would I have the courage outside of dreams to mount that hill again? I think we leave a part of ourselves in every house we have loved. I measure my years by the houses in which I have lived. So foolish to leave one's precious life in wood and stone. But perhaps that is the rent we pay for our memories, both bitter and sweet.

To deny the past is to limit the future. To deny the past is to deny the seed that brought life, determined our genes and characteristics, the teat which nourished, the culture which formed our soul, our mind, and forged our identity. Of course, we must all find our own way, our own selves. But we cannot deny what formed us, or else we must begin again, newly born without a past and, perhaps, lacking a future. Only a genius can make up a life without past influences or without the joys, sorrows, and all the emotions that are part of every family and which color our lives in every way.

PROLOGUE

Closed doors and windows let in neither light nor surprises.

My paternal grandparents left Russia when my father was a boy, and the family settled in Gloversville, New Hampshire. My mother's grandparents crossed America in a covered wagon and bought land in Sidney, Iowa. I reversed the direction to return to the continent of my ancestors. It took me half a century to discover there is more to life than an alto saxophone. Now I live in a country not my own, in a house haunted by friendly ghosts whose acquaintance I made over forty years ago.

I live in France, in a small village off the beaten path about seventy kilometers south of Paris in the grain belt. The principal crops are wheat, sunflowers, sugar beets, and colza. In the summer, a bright rectangle of yellow breaks through the sealike green of waving wheat. The roadsides are bordered with red poppies.

In the soft, quiet dusk of a warm early summer's evening in 1975, the door to the courtyard is open. The children are off on quiet pursuits; our collie, Snoopy, is licking her nettle-distressed paws in the sun-sweetened grass now heavy with dew; and Flash, spooky as only a Persian cat can be, is dodging aggressive barn swallows and asserting herself with insouciant fireflies. My mother and I linger over last year's cherries in *eau de vie*. She starts talking about her own family, reminiscing:

My ancestors came from England, Wales, Scotland, and France in the 1600s. My maternal grandfather, Joseph Hiatt, was only five years old when he crossed the country to Iowa in a covered wagon with his father and brothers. They settled 160 acres adjacent to Sidney. In those days, you could buy land for practically nothing. Later, Joseph Hiatt would meet his future wife, Minerva. She had been kidnapped when she was just a girl and sold as an indentured servant, but she had somehow managed to escape from this form of slavery. Minerva and Joseph Hiatt settled on a portion of land called "Hiatt's Addition," in an old house which became a local landmark. They had three children: my mother, Mina, my aunt Nell, and my uncle Alvo.

Mina Hiatt married into the Lankton family from Springfield, Illinois. Her husband, Charles, was proud of the fact that his father, John D. Lankton, often used to sit on Abraham Lincoln's knee. Although many women died in childbirth in those days, Mina gave Charles ten children, five daughters, and then five sons. Lloyd was the oldest son. The eldest daughter, Alice, died before I was born. Cecile was born next, Beulah was third, and Ruby was fourth. Ruby died during the horrible flu epidemic in

1918. I was the fifth child. Then came the twins, Joe and John, who were followed by Harold. By the time Chick, the tenth child, was born, our family had moved from Sidney to Shenandoah, Iowa.

When I was six, we lived in a new house in Sidney. The town had five hundred people then. Like all the kids, I spent most of my summers on the farm with Grandfather and Grandmother Hiatt: They had a big rambling farm and house. I was my grandmother's favorite, so I stayed there more than the others. I remember that they used a horse and buggy. There were other horses and, of course, some pigs and cattle. In the evening I would help my uncle Alvo bring in the cows to be milked. We had to cross a stream to get to the wood. My uncle had made a big swing from a rope so that when we came to the stream, we could swing across to the other side. Oh, it was fun! We loved that.

My grandfather used to do all the plowing and I would bring a pail of fresh water to him in the fields. In the summer, I followed him behind the plow pulling up the cold earth. I ran barefoot behind him and if he plowed up a snake, I'd run like hell back to the house. Grandpa used to say that he had known Jesse James when he was working in St. Joseph, Missouri. At that time, my grandfather was an interior decorator and did fancy painting. The lead in the paint was what probably killed him.

That was such a beautiful farm. We could see it across the valley from our house in Sidney, and when it caught fire we watched it burn to the ground. There was no fire department in those days. The farm house was rebuilt, but my grandmother died soon after.

We moved to Council Bluffs, Iowa, across the river from Omaha where I met Cecile Wilson, Ida McAdams, and her sister, Cecilia, who became my best friend. The McAdamses moved to Chicago. In 1917 Cecile Wilson and I went there to visit them. The night the train pulled out of that old station, everyone came to see us off. None of them had been as far as Chicago. There was a theater in Omaha called the Brandeis where all of the big shows played. Harold Ross, one of the boys who had come to see us off, had taken up theatrics in school. He said, "We may see your name in lights one day on the Brandeis Theatre." I was eighteen. They didn't know I wasn't coming back.

In Chicago, Ida McAdams had the coatroom in a club on Clark Street. We lived upstairs in the hotel. She asked if I would help her in the club for a while. It was a great spot: the comedian Joe Frisco and the Original Dixieland Jazz Band, which had just come from New Orleans, were working there. That was before the band went to Reisenwebers in New York

City, where they became the hit of New York and made a fortune. I knew all of them.

Cecile Wilson had been in show business before. She was going to see a producer she knew named Boyle Wolfaulk. He was producing a show that was going to the West Coast to play in Vaudeville houses. It was a condensed musical with soubrettes, comedians. . . . (Your father had sixteen shows like that when I met him.) Boyle Wolfaulk asked me to come and rehearse. When I protested that I hadn't been in show business before, he said, "Come along anyway." He had a few girls trying out who were professional dancers. By the time the show opened, I was really the only girl who was an amateur. Bobby Roberts was the juvenile. He was quite well-known in those days. Joe Roberts and his wife played the leads. They were good friends of Buster Keaton's and he came often to see them. That show went to the West Coast and we were on the road for quite a few weeks. We returned to Chicago by train on the southern route bordering Mexico. I still remember what a long hot ride it was! When we returned, the show ended.

Somebody told me to go see a producer by the name of Eddie Beck. He gave me a job in a new show at the Marigold Gardens. That was a beautiful place. Rudolph Valentino and his partner were dancing there. He was very sweet; he was a nice guy, handsome and a very good dancer with a great personality. But today he wouldn't be considered handsome with his patent leather hair. He married his partner, who was the heiress of a cosmetic firm. Her name was Hudnut. Ruth Etting was in the chorus. Bobby Roberts, with whom I was friends from my last show, was also appearing there. Ruth Etting, who was kind of catty, thought we had a romance going. When I said he was just a friend, she said, "Well, if you don't want him, I'll take him." I stayed with that show about a year until it ended. The producer's wife, Cookie Beck, told me a friend of hers named B. D. Berg was producing a show at the Winter Garden.

His office was in the North American Building. I'll never forget. When I went to the office, Joe Burroughs, who was writing the music and lyrics for the show, informed me that B. D. Berg was at the rehearsal hall. He gave me a note to take and said I should tell Mr. Berg that Mr. Burroughs said I was very nice and sweet. B. D. Berg interviewed me and I told him what Mr. Burroughs had said. He told his choreographer Al McLaughlin that he wanted me in the show. Al asked how he planned to do that since all the girls had been hired and fitted for costumes. B. D. Berg answered, "Let one of them go and put her in." That's

*what he did. I had to sit there and watch rehearsal. He had his own cos-
tume company called Lombardi Limited which made the costumes for all
his shows. I had to have the other girl's costume refitted for me. Mr. Berg
and Paul Rahn, the juvenile, went with me to the fitting. I was told to be
at rehearsal the next day.*

*The show was called "Looping the Loop," a play about the Loop in
Chicago. It was a revue and it ran for nearly six months. I know because
B. D. Berg and I were married six months after we met. That was in
1920. One night, he had even fired me for being late, but he remembered
the home-cooked dinners I had made for him and I was rehired the next
day. He had condensed musicals on the Keith, Pantages, and Loews cir-
cuits. He had quite a few acts going at the same time. When "Looping the
Loop" closed, he produced another show that was going to the Coast. He
wanted me to join it, which I did. Oh, that was a great little show: Ned
Williams and Irene Williams, who weren't related, were in it. Cecile Renick
was in it too. They were all popular in vaudeville. The red-headed girl
who was the soubrette in that show, Skitch Renard, was crazy about your
father. She was burned up when I came along.*

*Soon after our marriage, Ben moved his offices to the Palace Theater
Building in New York. He produced a couple other revues for the Keith
circuit: "Quakertown to Broadway" and "Hoosier Girl." They each ran
an hour and a half and were followed by other acts.*

*After vaudeville went on the rocks, Ben opened an automobile busi-
ness on 52d Street and 7th Avenue. That's where I first met his brother
Mike, who was one of the greatest trick cyclists and had traveled all over
Europe. Their family was originally from Kovna, Russia. When they came
to America, they opened a glove factory in Gloversville, New Hampshire.
They must have had some money; anyway that's where they settled. When
I first met Ben, his father had died and a doctor had told his mother she
should live in the mountains for her health. So she went to Fallsburg,
New York, where she opened the first hotel there, which she kept going
for quite a while. She lived in a house just across the road from the hotel.
Ben gave up his automobile business and went to White Lake, New York,
near Woodstock. He rented a large casino right on the lake and put in a
revue. On August 28, 1922 he opened with Sophie Tucker, Mae West,
Lilian Lorraine, W. S. Hart, and me, Mildred Darling. (Some of the girls
in that show later went to work for Ziegfeld. They were beautiful.) He
hired a Dixieland jazz band which was great and could play anything. It
was a big show with comedians, an ingenue, a chorus of dancers, plus*

the band. They all had rooms at the casino, which was so big it could have covered a block. I've never seen such a big dance floor. There was a huge kitchen which served delicious food. Ben ran the White Lake Casino for a couple of years and then gave it up. It was just a summer thing, and he certainly couldn't have made much money trying to take care of that big staff.

We returned to New York. Ziegfeld had a call for a new show, so I went. But I didn't tell Ben, as he didn't want me to work anymore. I got the job and went to work for Ziegfeld in the "Midnight Frolics" at the New Amsterdam Roof in 1922. On opening night, I finally told Ben and he came with baskets and baskets of flowers. They were stacked all over the lobby of the Roof. Appearing in that follies were Leon Errol, Will Rogers, Gloria Foy, and Carl Randall, who years later stole my scrapbook. Downstairs at the Amsterdam Theatre, Marilyn Miller was appearing in "Sunny." While I was working there, I also made several films at the old Paramount Studios in Astoria, Long Island, with Mae Murry, Alice Brady, and Thomas Mehen. When Alice Brady had to dance a shimmy in a film, I taught her how.

Your father had a revue in Atlantic City with Fatty Arbuckle. He was as big a star in the movies as Chaplin, Keaton, all of them, in those days. Fatty became involved in a scandal with a girl who died. I never did find out the true story. He was supposed to have raped her. He was brought to trial. The rumor went around to the effect that he had put something up into her insides . . . or something like that. . . . But he was such a nice guy that everyone said it couldn't be true. He got out of it, but he was ruined.

When I left Ziegfeld I went to work in a Shubert show about golf called "Top Hole." Ray Raymond was the star. His wife, Dorothy McKay, was later involved in his death with her lover, who was Paul Kelly, another big movie star, who went to the penitentiary for manslaughter. William Randolph Hearst owned a building called the Beaux Arts on 6th Avenue, across from Bryant Park. Marion Davies, whom he kept for years, had an apartment there. Hearst was a big man . . . a huge man. The Bustonaby family had a restaurant on the ground floor with a large fountain. There was a grill on the 8th floor called the Gold Room. The washroom attendant made so much money there, he bought out the Bustonabys and took over the restaurant. Ben produced the shows, using Paul Rahn, whom I had first met in Chicago, and with the chorus doing the Charleston, which was just catching on. I used to be there every night, because Ben never left me home. Texas Guinan announced the shows and

*she'd say, "Give this little girl a big hand," rave about her, look over at me
and ask, "Isn't that right, Mrs. Berg?" Joe Farr had the band. He was a
violinist. All the movie stars came to the 8th floor grill: Rex Ingram, Mabel
Normand—men drank champagne from her slippers, Bob Neally—he was
the "NE" of the "NEDICKS," Barbara LaMarr—a glamorous star, and
Norma Bayes—she introduced "Shine on Harvest Moon" and gave your
father a big red Spanish shawl which we had on our piano for years.*

    *Ben left the Beaux Arts and took over a whole building on 58th Street
across from the Plaza Hotel. He opened a room called Club Grandeur. It
was 1924 and I was pregnant with you. We lived upstairs until you were
born. The day I brought you home from the hospital one of your father's
customers, Hunt Humphries, who made all the gas fireplaces, came to see
you. He called his wife and told her to buy some baby clothes. A few
hours later, their maid arrived in a white uniform, carrying a huge box
from Best & Company containing French baby dresses and bonnets.*

    *Your father had some great clientele at the Club Grandeur! Henry
Carrington and David and Louis Marx, the toy manufacturers, came.
Louis Marx was Daniel Ellsburg's father-in-law. Bobby Gillette, the
razor heir, was a good customer, and Billy Leeds, the tin plate heir,
who was married to Princess Zenia of Greece, would come home with
Ben after the club closed. They would bring the band because Billy
loved to play drums. He was at our house on his twenty-fifth birthday
and Mamie, our maid, fixed scrambled eggs and champagne for breakfast. He and the princess were separated and they had a little girl just
your age. He put his head down on the edge of the table to talk to you
and hide his tears. He had a big estate in Oyster Bay and Ben gave
him our police dog Lucky, because Billy had kennels and trained dogs
there. Sometimes your father would go to his estate after the club
closed for the night. One morning when the Dolly Sisters were there,
wanting to play a joke on him, they locked him in the wine cellar. They
quickly let him out when they heard him popping the wine corks. At
Atlantic City, Billy rescued a drowning girl and later married her. Years
after that he found out he had cancer and shot himself. People came
from all over, even Europe, to the Club Grandeur. Your father ran it
beautifully and had some of the finest people in the world as customers. He had a French chef and a head waiter named Rudolph. His
waiters stayed with him for years. Some time later Ben opened the
Palladium, a new club in a building he took at 15 West 56th Street, and he
bought us a big Spanish-style house in Yonkers.*

This was during Prohibition, but Ben had only private clubs with a charter membership, so he never had any trouble although the federal agents were always trying to get something on him. He always brought something home from the club. One night they stopped him and made him open his briefcase. It was full of oranges. Ray Calhoun, whom I went out with after Ben's death while Ray was still the sole distributor for Cutty Sark, sold his company, the Gatsby Buckingham Corporation, for a fortune just before he died. He had a beautiful yacht and a beautiful home in Fieldston. But back in those days, he had started out as a rum-runner.

Your father sure loved you. He bought all of your clothes. One time he went to Best & Company and paid $60.00 for one little outfit, a Scotch plaid skirt, a white silk ruffled blouse, and a little black velvet vest. He bought shoes with buckles on them for you in every color: red, blue, black patent leather. He had dresses made to order for you, six at a time. They were very expensive as they were pure silk with hand smocking. Your little bedroom was at the back of the house and was furnished with a light blue bedroom set he bought for you: a little bed with a big red apple on the headboard, a chest of drawers, a little clothes tree, and a dresser with pull knobs that were A B C blocks decorated with apples in the center. Ben had the band come home often, especially if we had company. They would play "Why Do I Love You" in the yard under your window. (Ben had picked that song for you, because it was his favorite.)

By that time, we had a penthouse club on Madison Avenue which your father wanted to reopen on Park Avenue. After Ben died, his brother Mike tried to run it for a while, but he didn't know beans from peas about running a club. He also lacked your father's terrific personality and sense of humor. Ben had everyone having a gay time. Customers used to send him telegrams saying, "We're coming to town. Don't forget to shave." He hated shaving.

Years later when I was working at the 21 Club, Dave Marx used to say, "We never had so much fun, before or after, as we had at your husband's place." But Ben really overdid himself. The day before his heart attack we were in New York at the club. He wanted to get home in time to listen to "Amos and Andy," because every Sunday he always listened to them and to the opera or the symphony. We stopped at a place he knew to pick up a case of beer to take home, and ran into some of his friends. He began drinking and lost track of the time. From there, he wanted to go to Charlie Lucas's. They kept sending champagne to our table as if we were royalty. We ended up at Nick Bate's "Merry-Go-Round" on 55th between Madison and Park. When we started home, I wanted to drive. He got mad and flew off to his brother Dave's place on 59th Street where he spent the night. He came home the next day terribly ill. He remained in bed until he went to the hospital where he stayed about three days. It was Sunday, his family had come to visit him, and I had brought them home for lunch. As soon as the phone rang, I knew. By the time I got back to the hospital, he was gone.

That was in 1932. The stock market had crashed and Ben died broke. I was left with an insurance policy and two small children. Your brother Jimmy was two years old. I went to see a concessionaire who had checkrooms in all the big clubs. He paid fifty thousand dollars a year for the concession at the Copacabana, things were that good in those days. He put me to work in the Cotton Club on 48th Street. I enjoyed it there. I worked with Cab Calloway; Duke Ellington; Bill Robinson; Ethel Waters; Peg Leg Bates; Tip, Tap, and Toe; Rosetta Tharpe; and the Nicholas Brothers. They had extravagant shows with beautiful costumes. Herman Stark was the big boss with Mike Best and Connie Immerman from Connie's Inn in Harlem. He probably had some racketeer backers. Herman's brother Louis had complete charge of the kitchen. Since he lived near us in Yonkers and didn't drive, he paid for the gas and I used to drive him home after work. Herman and Louis must have had a piece of Dickie Wells's place in Harlem, as Louis had to stop there on the way home every night. The West Side Highway hadn't been built yet, so we'd drive through Central Park, out at 110th Street, and through Harlem to Wells. Dickie's was one of the most popular after hours spots and we'd stop and have a few drinks. I was working at the Cotton Club when Bill Robinson had his sixtieth birthday. It took place after closing hours and everybody came. That was some party!

I'll never forget Cab Calloway's birthday party. They had given him a big cake which he had left at the club. Louis Stark said, "Well now, we'll have to stop at the Calloway's and bring Cab's cake to him." Cab's cousin and his wife were up from Baltimore and staying at his house in Fieldston. It was around Christmas; there was snow on the ground and the Christmas decorations were gorgeous. Cab's manager had bought that house in his name for Cab, because at the time that residential section was restricted. Cab insisted we come in. The wives were already in bed. Cab had a bar downstairs and he insisted we have a birthday drink. It was daylight when we left. I dropped Louis at his house and went home. Then, at some ungodly hour around nine or ten A.M., Cab and his cousin came knocking at the door. They had been celebrating all morning and said they had decided to come and have a drink with me. I always had something to drink in the house in those days. You were there and carrying on with your songs. They finally left and I assumed they had gone home. They went to Harlem instead and stayed up celebrating all day. When I went to work that night, Cab hadn't shown up yet. His wife called the club saying he'd been home when she went to bed and she was afraid he'd been kidnapped. I didn't tell them he had been to my house that morning. He didn't show up for work until late . . . very late.

I didn't know all the guys in the band as they weren't allowed out front during the breaks. I don't know where they hung out. But I knew Walter "Foots" Thomas, who played tenor sax. When my car broke down a few times, he drove me all the way to Yonkers; he was a nice guy. Sonny Greer, who was the drummer with Duke's band, used to ride his bicycle home at night up the Harlem Speedway. I knew Mae Johnson, one of the stars in the shows, who was called "The Sepia Mae West." Harold Nicholas was just fifteen when he appeared in that show, and his mother sat in the dressing room each night to make sure that one of the chorus girls didn't snatch him for his money. The Brown twins were beautiful girls in the chorus. They had made several movies and were a top act. Harold Arlen wrote many of the shows and some beautiful tunes came out of those productions. Ethel Waters introduced "Stormy Weather" in one of them.

While working at the Cotton Club, I met the general manager of the Lipton Tea Company, who offered me a job. I didn't want to work nights anymore, so I decided to take him up on his offer. However, friends of ours who were in the real estate business, the Piantidosis, asked me to work for them instead. George Piantidosi had been with Shapiro-Bernstein, the music publishers, and his brother Al was a songwriter. George's wife Josie had been the cashier at Lindy's. Everybody loved Josie. When Al Jolson used to pass Lindy's in the winter, he would make a hole in the frost of the window and stick his tongue out at her. George and Josie became our neighbors in Yonkers. I first met the Piantidosis in that Spanish house on Glenbrook Avenue where your brother Jimmy was born. Ben had built a beautiful bar in that house. The walls were covered in burlap and the burlap door had a big U.S. padlock painted on it. They heard that Ben was living near them and they stopped by one Sunday. It was during prohibition and Ben invited them in for a drink. We became good friends. I got a real estate license and went to work for them in their Riverdale office.

Cab Calloway had fallen in love with a beautiful Spanish girl. She lived with her sister who was fat, ugly, and simple. Cab drove by the office one day in his big car with his big dog and called me outside. He wanted me to find a house for her, so I showed her a few houses. (She picked a new house on Broadway just below the Yonkers city line. It had a ten-thousand-dollar price tag on it. Can you imagine how cheap real estate was in those days? Cab liked that house too. It was near his house in Fieldston.) She was a nice girl and we became good friends. She finally married one of the neighbors, a Syrian guy who lived in the house behind hers. . . . Well, Cab did give her a hard time.

Gene Krupa and his manager Frank Verniere, who were friends of the Piantidosi's, asked us to find land and builders for two new houses to be constructed next to each other. George found some land near our house. At the time, we were living as caretakers in that fifteen-room house with the pool table on Park Hill Road, which a millionaire had bought very cheaply during the depression for speculation. Frank's son Philippe had to start school before the end of construction, so his wife, Mary, and their son came to stay with us until their house was finished.

Gene's wife, Ethel, used to come to visit Mary while their husbands were on the road. Gene's band had a good thing going in those days: The band was very popular and they made plenty of money. When Gene was arrested, I heard the story that he had taken that fall for Frank. Surprisingly, Mary and Ethel remained friends through it all. In fact, Ethel didn't have very many friends. After she died, Gene sold the house to his sister and her husband.

Then George Piantidosi died and, although Josie tried to run the office, she couldn't really handle it . . . maybe because she was a closet drinker. That was why I decided to leave the real estate business. By that time, you were already living in New York, so I moved there too.

My Life in E-flat

PART I
VIVACE

1. ALLEGRO

That is how this entity "Me" came to be: pioneers and immigrants whose offspring would never have met if they had not chosen to be part of the subculture. My father, who had been a producer of vaudeville shows, ran one of the smartest penthouse speakeasies. My mother had been in one of my father's shows and in the Ziegfeld's Midnight Frolic. She was twenty years younger than he, and he used to pamper her!

In 1925, smack dab in the middle of the Jazz Age, they had me, their jazz baby, Beverly Dolores Berg (I changed that name as soon as I could), and I've been part of the jazz scene ever since. When I was four, my tears flowed every time I listened to "Melancholy Baby." Not knowing the meaning of 'melancholy,' I related it to my beloved collie who had just died.

When I was five, we moved to a Spanish-style house on Glenbrook Avenue in Yonkers where my brother Jimmy was born. A young boy was watching the movers carry our furniture into the house. When my tricycle was unloaded he challenged me, "Wanna race?" This was my first social memory. Henry Mook, who was four years old, was handsome with blue eyes, freckles, and a fine nose. He was my first friend. I competed fiercely with him and also with all the boys in the neighborhood for his friendship. He broke my heart daily.

My good friend Patsy Driscoll, whose father, Charles, had taken over O. O. McIntyre's syndicated column, lived next door. When she became ill with a severe mastoid infection, I brought her a bag of candy and took a piece of chalk to scrawl a message on the sidewalk informing the passersby that Patsy was ill and asking them to please be quiet. Her father wrote a column about it, entitled "Friendship." To my embarrassment, he mentioned the seven sticky lemon drops in a dirty paper sack that I had taken to their door. That was my first press notice. Patsy loved dolls and silly girls' games, although they held little interest for me. With Henry Mook I could fall out of trees. He even showed me his penis. That didn't make as much of an impression on me as discovering Bach with his mother, who lived two houses down the street from us. An upright lady, Mrs.

Mildred Mook gave piano lessons. She had been the first neighbor to come calling. A widow, she was the daughter of Mr. Kaltenbach, the president of Fleishman Yeast. Her well-ordered, serene house always smelled of flowers, furniture polish, and pfeffernusse spice cookies. The doors between the rooms were always kept closed, and this seemed to me the antithesis of our disorganized household. I don't recall any servants, but perhaps she had a cleaning lady. How vulgar we must have seemed to her.

Daddy's valet and chauffeur was Frederick von Braun, who had been a German count before the war. My nursemaid was named Mamie. She was referred to as my "mammy" although she had pale freckled skin and fine, straight gold hair. She stayed with us as part of our family until my father died and we could no longer afford servants. By then, Mamie's hair was white. After she left us, she lived in Harlem and my mother often took me to visit. Her apartment was as clean and proper as she was. When she was with us, she always wore a white uniform, and I have a photo of her holding me when I was a newborn baby. Lovely, lusty, buxom Flax was our cook. Mother always said she sang like a bird. One night during a dinner party, her jealous boyfriend showed up at the back door brandishing a pistol. She must have been very beautiful to arouse such passion. Daddy loved to entertain, and we always had friends coming, going, or staying. Mother had a robin's-egg-blue Pontiac convertible with a rumble seat. How *nouveau riche* we must have seemed to Mrs. Mook.

So it was to Mrs. Mook's lovely, quiet home I went to study piano when I was six. She was a strict teacher and, though I rebelled at times to the discipline, she was patient and loving. I soon became her best pupil along with Henry, and vied with him in fierce competition for her approval. I loved the lessons, which had opened a new world to me. At my father's club, where I had been introduced to such disparate culinary delights as honeydew melon, Roquefort cheese, and the chef's specialty, orange sponge cake, I had been allowed to finger the player piano and pretend it was me playing "The Wedding of the Painted Doll." Now I could press any keys I wanted to, and make my own music.

With Mrs. Mook, I began my musical life in the key of C. Mrs. Mook was definitely in concert. C is an honest key, the key of the piano and the bass, the center. It is rooted, the do of the well-tempered scale, the foundation of harmony and dissonance. There is a solidarity to C, yet it is adaptable. Bill Evans said, "I think of all harmony as an expansion from and return to the tonic. Why does a flat ninth work with a dominant chord? It has to do with counterpoint more than harmony. It is the ninth of the dominant moving through the flat ninth to become the fifth of the tonic."

Bill preferred the key of A for its brightness. Duke, Strayhorn, and Mingus liked the darkness of A-flat and often added another black note to write in D-flat, although both Duke and Bill recorded "Reflections in D." A-flat and D-flat, and their twins G-sharp and C-sharp, are not easy keys to play. Coltrane came back to B-flat and C. When Miles began to play on modal scales, he eliminated key signatures. This is logical because if one improvises on a chord change, one is in the key of the chord, not the key signature. I believe this works better for improvisation than orchestration. So we still need the dark keys and the bright keys and a home base. Bird brought me E-flat, the key of the alto saxophone, though he liked to play blues in C. Alto players are transposers, forever thinking in another key. What could Adolph Sax have been thinking of? E-flat is the minor third of C. That interval is the basis of all minor chords, the foundation of sadness, the blues, Semitic music. Am I not half Russian-Jewish? I was always partial to minor chords, although now I love major 7th chords and my black birds sing in F.

My first heros were Bix Beiderbecke and George Gershwin. When George died of a brain tumor in 1937, my mother had to take me to a doctor to convince me that the migraine headaches which turned me green with pain were not caused by the same growth that had carried George off in his prime. I also shed bitter tears the day Bunny Berrigan died. After seeing "Young Man with a Horn" (1950), I took trumpet lessons. I was the only girl in the sixth grade with a red rim around her lips.

After my mother went to work at the Cotton Club, my musical education was furthered by privileged evenings spent listening to the bands of Duke Ellington and Cab Calloway. Sister Rosetta Tharpe could rock that big room. Her energy seemed to make the tables move. Ethel Waters was a spellbinder, but Sister Tharpe with her rough, hollering joy was more exciting to me. Mrs. Mook introduced me to keys and chords. Bill Evans was my university. It has taken a lifetime for me to understand the complexity of music, and I'm afraid I have little patience with three-chord music (i.e. rock).

Daddy was twenty years older than Mother. He adored her and kept her in luxury. I was spoiled terribly and became the second jewel in his crown. My mother was 34 when he died. His fortune had been lost in the great Wall Street Crash of 1929. We were left with a small insurance policy and little else. Money management was not my mother's forte. If Daddy had been the last of the big spenders, Mother was an apt pupil. But she did let two of the servants go after Daddy's death, and the freeloaders soon followed. As Lady Day said, "When it's gone and the spending ends, they don't come 'round no more.

The insurance money was dissipated in four years, to the disapproval of Daddy's brother, my uncle Mike. He felt it was a sin to live on one's capital. My uncle considered my mother a spendthrift shiksa, and our new state of poverty just desserts. I was an ethnic mongrel from show biz folks. Now, I was not only different, I was poor. My middle name was Dolores, which means sorrow, and I was of Russian descent. Hadn't George and Ira written, "More skies of gray than any Russian play could guarantee?" Uncle Mike did take me on a Caribbean cruise, buy me clothes, and pay my tuition at private boarding school. I suspect he hoped to install a bit of Jewishness in me. I only remember the Panama Canal.

I tried the Protestant Church for awhile and got through the local grammar school. However, I became very Jewish during my high school years, which coincided with Hitler's persecution of the Jews. I wrote letters to the local paper and became an oddball. Although my Jewish father died when I was seven, my Protestant mother never forced any religion on me. Westchester County was WASP and anti-Semitic, so I stayed home from school on Jewish holidays to declare myself a minority. School became unbearable, and Uncle Mike came to the rescue. Although he disapproved, he paid my tuition at Oakwood, a Quaker boarding school in Poughkeepsie. The Quaker religion seemed sensible to me, as their church is a place of contemplation where nobody preaches. After all, they are called Friends. But even there I encountered prejudice. The Friends on campus became very upset by the friendship of an Italian girl and an African boy.

The only black people I had known were my mother's friends from the Cotton Club. They were bright, talented people with whom I felt at ease. I was taken aback one day outside the public library when I was terrorized by two brawny, tough black girls. I knew nothing about racism, although I had tasted anti-Semitism. I had a schoolgirl crush on Cab Calloway. One morning after the Cotton Club closed, Cab came by our house. He offered to give me a singing lesson. Mother's friend came in the room just at the moment when Cab had my tongue pristinely depressed by his finger in a spotless white handkerchief to show where it should be in order to get those full round tones for "Minnie the Moocher" or "Saint James Infirmary." He had promised to take me to a night club on my sixteenth birthday. This was a promise to a little girl, for if he had a romantic interest in our house, it was for my mother. I breathlessly spilled out the news of my good fortune and was laid low. "You'd go out with a nigger?" That was my introduction to a new form of hatred. I remember the pain it caused me and how I sobbed with the hurt of it. I couldn't know then how many fears it would cause me in my lifetime. Years later on 52d Street, I defied the redneck servicemen by hanging out with black musicians. I had one child out of wedlock, and two more with a black man. I never felt I was a masochist. But I did have a sense of what was right for me, and if it didn't fit into the mores of society, then society be damned.

Trixie Kiefer was my only friend, and her only friend was me. She was a quiet, unattractive girl from a conservative German family. We had nothing in common to warrant such a long, loyal friendship except that neither one of us was really accepted at school. I never felt threatened by her; she was safe. Perhaps her dull family life was brightened by the colorful tales I told of my nightlife. I wangled with any icky sons of friends just to get to the Chez Parée or International Casino. Later, it was to go to the Astor Roof to hear Tommy Dorsey's band, to get autographs from Buddy Rich and my idol, Frank Sinatra. Bunny Berrigan asked me why I hadn't asked for his, but he was very drunk and I, too young to handle that.

I got through tenth grade at Oakwood, that Quaker stepping stone to nearby Vassar. I didn't find it friendly! After that I went to Scarborough, a country day school, which was a thirty-minute train ride up the Hudson River from Yonkers. During the time that I spent at Scarborough, I was rushed by a very WASP sorority. We were required to write lyrics to an existing melody. I chose "Zing! Went the Strings of My Heart." When I finished my small, jazzy effort, I was faced with blank stares. Better I had put words to "America, the Beautiful" or "Betty Co-Ed." Thank my lucky stars, I realized that sorority life was not for me. I might have ended up in a cashmere sweater set and a string of false pearls. Once again, I was a misfit. No one cared about academic progress or even whether you showed up for classes, as long as your tuition was paid. And so the following year was spent in that haven for Westchester scions.

I lost my heart to a long-haired nonconformist with a marvelous jalopy that conveniently had no inside door handle on the passenger side. Then one of the more sophisticated girls I met at Scarborough told me about a fascinating musician she had met at the Picadilli Hotel Drugstore. His name was Johnny Bothwell and he played alto saxophone. After meeting

Johnny, there was no doubt in my mind that school was not where I wanted to be. I was accepted in a summer stock company in Pawling, New York, that summer, and joined Actors Equity. In the fall, I went to the city to live with my aunt Cecile, and enrolled at the Professional Children's School in N.Y.C. This was a school for professional theatrical kids who could mail in their work if their show went on the road. Milton Berle was our most famous alumnus. I decided not to spend all day in school when I could complete my work in an hour, and a half, and drop it in the mailbox. I made up an excuse for the school and set out on the rounds of producers' offices. One of my odd jobs while making the rounds was playing piano in the sheet music section of a large department store. I was there to play the songs that the customers were interested in buying. I've forgotten the hit of that season, but it was dumb. After playing it ten times a day, I decided this was not for me.

Walgreen's Drugstore was on the corner of 44th Street and Broadway. All the musicians from the bands playing the Paramount Theater came there between shows. How different were the bands of Tommy Dorsey, Harry James, and Charlie Spivak from those of Duke and Cab. No Walgreen Drugstores for the latter. I was later to find them at the nearest bar, where the ambiance was more honest and joyous. But I was still a fledgling, and spent hours sipping cokes there at the Picadilly. Popsie, who was later to become Benny Goodman's bandboy, road manager, and photographer of musicians, worked behind the counter at Walgreen's. No matter how much I ate, he always gave me a check for a nickel coke.

At a cattle call I was chosen by John Murray Anderson to be one of his chorus cuties in a new Broadway show called "Springtime in Brazil," starring Milton Berle. I suspect the choreographer had a problem remembering names as he gave everyone nicknames. I was dubbed "The Weird One." This baptism made me realize that I had nothing in common with the gypsies and chorus boys, and that my future did not lie on the Great White Way. The show opened and closed. Although I made the rounds of producers' offices and tried to be the new pretty ingenue, it didn't touch my heart. I left the offices of J. J. and Lee Shubert and George Abbot behind me. I had met Frank Socolow, Dave Kurtzer, Lenny Green, and Dave Allyn, who were all with Ted Weems's band at Roseland. But that's another story. With music, I believed I had found the road home at last.

In Zelda Fitzgerald's autobiographical novel, *Save Me the Waltz*, the heroine is asked why she doesn't study tap dancing with Ned Wayburn. I did, when I was five: But Eleanor Powell tap shoes, my parents' background in show business, and two seasons in summer stock were not sufficient to give me an edge. All my life I had felt myself to be a misplaced person, a misfit, an alien. I still felt I was a stranger in a foreign land. However, as a chorus girl, I learned a traveling step which was to carry me through life.

In March, I fell behind in my correspondence with the school. In June, I received a notice to appear for final exams. I never did. Some dancers I had met knew of an opening in a line going to New Orleans. The pretentious club wasn't as respectable as the Roosevelt Hotel, where Bob Allen was playing, but it was one step out of the French Quarter, where jazz, my passion, was born. Now that was back to the roots. I was soon hanging out with some of the hipper musicians from Bob Allen's Midwest territory band.

During my nightclub debut, my tag "Weird One" was exchanged for "Dimples." This was equally short-lived. I learned that we had been hired to dance a bit and then to mix, a euphorism for cheating the customers. We drank downs, orange blossoms (orange juice with a breath of gin), or if the customer was well-heeled, we were to order champagne cocktails (ginger ale with the bartender's same breath). This was my first experience of professional humiliation. I found many excuses to remain in the dressing room between shows and I was not popular with the club owner. But this was the club where I first heard that wonderful tune "Sunday," loved by Dixieland players. It was sung in the show by a young Lee Wiley–type singer who was dubbed "The Lady Baritone." Her husband was a handsome young man with a horn, a trumpet player who spat a lot. I worried about tuberculosis. My education was further expanded by the ladies of the chorus who provided my first information about venereal disease.

The wonderful dinners at Antoine's and the Court of Two Sisters and the delicious coffee and doughnuts at Morning Call as the sun rose and the market opened (my first open-air market, a miniature of *Les Halles* in Paris!) were soon overshadowed by the cockroaches which abound in New Orleans and the breath-of-bartender cocktails. My contract was for four weeks, but after three weeks I wanted to go back home to New York. I had saved $80, my first earned money, and I didn't feel like blowing it all on a train ticket. I persuaded two other debutantes to hitchhike from New Orleans to New York City. We were three sharp young chicks hitchhiking through the Deep South in 1942.

A car full of crackers picked us up. One of the rednecks, looking at my friend's lipstick, poked his buddy in the ribs and slyly cackled, "Y'all been eating blackberries?" She retaliated as we pulled into a gas station by questioning, "You have to pull up to the pumps? In New York, they bring the pumps to your car!" Nobody believed we were from New York. They thought we were country girls running away to the big city. We caught a ride to the outskirts of Athens, Georgia. It was early evening when a big limousine pulled up. An old man was riding up front with his chauffeur. This was strange to see in Georgia and we should have known that this would be no ordinary ride. We piled in the back seat, eager to get out of this desolate country. The old man immediately turned around and started grabbing legs.

We yelled as one, "Stop this car!" We got out on the deserted highway just the other side of Athens. After a long wait for a car to pass, we headed back to town, where we stood a better chance of catching a ride. A deserted highway in Georgia was no place for three young girls. We planned to have dinner and calm our frazzled nerves. We ate in a greasy spoon where some truckers offered us a lift. Two of us got into one cab and our friend in another. Ten minutes down the road the truckers pulled up at a motel. The end of the line. Horrified, we got out and went to collect our friend who had slept through the whole scene. She awoke, mumbling thanks for the lift. We were feisty, but danger was still a new experience for me. The truckers finally split, leaving us back on a highway in the deep Georgia night. Since then, I've learned all about men who are charming until you say "No!"

Riding down the Blue Ridge Mountains at sixty miles an hour in an army crash truck with a driver drunk with power was such a hair-raising experience that at Alexandria, Virginia, on a four-lane highway backed up with rush-hour traffic, we risked our lives when we spotted a car with New Jersey plates. The thought of leaving the South behind gave us the courage to endure honking horns and dodge cursing drivers to burst in on a startled young man and beg a ride HOME. He was going to Newark. We took the subway to Manhattan.

Any serviceman who passed through New York during World War II had two alternatives: he could find coffee and doughnuts and sweet young things at the neighborhood U.S.O., or he could stop by the Stage Door Canteen on West 44th Street, where Shirley Booth might jitterbug with him to the music of a name band, or he might have a table with Ray Bolger as his waiter. He could see a movie star, in town to promote his latest film, give a miniature show. All the best-known performers in town dropped in nightly, and the most glamorous women in the world donned a red, white, and blue apron and did their bit for the morale of the troops. Hollywood immortalized it in a movie of the same name where the soldier-hero left his heart with a girl named Eileen. I wasn't Eileen, but my Actors' Guild union card proved I was connected with the theater and this made me eligible to be a hostess. I was a political ignoramus and had hardly formulated any social consciousness, but I had no desire to be slobbered on by some first-time-away-from-home anybody in an anonymous suit. I was seventeen, pretty, and more interested in the glamorous civilians with whom I was rubbing elbows. Killer Joe Piro, who was in the Coast Guard, came in every night to Lindy to the bands of Harry James and Tommy Dorsey. He and I danced well together, and this was the only time in my life when I enjoyed dancing without a paycheck. When Joe danced, everyone would form a circle around the dance floor and Joe and I would dance until he exhausted me. Then he would pull another partner from the circle. He weighed about 110 pounds, but his energy always wore out at least three willing partners.

Most of the servicemen were polite and too awed by this world of glamour to make passes. One sailor did ask me to marry him and gave me a minuscule diamond engagement ring which I returned after I met my first alto player. A tall, shy, red-headed West Pointer invited me to the Point for a weekend. Shades of Ruby Keeler and Dick Powell. I read up on Flirtation Walk, packed my least flamboyant clothes, and went off to play Bryn Mawr. At the Saturday night prom, I met George Patton, Jr., whose father was conquering Europe. Junior didn't do too badly thirty years later at a gala in Vietnam where he showed the notches in his belt. That night he was unarmed, and though a bit of a stiff, he was handsome. I think he wore a saber. That's the kind of weekend it was. I was assigned a bunk in a dorm full of chic girls from Smith and Vassar. They looked at me as if I had just entered through the back door. Then they studiously ignored me.

I had always hated dolls, football games, sororities, and pajama parties where wealthy girls spoke only of clothes and fraternity pins. Here I was in the midst of all the vacuousness I had always detested. My date took me for a stroll on the fabled Flirtation Walk. He didn't try to kiss me. The view of the Hudson River was magnificent. When I took the train home to New York, the Hudson looked just as pretty, and I never looked back on that other world.

2. BEBOP

When I was eighteen, the hottest jazz I knew was the Benny Goodman sextet and Duke and Cab from my Cotton Club days. When I was looking for an apartment, or at least a room to rent, fate, or perhaps instinct, led me to 7 West 52d Street. Fifty-second Street, or Swing Street, was where all the jazz was happening. There were perhaps a dozen clubs on that block between 5th and 6th Avenues where jazz was played nightly from nine o'clock until four in the morning. Jimmy Ryan's had a Dixieland policy and Leon & Eddie's had a show which often featured the stripper Lili St. Cyr. Many of the clubs became the birthplace of bebop.

I rented a large ground-floor room, opening onto a courtyard in a brownstone near 5th Avenue, two doors down from the 21 Club. I found a roommate, a dancer I had met in a chorus line, and I got a job as a camera girl taking souvenir photos in all the clubs that lined the block. That tided me over between dancing gigs, and my time was more or less my own. The darkroom boy was Morris Levy, who was later front man of Birdland, where his brother Stan was killed at the bar. Soon we had acquired two more young, pretty roommates and our room was always so crowded with admirers that we considered charging an entrance fee. Life was so exciting that none of us worked more than we had to and we were always broke. Bands working in town stored their instruments with us, and friends of friends dropped by to get high.

From that room, I moved by myself to a small, windowless garret on the fifth floor. The only light came through the skylight. It was so depressing, I dubbed it the "Suicide Room." All the junkies on 52d Street got hip to the hall toilets to fix in, and we had some of the biggest names in jazz using the facilities nightly. But outside, the creative energy was palpitating. Monte Kay and Mal Braverman, who were doing publicity for the clubs, ran Sunday afternoon jam sessions, first at the Onyx and later on Columbus Circle. Tommy Young and Billy Xstine, as he was billed then, were at the Yacht Club; Billie Holiday and Joe Guy were at Tondalayo's; and Coleman Hawkins, Don Byas, and Benny Harris were at the Three

Deuces. After they closed, Don joined Max Roach, Oscar Pettiford, and George Wallington at the Onyx.

After leaving the "Suicide Room," I lived in a two-bedroom apartment with my mother, who had moved to New York. Our house in Yonkers had always been full of musicians and friends of my parents' and now, in our apartment at 7 West, Mother was surrounded with my friends, the beboppers. I'm not sure they were any more outrageous than the musicians in Duke's or Cab's bands, but perhaps it had been easier for my mother to deal with a little girl than a grown daughter. She had always been color-blind and liberal, but she was a puritan regarding sex. We managed. She worked in the checkroom at the 21 Club, so she never came home until after midnight. She always respected my love of music and the talent she thought I had. She was disappointed I hadn't done more with it, whatever it was: I could have become a star.

I waited for the doorbell to ring at 7 West, for friends who were as passionate as I for this new music to tell me about a jam session, a band rehearsing, or a hot new musician in town. We were all obsessed by this new, electrifying music. It was all that mattered to us. My lovers were plentiful and easy to come by. However, they took second place to the music. I never had a lover who was a musician I couldn't respect. The music was my consuming need. It occupied me totally and was the most important thing in my life. My buddies and I ran from club to session to rehearsal. We shared our records and learned all the solos of our bebop heros. We were witnessing, as well as participating in, a musical revolution. My doorbell never stopped ringing. Friends and musicians dropped by and the music continued. Music filled our days and nights. It was a good time to be young, to participate in that important period of musical and political history.

There had never been such a concentration of clubs presenting jazz since Storyville. There were always five or six clubs with bands alternating nightly during the war years. Along with the booming business, World War II brought a bit of the Old South to 52d Street: apple-cheeked soldiers straight from the hills, and sailors, many shod for the first time and too young to shave. They brought prejudice, unchanged since the Civil War, and were outraged by the sight of so many pretty girls in the company of black men. The Axis and the Allies had their war. We had ours. I was on the side of the beboppers, who were the underdogs. They were fighting not only racism, but also hostility to their music, which aroused strong passions. The radio stations in California had banned bebop from the airwaves, lest it pollute the American way of life. Well-established musicians like Louis Armstrong and Cab Calloway ridiculed it in the press. I loved the fight. I was rooting for little Benny Harris the night he knocked a drunken sailor into the gutter. Benny must have been a foot shorter than the sailor, and I exploded in glee when a taxi backed over the big oaf. But all the battles didn't end in victory for our side. One night, the uniformed side attacked Dizzy Gillespie and Oscar Pettiford in the subway on their way uptown after work. Both Diz and O. P. were stripped naked, and left to make their way home as best they could. Although they laughed about it the next day, this imaginative scenario wasn't really funny.

Coleman Hawkins was always a dapper gentleman. He had a lovely lady with violet eyes. Ben Webster, a big bear of a man, was a father figure and my protector. He was the buddy of a guitar player I was hanging with, and woe to anyone who fucked with me. I invited him to my apartment one night when two of my girlfriends were there. He chose the plainer of the two because, he said, the prettiest one had dirty feet. Funny that he was so meticulous, after he had peed on my mother's couch one night when, drunk, he had fallen into a very sound sleep. Ben and I remained friends until he died, an expatriate in Copenhagen. I remember one day in a musicians' bar in New York when he had called me the plain one. He was always a gentleman, well dressed and wearing a hat. In later years, he sat in a chair to play. I always felt he was lonely. Thelonious Monk, in those days, wore a beret and a "Free France" button. He always seemed mysterious and older.

The first albums I ever bought were those of Lady Day and Pres (Lester Young). He was the giant at that time, and I was terribly in awe of him. Sensing his private nature, I never intruded upon it. Later, when I was pregnant with Kim and felt more comfortable around him, I told him that if the baby was a boy I intended to name him Brew Pres, after two saxophonists (Brew being Brew Moore). He responded, "Oh, please . . . I have enough problems!"

The White Rose Bar, where drinks cost twenty-five cents, was the place where everyone used to hang out between sets. We stationed ourselves out front where we could watch the glamorous people we admired, such as Billie Holiday drinking brandy alexanders, with her were her Chihuahua and her boxer called Missy. Don Byas, Clyde Hart, Big Sid Catlett, and Hal "Doc" West, who were playing at one club or another, would stop in for a drink. We would sit on a ledge in front of the White Rose, and when there was no action between sets we used to sit on the steps of the brownstone, where we could hear the music from the clubs. The cops came by often to chase us away, but as soon as they left we went back. In *Collier's Magazine,* Robert Sylvester wrote about the clubs on 52d Street and he interviewed me. In his column, he called me "The Queen of 52d Street."

I was working as a checkroom girl in the Yacht Club. All of the concessions were run by a syndicate, and they switched the girls around according to what was needed. A handsome, slim, light-skinned black man would come in every night and stand next to the checkroom, talking to me. He told me his name was Danny Brown and that he was an artist. One night, he walked me home and studiously kissed me. Then he told me that he didn't earn his living as an artist. If I were willing to help him out financially, he would take good care of me. This was a line worthy of any of today's TV series, but I was so naive at the time that he had to spell it out: He was a pimp, and everyone on 52d Street had been laying bets on who would be first to turn me out and turn me on. Danny Brown had a certain class, and we remained friends of a sort, in spite of the fact that I could do nothing for his financial condition.

Our apartment was on the second floor of 7 West, which was old and inadequately wired. Periodically, there was the smell of smoldering electrical wiring. I have an unreasonable fear of fire, no doubt because as a baby I set my crib on fire with a Seder candle. I often called the fire department and they were getting uptight. From our window we could look across the courtyard to an apartment in the back. One night I thought I saw red flames coming from it. I sprinted downstairs to the hall phone and called the fire department. When I ran back upstairs to check from my window, I saw that the flames were a red light bulb, and realized that the smoke had been better than the fire. At that moment, eight firemen, fully equipped with hoses, brandishing fire axes, helmets agleam, burst through the front door demanding, "Where's the fire?"

Another late night, I was using the hall phone. Someone had unscrewed the light bulb. As I was dialing, a strange black man appeared out of the shadows, mumbling something. I hung up the phone and ran upstairs where Dave Tough was waiting. A few hours later, we heard screams coming from the girl who lived downstairs. Dave weighed about 105 pounds and I out-weighed him by five pounds: altogether that made 215, so we went to her rescue. We were either stout-hearted or foolish. She had been raped by the man I had encountered in the hall earlier. In her panic she did get off some great lines:

"I told him I didn't want a black baby. He didn't even take off his shoes. I asked him how could he enjoy it? And I had just bought *Native Son!*"

I met Dave Tough when he was playing drums with Woody Herman's First Herd. He was older than the other cats I knew, better read and very sophisticated. Dave was my first intellectual. Between the wars, he had been an expatriate in Europe, hobnobbing with the Prince of Wales at Bricktop's in Paris. He was gentle and sensitive, with a sex drive brought low by alcohol and barbiturates. Nonetheless, he seemed in need of human comfort. Dave had a fragile ego, unable to withstand the buffeting blows of life. He often took me out to dinner and I went to the Hotel Pennsylvania every night that the band played there. One evening he seemed particularly agitated, and asked if I would spend the night with him in the band room. There had been nothing between us sexually, but I understood his need and agreed. As we prepared for bed, he told me he was married, and said he didn't want to hurt me, nor his wife. He dressed and left. I saw what he meant, but decided to stay there. Some hours later, Dave returned. He told me he had taken the subway to Newark where he lived, but he loved me and he had to come back. While making the round trip, he had written the first of several treasured poems I have.

The following morning as we left the room, a tiny, angry wraith ran down the hall and gave me a resounding slap across the face. It was Casey, Dave's wife, wielding her marriage certificate. I was too startled to react, even though I realized that she was right and I was wrong. Dave refused to leave me, and we took a room at the Belvedere Hotel. He was in bad shape and more in need of a nurse than a lover. He was an alcoholic, although he drank nothing stronger than Coca-Cola all the time I was with him. He did take pills though: cackers to sleep and uppers to wake up in the morning. Each night he carefully arranged a selection on a chair by the bed. He was in no condition to work. This was the fault of his nervous system and not me. However, Woody thought I had Dave holed up, and blamed me for Dave not showing up.

Dave had bottles of pills by the hundreds in the bathroom medicine cabinet. One day I found two Nembutal carefully wrapped in waxed paper and secreted inside a jar of my cosmetics. When I asked him why, he said he didn't want the maid to find them. He really wouldn't have been any use to Woody, who was pushing a powerhouse band at that time.

Max Kaminsky, in his book *My Life in Jazz,* speaks of the hard feelings between the boppers and the moldy figs during the forties. He assures us that the purveyors of the whole tone scales, weird harmonics, and out-of-tune beboppers broke the hearts of Louis Armstrong, Lips Page, and Dave Tough. Kaminsky wrote, "Dave fell for the new music. . . . if he had given it time, he would have heard the barrenness of so much of it, and how a great deal of it was only exchanging old clichés for new clichés." Not so. Dave really loved what was happening and when he won the *Downbeat* Poll, he came to 7 West to show me. He was working at Eddie Condon's Dixieland club in the Village. It was at the end of his life and he had become too ill to make gigs. The only people who would hire him were his friends from the old days. He protested that the award should have gone to Max Roach or Art Blakey, and with a small smile said he would have to sneak the *Downbeat* into Condon's under his coat. I never heard a bopper put Dave down. However, I had no patience with Dave's passivity to life and we drifted apart. He always cared and kept in touch. A few times when I was on the road he showed up at my mother's, beaten up and dirty, to recover from a drunk, until one winter night, too sick or too drunk to make harbor anywhere he died on the frozen Newark streets . . . on his way home to Casey, I hope.

Joe Maini's cellar pad was deliciously depraved. It was in that dreary Upper West Side of New York, now infamously known as Needle Park. Rows of brownstones that had seen better times, but now fallen into disrepute, served as transient rooming houses to people who were moving up . . . or down. That style of architecture stretches endlessly from Broadway to Riverside Drive. It was a particularly hopeless section. Musicians always seem to anticipate needle parks.

Descending to the cellar in a makeshift elevator (I was a stalwart girl to take that first ride), one had to wend one's way through a labyrinth of spooky, dimly lit corridors, stooping to get under the snaked heating pipes, through passageways which led to an inferno of oil burners that provided areas for strange young men from the FBI to lurk. They must have been assigned to watch the comings and goings to the Maini pad, take notes, tap phones, and bide their time. If one possessed a strong heart, one finally came to the door at the end of the long hall.

In Joe's pad, there were draperies over everything. They were dark and mismatched, and added to the gloom, which was relieved only by a bit of grayish light creeping through a carelessly draped street-level window. The room was large and low-ceilinged, containing the nondescript tables and chairs of furnished rooms, an unkempt mattress and springs, unwashed dishes, and bent, blackened spoons, a wire recorder, a piano, and a set of drums. Joe lived here with Jimmy Knepper, Joe Albany, Dean Benedetti, and Roy Hall. But there were always several unknown cats in various stages of undress and highness, and to whom you were never introduced. A brief nod and a muttered "man" sufficed. But, there was music . . . wire music, live music . . . so you could close your eyes and forget for awhile, the trip out.

I heard Willie "The Lion" Smith once at a rent party in Harlem. I don't remember the circumstances of my being there anymore; the only thing that mattered was the music I loved, bebop. His music remains in my memory. I also remember his derby, his cigar, the old upright he played, and the reefer (the best in New York at that time).

In the thirties, black musicians had been raised by a generation once removed from slavery. Jim Crow might have seemed the natural order of life and the music conformed to the white standards of entertainment. It was, for the most part, earning a living, and not creating art that concerned musicians at that time. During the years of World War II, the young musicians were more sophisticated and better informed.

In the twenties and thirties, jazz was more extroverted, with an obvious beat and feeling. Beboppers made the transition to a more complex form of music. They were the introverts who turned their backs on the audience, eliminated long announcements, and forced the audience to listen to the music. Because they felt rejected both as blacks and as musicians (their new music was reviled), they often withdrew into heroin and racial hatred. The only people of color I had known in my adolescence were the entertainers . . . musicians and friends of my mother. To me, the only thing that made them different was that they were talented, exciting, and glamorous.

I think now of all our giants who died, never knowing that they would be celebrated in our culture and memory. One could construct a monument to the victims of the bebop revolution. True, some were victims of self-indulgence which resulted from the rejection, the mockery, and the long exile of the artist whose creation was too advanced for his public. Oh, how many names in history must be engraved on that monument? It would have to encompass more than beboppers.

The black giants were held in awe by the white musicians who were, after all, experimenting with what was a primarily black concept of music. Here was one way the black musician could strike back at the white musicians he felt had taken his music, commercialized it, and profited from it. In all other ways, a black musician was frustrated. Making a white player insecure about the thing most dear to him was a wonderful revenge. The sad thing was that the victims were really the allies. So the music became polarized. Whereas black musicians had used drugs to anesthetize life, the white musicians used drugs to emulate in order to show that they, too, were rejected and harassed. They became funky-butt apers of the saddest part of the black experience. The bebop era became the generation of the sneer. It was fashionable defense to sneer at anything white. Rejected white musicians joined in. They, too, belittled other white musicians. But, in reality, it was themselves they were rejecting, and they were left with only false values. Many found a junkie fraternity which transcended color.

The more sensitive and musically advanced musicians of the swing era joined the bebop revolution. The ones who couldn't found allies in the press and formed their own clique. The next black generation, the cool ones, found racial pressure had lessened after the war. As they became more integrated socially, their music also became more integrated with white music. But they lost that wonderful, driving swing of the thirties as well as the originality of the forties, and their music became bloodless. Interestingly, with the increasing prominence of black awareness, jazz has become, once again, black music, deeply infused politically. The true black music, the roots, spent some time in England and returned to the U.S.A. as white music. With the commercial acceptance of rock and roll, black musicians have once again reintegrated; the same is true for rhythm and blues (as Jon Hendricks remembers it), and a new fusion was born. However, I can't help thinking that this one is also destined to be a dead end.

Now our heroes have been assimilated into our general culture. Lester Young, Fats Navarro, Bud Powell, Art Tatum, and Bird changed our music for all time. But what about Booker Little, Tiny Kahn, and Sonny Berman? Their names are known to a small public.

3. YATAG

When Don Byas left Max Roach, Oscar Pettiford, and George Wallington at the Onyx, I thought he would be irreplaceable. When I asked the press agent to tell me who was coming in, he replied, "You don't know him. He's a saxophone player from Kansas City."

"Is he cute?" I inquired.

"No. But you'll dig him." That turned out to be the understatement of all times. That saxophone player from Kansas City never did make it to the Onyx gig.

When he did show, Bird brought a new music to 52d Street, and it displaced swing, which was a foot-tapping, happy, partying music. You could still tap your feet to Bird's music, but you had to think about it first. It was intellectual. It had more freedom than swing. It could soar in flights of uncontained joy, but it also bared all the pain of the soul of black America. There were no compromises in this music: it was straight ahead, and ended forever the era of the bandana head. The music met with hostility, not only from white audiences who sensed its message and felt threatened, but from older black musicians who had to reflect on the expression "plantation nigger." These musicians had been hard boozers, but this new breed looked and was even more self-destructive.

When I read the following passage by Jung, I immediately thought of Bird:

> Great gifts are the fairest, and often the most dangerous, fruits on the tree of humanity. They hang on the weakest branches, which easily break. In most cases . . . the gift develops in inverse ratio to the maturation of the personality as a whole. A gift is not an absolute value, or rather, it is such a value only when the rest of the personality keeps pace with it.

Bird strived for normalcy and was happiest when, a few years later, he had a band with bad violinists. They were all white and legitimate. I would come to find this aspect of his personality innocent and touching. But even Bird wasn't free of prejudice. He didn't like West Indians, Jews, or "faggots," although he thought female homosexual acts were cute and innocent. He was seemingly blind toward racism directed at him and always carried himself with dignity. He seemed older than his contemporaries, and had a strange power over people which came from an innate understanding of psychology. He was unread, yet a mine of diverse knowledge. It would take another generation to reject the premise that white is right, but Bird had opened the door.

When I met Charlie Parker, he was twenty-three and I was eighteen. Someone brought him to 7 West and, although he wasn't handsome or physically attractive to me, his magnetism and experience were different from any of the men I had known. He had been married twice, had a young son and an old habit. I liked him. He was sweet, gentle, and always cheerful with me. He soon became my confidant and best friend. Insensitive as I was to his love for me, I would confide my latest passion. He never reproved me. One night I was dozing on the couch in someone's 52d Street pad. Bird dropped by. He sat on the edge of the couch and whispered the love he had kept silent. It startled me into thinking about him in a different way. It also frightened me because his feelings were deeper than mine. I wasn't ready to get deeply involved, so we kept it light. We hung out. He dropped by or I went to the club. We smoked reefers together and were buddies.

Bird was becoming very controversial, musically. He couldn't be ignored and his music aroused deep reactions. Those who understood it became his disciples. However, his music was difficult to understand, and threatening to the established order. But Bird never hesitated. He was always sure of his musical course and he knew he was special. Even in his worst moments, he remained strong, manly, and in command.

Flaubert said, "Be regular and orderly in your life, like a good bourgeois, so that you can be violent and original in your work." Bird was none of these, except original, both in form and structure. He changed the pattern of improvisation, phrasing in a new way, and forever influenced all music which followed. Critics always said that Bird had been influenced by Lester Young. This annoyed him, and he asserted Buster "The Prof" Smith was his influence. Until Bird, Pres had been the king of swing for me. But Pres phrased behind the beat. How could they think Bird came out of Pres? Bird had a trumpet player and a pianist who played behind the beat, and it bugged him. He said that he didn't dig rushing either, that he felt the placement of time right on. Nevertheless, Bird loved Pres, and told me he would go night after night to hear him in Kansas City. Pres would sit on the bandstand with a joint between each finger, and when he smoked one, he'd move each one up a finger.

Bird was so engrossed with music and drugs that he had little time for women. I knew that if I opened my heart to him, he would love me for-ever. But, at eighteen, I was too immature to settle my future and I was afraid of his intensity. I knew this could be no casual affair with me in command. Life was fun. I had just attained my independence and the world was big and exciting. I had a thirst for freedom and wanted to sip at many fountains. I knew that Bird would be too heavy to handle lightly. Still, I was drawn to him and wanted his approval. How much I wanted it, I wouldn't know until I felt his freeze. But Bird seemed to be content just hanging out.

On my twenty-first birthday, I went to the Three Deuces around mid-night. Bird was working there with Diz, Max, Al Haig, and Curley Russell. During a solo, he spotted me and interpolated "Happy Birthday." Then he grabbed Diz's arm and told him to play "All the Things You Are," which he always called "YATAG." Like all the good players, he knew the lyrics of this song, and "You are the angel glow" was his favorite. That was a lovely birthday present. After the gig, we went uptown. First we went to Bird's pad on 149th Street where he rolled a joint as big as a cigar, and insisted that I smoke it all. There was strong pot around in those days: Mae's, Chicago Light Green. . . . Then we walked along Upper Broadway, which was just waking up. A few people were waiting for the trolley to take them to work, sitting on the benches in the island which divided uptown and downtown traffic. (They still had trolleys in those days.) Bird lit a railroad flare, which was his special surprise birthday gift for me. I had no idea where he found it, but it set off a startling light in the early dawn. Mixed couples were apt to be met with hostility, and we were attracting a lot of attention with our hissing cerise torch. . . . Besides, I was stoned. "That's beautiful, Bird. I'd love to have a dress that color, but let's split before the fuzz comes," I pleaded. We ran up Broadway hand in hand, followed by hostile glances from the gray people we left behind to watch my sputtering end of a perfect birthday.

When Bird was living on 149th Street and Amsterdam Avenue, Miles Davis, who had become his protégé, had a room on the floor below. The one-room pad I was living in at the time was getting too small for me and my three roommates, so we scouted around for a new pad. We heard that two studio apartments were available on 152d Street, between Broadway and Riverside Drive. On our first night there, the bedbugs attacked. When our unsympathetic landlady implied that we had brought them with us, we should have been forewarned. We had paid a month's rent, so we bought sulphur candles and split for the day. The candles took care of the bedbugs, but did nothing for the other tenants. Lower-class Irish, they were frustrated that their striving for upward mobility had brought them no further from Harlem than the other side of Broadway. Their children tortured cats for amusement, and they were the worst sort of bigots.

It was at that time that Bird and I more or less slipped into a romance. Bird was serious. I wasn't. We took the subway downtown to the Three Deuces, where we were both working. We went to the movies together or grabbed a bite to eat. Three blocks down Broadway, near 149th Street, there was a soulful establishment called Belle's. Its three rooms catered to all gustatory needs: a bar, a restaurant, and an ice cream parlor. Bird had the sweet tooth of many heavy drinkers and all vipers. I had always been a malted freak, so we did our sipping in the ice cream parlor. Sippin' at Belle's was always a delight, especially with Bird and Miles.

The 152d Street racist and cat-torturing society eventually won. One of our neighbors threw a bottle out of the window at one of our gentle-man callers, and scored a direct hit, although it wasn't serious. However, the "perpetrator of the assault" had called the cops, and Commissioner Valentine's vice squad was soon on the scene. Of course, they thought my roommates and I were four young hookers with our two black pimps. One of the cops even told me he knew of a good setup on the other side of Broadway, and he would take care of me. Between the bedbugs, the neighbors, and New York's finest, my spirit had been badly battered. That was when I moved back to 7 West into the second-floor apartment with my mother.

I started having a light romance with a piano player named Dense Thornton. He had a room in a large uptown apartment that belonged to Doris Green. I knew that Doris worked in one of the 52d Street clubs, but I didn't know that she was torching for Bird. But one night, I was late for a date with Bird because I had fallen asleep in Dense's room. By the time I got downtown, Bird had finished work, and Doris had already seen to it that he had the word. It really surprised me that he felt so hurt and was so unforgiving.

That week, I had to leave for a dancing gig in Montreal. By the time I got back to New York, Bird had gone to California with Dizzy to work at Billy Berg's. I found out I had gotten pregnant in Canada. I was still so young that I was afraid to tell my mother. I kept putting off a decision. I finally decided I wanted this baby, even though I didn't love its father and would never see him again. He was just someone I met when I was dancing in Canada, a sportswriter who went under the name of Bill Anderson although his real name was Bill Facus. I wanted to work my way west. I missed Bird, although I didn't realize I was hooked on him.

I got a gig in Chicago, and when I opened at the Brown Derby, I was two months pregnant. The star of the show was Joan Barry, who had taken Charlie Chaplin to court in a paternity suit. Opening night was attended by the previous ladies of the chorus who had been a six-year fixture at that club. After the first show, someone came into the dressing room to tell us that some gentlemen wanted us to join them at their table. Who did they think we were? We were a high-class line from New York, not a bunch of B girls! The bosslady was a tough redhead who fronted the club for her Mafia boyfriend. But our contract was firm, so she promptly re-engaged the old line . . . for the mixing. We did the dancing. The engagement ended a month later, and those girls never understood why we were so dumb that we preferred dancing to bilking the johns.

While working at that club, I was "discovered" by an old-time, famous producer-entrepreneur who was living in Hollywood and promoting starlets. Yvonne De Carlo was his best-known discovery. Nils T. Granlandt liked exotic types, and told me if I came to California and looked him up he'd find work for me. Not thinking past my third month of pregnancy, I decided to blow what money I had made on the gig and buy a ticket to the Coast with my girlfriend. I was heading west to California and Bird. When we went to Union Station to catch the train, it was overflowing with servicemen. We discovered we couldn't afford a berth, and so we made the three-day trip sitting up in a dirty coach.

Hollywood! It seemed everybody was on the Coast in 1945: Pres, newly released from an army stockade, Mulligan, Joe Albany, Howard McGhee, and of course Bird, who was sharing a small house with the tenor player Gene Montgomery. The day I tracked him down, he was alone, playing his horn, and I followed the sound. We had a tender, friendly reunion. The first time we had made love was in his room on 149th Street. It was a hot summer afternoon, and I had gone there to bemoan my latest tale of disillusioned, romantic woe. I had no intention of becoming his lover, but I had allowed myself to be consoled. Now I had to tell him not only that I had had another affair, but that I was carrying a child. Bird put down any thoughts of resuming our romance when I told him I was pregnant.

My friend Claire and I became part of the crowd of young, black players who made that house their headquarters. We were living a split existence: into the Hollywood fringe by day, and late nights in the black jazz clubs along Central Avenue. It was precarious because the two didn't mix. Our first day in town, we had gone to a flick at Grauman's Chinese Theater. We didn't have a room yet, but it was important to hit Hollywood via that famous monument. Then I had called my producer friend, Nils T. Granlandt, who was tied up. However, he gave us the number of a friend who was in the real estate business and also owned a restaurant: a room and a free meal! So we called Clem; that was really his name. He invited us to join him for dinner at his restaurant. We explained that our trunks were still at the station and we weren't very presentable, but he reassured us that there would be no problem. After three days on that dirty train in the same clothes, we went to meet him. We needn't have worried. It wasn't the grand restaurant we were expecting. It was a Greek luncheonette. The lodgings were better: He put a nice house in Hollywood at our disposal. The house was up for sale, and all we had to do in exchange for this munificence was to show the house to prospective buyers. But we were keeping late hours hanging out with the cats and we never answered the door until after noon. We soon lost our little nest. We found a room to rent in a married couple's house. The husband was always hitting on us, but there was a kumquat tree in the yard which helped fill our constantly hungry stomachs.

We met a drummer, Chuck Thompson, who had an old black bullet-proofed gangster car. We tooled around in it, hoping to avoid the L.A. police who didn't take kindly to mixed couples. The car, loaded down with all the cats, Gene, Shifty Henry, Wardell Gray, and Sonny Chris, would swing down to the Finale, where Bird was playing with Joe Albany. One night, when I walked in with another Clem we had met, Bird interpolated "We're in the Money."

Clem 2 was one of those inexplicable California dudes. He gave Claire and me a ride one night when we were hitching home from the Trocadero, where Nat Cole was playing with his trio. When Clem found out that I knew how to read and write music, he told me that, although he was a songwriter, he could do neither. He needed someone always at hand to jot down his immortal melodies before they were lost forever. I was hired. The gig was to hang out with him. It didn't pay much, but it had fringe benefits such as transportation and an occasional free meal. He was tone-deaf and sang in the cracks. I would sing back an improved approximation, and he would always agree that it was exactly what he had just sung. So I would write down a bar or two; his inspiration didn't come in long phrases. He had eyes for Claire which he manifested in palm sucking. He had a motherly protectiveness towards my pregnant condition. We both had him covered. Clem was erratic and a bad driver to boot. In sheer terror, I would yell, "Stop the car! I'm getting out! I can't make it!" He'd coax me back with the promise of a grand dinner at the Brown Derby. I would Sarah Bernhardt some more and he would beg, "Think of little Pres." That's the name I had decided upon. One night, Clem took us to Chasen's after we had smoked some shit. We didn't know it had been doctored with morphine paste. Chasen's was very hot, crowded, and plastic. I realized I was about to black out while we were in the mob, waiting for a table. Elbowing my way to the door, I told Clem that I needed air. We went outside, losing our place in line. I sat on a chair, head in hands, trying to get myself together. Clem was in a pique, "Straighten up! George Raft is looking at you!"

Clem was generous and got his kicks by grooving everyone. He got Miles's horn out of pawn. When his car was crowded with cats, he'd stop and disappear into a drugstore with an air of mystery. Everyone would complain, "Oh, man, what's he doing now?" Clem would emerge, his pockets bulging with packets of all brands of chewing gum, cigarettes, candy, or dexies. With ritual care he would pass out one of each to every-body, one at a time, prolonging our gratitude. We'd arrive at Gene's house, and Clem would go-fer: chicken dinners for all. We must have treated him cruelly, but I think he was a lonely person whose only talent was his gen-erosity.

Bird was always my magnet, but I was grooving, hanging out and hearing a lot of the good new music. He was friendly but distant. I was in my fifth month of pregnancy and could no longer put off plans for the impending birth of my child. I still hadn't seen a doctor, and my Holly-wood career had obviously been aborted because I hadn't been. When I called Bird to tell him I was going back east, all he said to me was "Have a nice trip." The ultimate putdown. Claire and I were not unhappy to be leaving the land of Orange Julius, and when my mother wired me the money, we caught the first possible plane. I was six months pregnant and happy to be back in the Apple.

4. THEME

The day Kim was born, I got a call at the hospital telling me that Bird was dead. That rumor had reached the East Coast. Actually Bird had suffered a complete mental and physical breakdown while playing "Lover Man" at a recording session for Ross Russell, who owned Dial Record Company. Bird had lost control of his motor functions, and had been taken back to his hotel where he later appeared naked in the lobby, demanding a telephone. Bird was again taken upstairs where he fell asleep with a cigarette, setting fire to his room. He was then arrested, and Ross got him a lawyer who bargained with the judge, arranging for Bird to be committed to Camarillo State Hospital instead of jail. Bird thought Ross had had him committed, and never forgave him for that, nor for the release of "Lover Man."

Some years later, Bird rerecorded that tune, beginning with the same halting phrase before soaring with his recovered strength. He took me into a listening booth in a record shop, and proudly played it for me. I wonder if Ross was wrong to have released that document of a man in agony. Certainly it is touching and beautiful, but Bird was a private man, and "Lover Man" laid bare his tortured soul. His association with Ross, from 1945 through 1948, encompassed perhaps the most turbulent years of Bird's life.

I went back to dancing, leaving my baby daughter, Kim, in my mother's care while I was on the road. At last, I made the big time! I got a gig on Broadway, two doors down from what would later become Birdland. It was a theater/restaurant, called Iceland. (After the club folded, it was reopened as The Band Box and featured jazz and big bands.) In our show we had beautiful costumes, and I would ask a handsome young trumpet player in the band to zip my gown. Bill and I began dating. One night we went to see *Gentleman's Agreement,* a film about anti-Semitism. As Bill was walking me home, I confessed that I was half Jewish. So was he, he said, hugging me with relief. Another night he asked if I would stop smoking pot for him. I simply replied no, that it was part of the me that he loved. When he asked me to marry him, it seemed like a good idea. I was still afraid of locking up with Bird. Bill and I were compatible and he would be a good father to Kim. We went through a quickie ceremony at city hall, where I became Mrs. Bill Heyer. He moved into my mother's apartment with me. We dug each other, but I didn't love him any more than any of the other men I had had crushes on up till then. We got along well, but it was a disaster. Although he really tried, we never had a real marriage. We were perfect roommates, but not ideal partners in marriage. After less than a year, he went home to his mother in Newark. He had loved me more than I had loved him.

I received a letter from Ross Russell on the Coast. He wrote that Bird was coming back east, and asked if I could line up a gig at the Three Deuces, which I did. The night that Bird arrived in town, I wanted to see him so badly that I ran around uptown to all the places where he might be. I didn't know that our old friend, Doris Green, had gone to California when Bird was in Camarillo. She had taken care of him, and had now accompanied him back to New York. I never found Bird that night, but the first time I saw him walking towards me on 52d Street, I felt as though someone had punched me in the stomach, knocking all the wind out of me. That's how Bird affected me ever after. I was hooked. When we first met, Bird walked bent over with an uptown bounce. He used to tease, "When are you going to marry me?" I would reply, "When you straighten up." After Camarillo, he walked upright.

After Bird's return from California, I often saw him with Doris, driving in his Cadillac. He always stopped to speak. In 1949 Bird went to Europe for the first time to play at the Paris Jazz Festival. He experienced another world. He told me how well his music had been accepted and how kindly he had been treated. He had been invited to dinner at the home of an aristocratic lady. She had tapestries on the wall and a wreath of roses was laid on the table. Bird, on his best behavior, spoke of his love for Omar Khayyam's poetry. Madame Berdin, who had a leather-bound first edition, went to her bibliothèque and placed it in Bird's hand. "For me?" he asked. "Of course," she responded. Obviously, she hadn't meant to part with it. Noblesse oblige. Bird had also met the great saxophonist Marcel Mule. He came home bearing gifts, music and records. He had been idolized and he had a new dignity.

Don Lanphere was the new tenor player in town. With Kim, I moved into his apartment on East 98th Street between 5th and Madison Avenues. We bought Buddy Stewart's furniture. Buddy and Dave

Lambert were the first bebop singers. They worked and recorded for Gene Krupa. The apartment was near Central Park and I didn't realize how close we were to Spanish Harlem, junkie heaven, and Bird's connection. Bird was not timid concerning my attraction to any other man, and he dropped by often on his way to score. Don and I slept on separate daybeds. One night Bird tucked me in. I felt his magnetism and his love. Don was on the road with Woody Herman, and I got a dancing gig at the Old Roumania in the Village. There was a girl working in the line who told us about her children, but she never showed photos. She was married to Kansas Fields, a black drummer. I was having a hard time resisting Bird, and confided in her. Bird and I had planned a rendezvous one night after the show. Seeing the secret life that Mimi Fields was living, and thinking about Kim, I sent Bird a telegram saying no. I drank too much that night, went home, and fell asleep. The doorbell rang. It was Bird. He claimed he hadn't received my telegram. Of course he had. I staggered back to bed. He lay down beside me. In the morning we made love. He went out to buy food and when I awoke, he had made a big mixed salad. Once again we were lovers, but I was still not ready for a permanent commitment.

The narcotic squad was watching Bird and since they saw him coming often to our apartment, they thought we might be pushers. One morning a friend who lived on the next block brought his son to our apartment. We were going to take the children to Central Park. The house was not clean and all my belongings were in boxes, as I was planning to move out. The narcs came. They looked at my albums and when Kim emerged, naked, from her room, they said, "That's *The Rite of Spring*." A friend had left jars of lemonade homegrown, which were in the kitchen cabinet, and I had a few joints of good grass in a drawer. I flushed everything down the toilet on the advice of the narcs, who realized I was not a pusher. When Bird came by that night he reprimanded me: "Did you have to throw away the good shit?" That was my second run-in with the police. Once again, it was time to leave a dangerous area and go back to 7 West and my mother.

I have always been convinced that pot is innocent and nonaddictive. I thought I would be an old lady in a rocking chair still getting high. However, it has been many years now since my daughters and I have smoked. I can't seem to fit it in between my cigarettes and wine. I'm not sure I am healthier for that.

Still resisting Bird, but yearning for him, I was running a high fever one night. I called him from the hall phone at 7 West and told him I needed him. I wanted him.

Several months after Bird returned from Paris, I awakened one dawn hearing someone whisper my name. I was sleeping in the first bedroom at 7 West and my mother was asleep on the couch in the living room. She must have forgotten to lock the door. Anyone entering my room had to pass her first. I awoke and saw Bird standing next to my bed.

"Come with me," he pleaded.

"No, I can't. My mother is in the other room. If she sees I'm gone, she'll probably call the cops and say her daughter has been abducted."

"Come with me now!" insisted Bird in a louder voice.

I realized Bird was not to be deterred; I must humor him or face an ugly scene. While I got up and quickly threw on some clothes, Bird went down to wait for me in his Cadillac. That car was his answer to all the honky cab drivers who had refused to pick up a black fare.

Bird was planning to drive to the airport and board a plane for Paris. I pointed out that I had a four-year-old daughter upstairs, and besides, I wasn't really dressed for a trip to Paris nor did I have a passport. Had I been more stout-hearted, we would have eaten dinner in France that night. Instead, I talked him into taking a ride to my old stomping grounds in Westchester. Bird pulled the car into a leafy byway and we made love. He went to pick some berries for my breakfast, and returned bearing gifts. He had not only picked some blackberries, but also some pot he had found growing there. Unfortunately, a highway patrol car drove up, and Bird quickly threw the pot away. We drove to the cemetery where my father was buried. Four years later, we would make that same drive to bury our daughter, Pree.

On May 29, 1950, until death did us part, I acknowledged the inevitable, and Kim and I became Bird's family. We moved into his apartment on East 11th Street. My mother thought Bird had bewitched me.

Bird had a Swedish tour coming up in the fall. He had great respect for the Scandinavians. It was important to him not to be strung out: he wanted to be clean when he left for Europe. He kicked his habit shortly before he left. The morning we saw him off, he was feeling shaky, but confident that this was a new start for him. However, his body wasn't as strong as his mind, and he satisfied his cravings for drugs with alcohol. While he was in Sweden, he was invited by Charles Delaunay to do a concert in Paris for French radio. They sent a plane ticket and promised an advance. The story of what happened became muddled, but Bird claimed that when he arrived in Paris he was broke and couldn't get in touch with anyone for the promised advance. I'm sure he drank and partied for a few days.

His health had deteriorated, and he finally returned to New York without ever playing the concert. Leonard Feather was with me at the airport to meet Bird. We went to a Chinese restaurant on 52d Street for lunch, where Leonard asked Bird if he would tape a broadcast. While they were on the air, Leonard called Delaunay in Paris. Charles remarked that Bird was in Paris to play a concert. Bird got on the phone and, very sweetly, said he'd had a good flight home.

Bird looked unhealthy; he was sweating and in pain. After seeing a doctor, he was hospitalized immediately. During his several days in the hospital, many tests were administered. They found a bleeding ulcer which was brought under temporary control. They also discovered an abdominal lesion which could not be treated. It was probably the result of the prussic acid Bird had swallowed in Camarillo. According to Bird, he had put it in chewing gum during his depression. After his release from the hospital, Bird stayed relatively clean. He was often in pain, and there were times he sought relief in heroin, but he never had a heavy habit again.

While Bird was in Sweden I learned that I was pregnant. Bird was joyous. My having his baby assured him of my love. Before Pree was born, we moved to a large apartment on Avenue B and 10th Street. For the first time in his life Bird had a stable family life. He played his role of husband and father to the hilt. He adored Kim and took his paternal duties seriously.

Our apartment was in the Ukrainian section of the Lower East Side. It later became known as the East Village. It was an area full of poverty, peopled by Hassidic Jews with side locks and by gypsies, and was a melting pot for refugees. Our building was across from Thompkins Square Park and each of the five families living in it occupied an entire floor. We occupied the ground floor, which had a separate entrance and opened onto a large courtyard in back for the children and all the animals we would eventually accumulate. We redecorated the apartment. We bought blond wood furniture, put up Steinberg birdcage wallpaper from Sloans and painted the living room charcoal gray.

The neighborhood bars were a neverending delight to Bird. He spent hours in them, chatting with the old men, learning Russian phrases, talking politics, eating piroshki. When the children were old enough,

I would send them in to pull at Bird's sleeve and say, "Daddy, oh Daddy, come home now." He would walk with us to the A & P on 13th Street, help us carry the groceries home, and then return to the bar. None of the old men there was aware that he was "Yardbird" and they called him "Charlie." Only the insiders called him "Bird." My mother did because she couldn't call him "son," although I knew there were times when she wanted to. Bird knew everyone in the neighborhood. One night while we were waiting on the corner for a bus, we saw an old couple. They were thin, bedraggled and whining gutter-cats who were so drunk that they were holding each other up. I turned away in disgust and felt like crying. Bird knew them by name.

Before Bird kicked, he would have to go uptown every night. One of his connections was on 110th Street, just east of Central Park. It was an unsafe area, so Bird had bought me a switchblade and showed me how to use it because he would leave me in the car while he went inside to cop. Most nights, once he was inside, he would nod off and forget the time. I remember with dread sitting in the car as dawn came, frightened and barely able to stay awake, hoping the cops wouldn't drive by and pull up to ask me what I was doing there. Another time while Bird was out, the phone rang and it was an albino pusher I knew. He told me that Bird had just finked out on him, and that he was out to get Bird. After Pree was born, Bird kept all that dirt away from our home and was very protective of his family.

When Pree was a baby, we used to put her in her carriage outside in our fenced-off entry. Joe Albany would come by and stand on the sidewalk holding long one-sided conversations with her until Bird would go out and tell him to leave. Pree couldn't talk but they seemed to have an understanding. I felt sorry for Joe, who never forgot that Pree's name had been taken from one of his songs. At that time, Joe was in an almost catatonic state which was to last many years.

After Pree was born, we had a vacation in the Berkshire Mountains near Pittsfield, Massachusetts. It was too late in the season for the concerts at nearby Lennox. Bird and I rented a cabin on a mountain top at a typically American rustic place called Holiday Hills. Bird loved it. For the first few days, he was content to sleep or tell me how junkies dream their lives away, nodding and dreaming of this kind of life. But on the fourth day, he provoked a quarrel which would allow him to escape. After dinner, he jumped in the car, leaving me alone and terrified for several hours. When he returned, he was drunk. He had found a hick roadhouse and had sat in with the band playing a borrowed tenor. I wondered about the reaction of the musicians when Bird suddenly appeared at that place in the middle of nowhere. Our last three days were less than ideal. On the way back to New York, when we stopped for gas, I ran into a bar and downed a defiant daiquiri. But for Bird the vacation had been a grand success and he told everyone about his flight into reality!

A year after Pree was born, Bird, wanting a son, made Baird on the couch one afternoon. Baird so resembled Bird that he used to brag he had spit him out. Bird had an idealized view of family life that he tried to maintain despite the drugs and drags of life. Where did his old-fashioned ideas come from? I knew they weren't gleaned from a nineteenth-century novel, because the only book I ever saw him read was a book on Yoga that someone had given him. His views may have come from his mother, Addie, who called herself "Parkie." His father had been shot by another woman, so perhaps Bird had decided to be a different kind of father. When I bought a new strapless bra, Bird admonished me, saying, "Chan, you're a mother now, and you shouldn't go around exposing yourself!" But, after count-less backstage dressing rooms, I was casual about my body, even in those unenlightened times. Bird reproved me for walking around the house na-ked in front of our son Baird, who was only one year old! I have never been at ease wearing any sort of footwear, so even in mid-winter I would try to sneak out of the house without socks. When Bird and I would be halfway down the block, he would notice and order me home to put socks on.

The Rockland Palace was a large ballroom in the Bronx. Bird was booked there to play at a dance to raise money for the defense of Ben-jamin Davis, secretary of the American Communist Party. Bird had his beloved strings and his favorite rhythm section: Max Roach, Teddy Kotick, and Walter Bishop, augmented by Mundell Lowe. The communists paid better than the capitalists and this was one of his highest paying gigs.

It was my first night out after the birth of Baird. Bird taped the micro-phone of my Brush Sound Mirror recorder to the house microphone, which resulted in a faithful reproduction of his sound. Bird, the proud father, was beaming and his music soared. He played so astonishingly that night, that when Paul Robeson joined him on the stand after "Lester Leaps In," I forgot to turn on my tape recorder and missed his acapella "Water Boy."

Driving through Central Park one night, Bird stopped his Cadillac at the posh Tavern on the Green and insisted we go in. I don't remember if we had dinner or just a drink, but I do remember Bird inviting me to dance. He actually wanted to get on a dance floor with me in that hotbed of conservatism. In those pre-emancipated days, we attracted a lot of attention just walking down the street. We danced a very old-fashioned Peabody. As we danced, I was so hard pressed to keep up with his long, sliding strides that I didn't notice the reaction of the customers. Also, the band was so delighted when they recognized Bird that the saxophones forgot to play. I was happy because it gave Bird so much pleasure.

There is a happy maturity in the music of Bird during those years, from 1951 to 1953. He had entered this phase of domestic stability and his children brought much joy to him. He dug Sundays best of all. I would cook a roast, and my mother, brother Jimmy, and Aunt Janet would come for Sunday dinner. It was all very middle class, except for our table which we had had made in the form of a G, or treble, clef. The indentation was the perfect spot for the high chair.

On his birthday in 1954, Bird bought a large piece of white cardboard and some watercolors. He traced the letters to spell "Happy Birthday Bird" and had me paint them. When my mother arrived for the birthday dinner I had prepared, Bird proudly told her that I had painted the birthday message for him!

Bird loved kids, even the little neighborhood hoodlums, and he was especially gentle with old drunks and derelicts. In spite of his acquired cynicism, he liked people, all kinds of people except bookers or agents. His rapport with ordinary people led me to believe that he would have been happier had he been born white and untalented. Even the music he listened to was square. He bought records of Kay Kyser's "Slow Boat to China," which he played often, and Mario Lanza singing "Be My Love," which he would imitate, singing in an exaggerated, fractured tenor. The only record he bought which was even close to being hot was Peggy Lee's "Lover," which he would play over and over until my mother would freak out. Probably one of the things Bird was proudest of was that Mitch Miller had played oboe on the string dates and that they had been arranged by a Hollywood hack.

Bird loved magic shops and was always bringing home corny magic tricks for the children. He adored exploding matches and those buzzers that you conceal in your palm to give a slight shock when you shake hands. One of his gifts was a jar marked "Peanut Brittle." When it was opened, three long cloth snakes popped out to slither across the floor. I found them slightly sadistic, but not Bird. He was childlike in his passion for gadgets.

When Bird thought he had been particularly naughty (his own conception of naughty, but not the naughtiness to which I objected), he would stop at the corner drugstore on his way home. He would buy me a horrific ice cream sundae with "the works": sickeningly sweet chewy nuts, thin syrup, and gobs of warm whipped cream. With a beaming smile splitting his broad face, he would throw his hat through the door, signaling apology.

It is poetic justice that Bird died watching jugglers on Tommy and Jimmy Dorsey's TV show. Bird had a child's heart and the soul of a giant.

5. *Interlude*

Bird was using drugs again and we were always broke. On July 17, 1951, Pree had been born with a congenital heart problem and she was chronically ill. A year later Baird was born, a healthy, strapping son. We had a maid to help with the children, Bird still had his Cadillac, but all the money was going to the pushers who hung around Bird like pilot fish. Bird had taken a bust. At his trial, the judge said, "Three months. Suspended sentence." And a lecture followed, "Mr. Parker, if you ever have the urge to stick a needle in your arm again, take your horn out into the woods somewhere and blow." But even if Bird had followed that white man's advice, he would probably have been arrested! How easy it is to pontificate.

After his fall, Bird couldn't get a cabaret card to work in the clubs in New York City. That is deadly to an artist, especially a genius like Bird. Few contemporaries could match his brilliance. His agency sent him out of town with local rhythm sections. For one gig in Rochester, he had a pianist who could play "Stardust" in only one key! One day two detectives came to our house, and offered Bird a cabaret card in exchange for names. Bird refused. Billy Rowe, a big wheel in Harlem, had also said he could get Bird a card; and the Birdland gangsters claimed they could put in the fix for one. But nothing happened and Bird couldn't work.

We decided to apply for welfare and see if that would push a card through. One day we took Pree and went to the A.D.C. Board. The woman who took our application at the relief board must have thought we were crazy when we told her we had a Cadillac and a maid. But we had no money. Bird explained that all he wanted was the right to work, that Pree was chronically ill and needed constant medical care. Our application was denied. We went next to the Legal Aid Society. We had a sympathetic lawyer, but since he worked for the city, he could do nothing for us. On his own, he found us an outside lawyer who was trying to have that most unjust law repealed. Bird wrote a letter to the A.D.C. Board and asked to serve his sentence so that he would then be able to work. However, that would have been impossible since anyone with a narcotic conviction was banned from working in New York clubs. Nevertheless, somebody must have been moved by Bird's letter because he became the first man in the state with a narcotics record to get a card.

Besides using shit, Bird was drinking heavily. The combination made him a crazy man, evil and violent. When it got too much for me, I would take the children and flee to my mother's apartment. My friends began calling me "Portia" after the heroine of the popular soap opera "Portia Faces Life." In fact, it was more of a tragedy. After one of my night flights, I realized I had forgotten some things I needed for the children. I was afraid to go back home to Avenue B, so I asked my brother Jimmy to go. I also asked him to bring me the tape recorder that Bird had given me because I really dug it. I was afraid that, in his anger, Bird might pawn it, or permanently damage it. Later on, after Jimmy's return, Bill Heyer, my ex-husband, dropped by. He set his trumpet down in the kitchen and came into the living room with me. We were listening to some tapes when suddenly someone started knocking on the door. It was Bird demanding to be let in. I panicked. He radiated such authority that everyone was always cowed by him. Bird had a way of arousing extreme emotions without doing a thing! Without opening the door, I told him that if he didn't leave me alone, I would call the police. He replied that if I wanted the police, he would be happy to get them for me. Soon Bird returned with the police; I let them in. I didn't want a scene so I asked Bill to go into the back room. He neglected to take his trumpet. When I opened the door, Bird walked imperiously through the apartment to the first bedroom where he saw the suitcases and the crib. Of course, he saw Bill's horn in the kitchen. With an expansive wave of his arm, he told the bemused policemen, "I want all of these things confiscated. They belong to me." The police, reasoning with him, said that he had no use for the crib or the baby things. Bird finally settled for the tape recorder and left in triumph.

But Bird was a family man. In his constant striving for normalcy, his family, his in-laws, and even his home were part of that white world which had been denied to him as a black man in America. I know it tore him apart to have a habit which he had to hide from me. I knew very little of that part of his life, but I did realize the conflict within him. One Christmas, when there was no money in the house, Bird sold his car to buy Kim her first bicycle. But, as he had once said to me, he already had five Cadillacs in his arm.

Bird's health was getting progressively worse. He had ulcers that caused him constant pain and he was beginning to swell from edema. One doctor lectured Bird on the effect of alcohol on bleeding ulcers, and prescribed a liquid medication for the ulcers with codeine for the pain. There were dozens of bottles of the liquid in the house: it was the codeine that interested Bird. Another doctor diagnosed a liver and heart condition. Bird was a constant patient at Bellevue Hospital. He even asked to take shock treatments as an out-patient! None of this slowed him down. A fix allowed him to forget the pain and keep going. But I was never sure how sick Bird was, or to what extent he was exaggerating in order to get narcotics. Although he was constantly told by doctors how sick he was, I don't think even he believed it. Bird had such a huge appetite for life that it was impossible to believe he wasn't immortal.

Bird had always had the capacity to go for days without sleep. Now, he began falling asleep on the bandstand, with photographers snapping the pictures which became collectors' items. Once, when he had fallen asleep in a doctor's waiting room, the worried doctor offered to give our children a free examination. There was the sleep in a chair, nodding with a cigarette burning his fingers, the sleep in bed, still holding that ever-lethal cigarette with his eyes closed and snoring. When I would protest, he would smile and say, "Just resting my eyes, Pudding." Bird was on a down-hill ride.

One night when we were at home, Bird was very agitated and disturbed. He must have been looking for a pretext to get out of the house and go to Bellevue Hospital for observation. He called the police, and asked them to come get him because he was going to kill his wife. He then told me to turn off all the lights and run screaming out into the street. I turned off the lights, but went into the bedroom and shut the door, hoping to remove myself from this latest insanity. Ten minutes later, when the police still hadn't arrived, I heard Bird call them again. This time he said he was going to kill his mother-in-law. (My mother wasn't even there, but safe in her own apartment.) Soon I heard voices in our hallway. I thought it was the cops, but none came to our door and Bird just sat waiting. A few minutes later, the police entered with two teenagers, whom they had found in our hall, in tow. Bird immediately took charge of the situation with great authority. In his best Captain Midnight style, he told the police that he often carried large sums of money and had observed the kids following him. He claimed he had called the police with his murder story so they wouldn't waste any time coming. He then dismissed them all with a grand gesture, saying, "Take them down to the station and book them. I'll be down in the morning to press charges." The capper was when Bird had me wake the children, dress them and take them to my mother's, saying he had to go uptown to find out who was putting the heat on us.

All of the neighborhood cops knew Bird, so that when he was drunk out of his skull, a few months later, he was escorted home by two blues. When I opened the door, Bird beamed and said, "Well, we caught two more of them." Still another night, Bird had been in the bathroom an unusually long time. Bird used to lock himself in the bathroom to shoot. When I couldn't rouse him by banging on the door, I finally called our upstairs neighbors, the Feldmans, to come down and take the hinges off the door. Bird had nearly OD'd.

Bird was out roaming the night our cat, Eurydice, had kittens. The first kitten, which sounded like a bird and looked like a mouse, was born at 5:00 A.M. Bird came home and, delighted by the miracle of birth, woke me up to talk about it. He wasn't juiced. He went out again and I went back to sleep. Around 8:30, the long-suffering Feldmans from upstairs woke me with the news that an ambulance had just taken Bird to Bellevue. When I arrived, Bird was in the receiving room. His face looked like chopped meat. In the Russian bar down the street, two old men had hit him from behind with a chair and then beat the shit out of him. The hospital had found a switchblade among his personal effects. When I told Bird about the lecture I had received when the nurse returned it to me, he looked at me and chided, "If I had wanted to use it, you don't think I would be here now, do you?" Despite the oxygen tanks all around him, Bird demanded a cigarette. Eurydice had her third kitten at five that afternoon.

Once, when I returned from one of my sojourns at my mother's, I found a loaded gun under the pillow. It was the police .38 that Bird had bought on one of his tours in the South. While trying to unload it, I somehow got it cocked. I didn't know how to delethalize it, so I filled the sink with water, submerged the gun, and left a note saying, "God, you're weird!" Bird had a childlike fascination with guns. He bought a German World War II Walther from a friend, and we also had a 12–gauge shotgun, along with my brother's .22. On another occasion, I returned home to find a hunting knife imbedded in the headboard of our bed.

A few months later, Bird came home one night and went into the bedroom, closing the door behind him. When I entered the room, he hid something behind his back. Instinctively, I knew he was playing cowboy that night. He was holding a gun. He promised me that he would throw it away. He went outside and rattled the garbage can, but I wasn't fooled and demanded that he really did get rid of the weapon. With a beatific smile, he insisted that I dispose of it. The next morning, while I was walking to the East River carrying the damn thing in a paper sack, I kept looking anxiously over my shoulder. I could hardly believe it was real as I asked myself once again, "What am I doing here?"

Life with Bird wasn't all fear and violence. Once he said to me, "I wish I was a lion so I could tear you to pieces and eat you up. Then I wish I was God, so I could spit you up and put you back together again." In a crowded taxi, Bird had me on his lap and Kim was on mine. Kim joked, "We're a sandwich, Daddy. Have a bite." Bird smiled at her and replied, "Bird doesn't eat sweets, honey." After I lost Bird, all his sweetness and tenderness came back to haunt me. If I had something in my eye, he would look and say, "I don't see anything but pretty." When he kissed me, he would tell me, "That tastes like more." Nobody except George Brent in "Dark Victory" could pull off the line that Bird laid on me when he gave me a wedding ring: "A little bit of gold and a whole lot of sentiment." He described our lovemaking as "an express train to heaven." He would touch me and tell me, "These are the notes I'd like to play." In his sleep, his fingers moved on my arm as if he were dreaming I was his horn.

Bird adored cowboy movies, the cornier the better. When he spied Gabby Hayes on a train, he got his autograph and proudly presented it to Kim. She was too young to understand autographs and, thinking it was a coupon, asked, "Where do you send it? I don't know how it's supposed to go. What's it for in the first place, anyhow?"

Bird was more sophisticated in the art of human relations than most of the musicians I knew. He studied the workings of people's minds and emotions, and was well aware of the feelings that others were experiencing. He realized that most people were concerned only with the impression they were making, and he capitalized on this. Perhaps that was why most people were afraid of him. It's why he could crush with a look. That was his armor, what made him strong. One night, a drummer Bird had hired for a gig started asking personal questions: "Whatever happened to that chick named Chan you used to run with?" The other musicians were aghast and expected Bird to knock him down. But Bird, in complete command as always, replied sweetly, "She's the mother of two lovely children."

But Bird was also very impressionable and was influenced by an assortment of odd, white fans. One of them convinced Bird to try

Reichian therapy. At his first session, he was told he must buy an expensive orgone box. When he told me, I derided the idea that sitting in a box could help anyone. That was the end of Reich.

Bird was fertile earth. In two years our household expanded to include three kids, three Maltese terriers, and two cats. But the final straw was Mossedegh, a beautiful but overbred Afghan hound we called Mo. The tiny Maltese were feisty and had her bluffed, so there was constant snarling and yapping. If Mo had been put in an orgone box, it certainly would have solved our problem! She loved water and would jump into the draining bathtub or find a mud puddle in the courtyard. Then she would lope through the house and leap on anyone sitting on the couch. But she preferred the living room as a toilet facility and ignored the courtyard for that! She had no sense in her lovely pointed head and we couldn't housebreak her. One rainy night, I finally gave Bird an ultimatum: either the dog went, or I would! Bird took Mo and went out, leaving me to stay with the kids and the rest of the animals. A few hours later, the manager of the Downbeat Club called to say that Bird had brought a dog into the club, tied it up, and left. Could I come and retrieve it? Since I couldn't leave the children alone, I called my mother who took a cab across town, picked up Mo, and took her back to her apartment. When Bird returned he told me, "Well, I found Mo a good home."

One morning we awoke to the noise of firemen breaking into our apartment and the smell of smoke. The fire was soon traced to its source: a built-in metal wall hamper in the bathroom. Fortunately, it was empty, except for a charred washcloth. Perhaps Bird had mistaken it for an ashtray. But a pair of Bird's trousers, which were hanging on the metal hooks above the hamper, had also started to burn and the cuffs were beyond repair. They were part of a new amply cut suit, so Bird had a tailor shorten them. The tailor cut them at a strange length, a bit longer than Bermudas. When Bird wore them with the suit jacket, which had padded shoulders and a 50s drape, his large body and thin shapely legs made a strange-looking figure. No one in New York wore shorts at that time. Heads turned!

Bird was wearing this style-setting suit one afternoon when we ran into Moondog on the corner of 52d Street and 6th Avenue. Moondog was a familiar figure on the New York sidewalks. He was a blind, bearded, robed mystic who sat in doorways around town. He played drums and accepted contributions. He was often accompanied by a pretty young acolyte who picked crumbs from his beard. Bird always stopped to chat with him. That day, he told us that his wife had just had a baby girl. Expecting something exotic and Eastern, I asked what they had named her. To my disappointment, he replied, "We were going to name her May, but she was born late, so we call her June." There was a convention of Jehovah's Witnesses in town: typical clean-cut middle Americans, the ladies in hats and white gloves and the men with short, bad haircuts and neat suits. Being stared at with Bird was nothing new to me. But with Moondog in his white robe as an added attraction and Bird in his silly suit, we soon raised a crowd. We continued chatting with Moondog, whose arms were full of groceries. When Bird walked him to the corner to help him on a bus, one of the ladies approached me timidly. Indicating Moondog, she politely said, "Excuse me, but what is he?" Ah, how to explain Moondog? I suppose I could have shaken her up by answering, "Jehovah." Logic prevailed and I simply said, "A blind drummer." On second thought, that response was probably just as puzzling.

6. CODA

In 1953 Baird was less than a year old and Pree was just two. Bird and I were having problems with our relationship, and I was pregnant again. I was not in good health: I weighed 103 pounds, had chronic bronchitis, and was working on my sixth pneumonia. A doctor I had seen in a sleazy office on 125th Street across from the Apollo Theater had diagnosed probable tuberculosis. Bird even excused his late arrival at the "Chi Chi, Kim, Laird Baird" date by saying I had TB. Bird was drinking heavily. After a bad scene, I took the children and fled once again to my womb on 52d Street. Three days later, Bird had sobered up and realized the physical condition I was in. When Bird walked into my mother's apartment, he had brought along my cat Orpheus, who had been hanging out in the alleys along Avenue B. When I saw that mangy cat, I knew I would have to bathe him; he was a scummy sight! I had never bathed a cat, and I knew they didn't take very kindly to water. I held the cat's legs firmly, hoping to avoid his sharp claws. The minute he hit the water, I realized my error. Orpheus looked down at my arm and sank his teeth into it, effecting his immediate release and leaving me with an infection which sent me to the nearest hospital that night. By then, the wound was swollen and full of pus. The intern cleaned it and prepared a tetanus injection. When he asked if I suffered from asthma, I replied that I had hay fever and was prone to allergies. He decided to see how I would react to a minute amount injected under my skin. An ever-widening red circle started to creep up my arm, and the pain was intense, so he decided against the injection. For the rest of the night, I lay in pain, burning with a high fever.

My mother convinced Bird that I wasn't physically strong enough to have another baby, having had the others so close together. Although Bird had wanted the baby, he found someone who would abort me. I was underweight, and still running a fever from the lung infection and the cat bite. I must have looked like death when we went to the Harlem apartment of Bird's connection, where a chick with a catheter was waiting. She took me into the bedroom, laid me on the bed, and, without formality, inserted the catheter into my womb, telling me I would expel the fetus the next day. I went back to my mother's apartment to wait. Nothing seemed to be happening and I even went out. I remember Bird running me up and down the stairs on 52d Street that night. In spite of his wanting the child, he was almost cocky, like a boy who had knocked up his girl. The pain started the next morning while my mother was out shopping. I gave birth to a dead male fetus. The cord was still attached to me when my mother returned. I was sobbing hysterically. My strong, practical mother cut the cord and helped me to bed. For some reason, I insisted she save the fetus to show Bird.

In my weakened condition, I didn't have the strength to expel the afterbirth. The abortionist paid me several visits that day, pressing firmly down on my abdomen. I was yellow and hemorrhaging, getting weaker by the hour. She was becoming more and more worried. She finally told my mother that I would have to go to the hospital. The doctor who examined me said I had gangrene, and asked who had done this to me. He never believed my story of a miscarriage, and even asked me once more when I was on the operating table. When I was well enough to return home, I asked Bird to take my cat Orpheus to the SPCA to be examined for rabies. Bird returned without the cat. He had told them to destroy Orpheus. I was able to call in time to save the cat. When I asked Bird why he had done this, he replied, "You killed my son, didn't you?"

When Pree was two years old, she still couldn't walk, and crawled by dragging both legs in tandem. She couldn't keep food down and had projectile vomiting. She was constantly full of mucus. (From what I've read of the symptoms, I now think she must have had cystic fibrosis, a disease which often went unrecognized at that time.) Pree was admitted to the hospital for observation. She was released after two weeks, the doctors unable to diagnose her problem. I found a pediatrician who was a heart specialist, and she discovered that Pree had an open heart valve. This was before open-heart surgery.

I loved Pree dearly, but it was almost as if Bird wouldn't admit her existence. Perhaps a doctor had told him what they couldn't tell me. I think he knew better than I that she couldn't live. By not acknowledging her life, he may have hoped that it could quiet some of his pain at her inevitable death. It didn't. He recorded tunes he named for Baird and Kim. Although I pressed him, he never wrote a song for Pree. He called Kim "Shorty Boodle," "Princess Wet-the-Bed," or "Princess P.P.," and he called Baird "Thunder." But Pree was always "Pree." He was hurt because I had given her no middle name, as I had the other children. In spite of my explaining that I liked the sound of "Pree Parker," he always felt it was a slight. A strange, ethereal kinship existed between Bird and Pree, a sort of doomed understanding and mutual tolerance.

Pree was a beautiful, unearthly child. Her skin was luminous. It had an amber light radiating through it. Bird objected to my keeping her hair cut short. However, it was a practical necessity, as she spent most of her time in bed and it was difficult to keep it unmatted. Bird told me I didn't know about black hair. Pree had an uncanny ear, though she had trouble forming words: "shoes" came out as "fews." Every day at the exact hour, she would pull herself to the radio and turn on "Dr. Jive," moving her head in time to the music. Sometimes she would put on a symphony and sing the underparts.

I always felt that Pree was an old soul who had lived before. Her birth had been long and painful and her life was a constant struggle. The simple act of swallowing food was nearly impossible. It was as if the nourishment of this world was incompatible with her needs. She had difficulty communicating verbally, but we understood each other by a look, or a stronger sensation. At night after Kim and Baird were asleep, Pree would pull herself erect in her crib and hold her arms to me. I would take her into my bed and hold her quietly. In our silence, I felt a great communion. She had an old, wise look, always understanding and unsurprised, as if she had been through all of this before. She understood and accepted. Even as she lay dying in an oxygen tent, Pree regained consciousness for one fleeting moment, and looked at me with that accepting expression meant to soothe me and tell me something I must never forget. There is a reason for everything. Life is not a random act. We have a destiny, and rebirth is our pattern.

Pree, who was in a coma, had stopped breathing in the taxi on the way to the hospital. But her breathing resumed. At St. Vincent's Hospital, the nuns asked if they could baptize her because she was so sick that she might not recover. Then they placed Pree in an oxygen tent, and I stayed by her side all day. The doctors explained that she had vomited in her sleep the night before and that some had entered her lungs, which they had cleaned out. Other than that, she was left alone. That evening, I went downstairs to call Bird, who was in California. I told him Pree had been hospitalized. I grabbed a sandwich to take back to her room. Around nine in the evening, she stopped breathing again. I screamed for a doctor. They brought a resuscitator. It didn't help, and they prepared to do a tracheotomy as I stood, helpless, at the foot of the bed. I was silently mouthing, "Even if you must grow up and watch your child die, live. Life is good, Pree, Live!" There is an old expression which says, "There are no atheists in foxholes." Yet I stood in that hospital room watching Pree die and I couldn't believe in prayer. One of the nurses finally noticed me, and I was asked to leave the room. I begged to stay, promising I would not become hysterical. They forced me to leave. I knew I had lost Pree, even before they came down the hall to tell me. They gave me the robe and booties she had worn to the hospital. My mother had arrived, and she took me home. No one could convince me to stop clutching Pree's robe. I held onto that robe for days, until Bird arrived. He finally managed to persuade me to let go of it. I still have them.

The night after Pree's death, the telegrams began to arrive:

March 7, 1954   4:13 A.M.
MY DARLING, FOR GOD'S SAKE HOLD ONTO YOURSELF.
CHAS. PARKER

March 7, 1954   4:15 A.M.
CHAN, HELP. CHARLIE PARKER

March 7, 1954   7:38 A.M.
MY DAUGHTER IS DEAD. I KNOW IT. I WILL BE THERE AS QUICK AS I CAN. IT IS VERY NICE OUT HERE. PEOPLE HAVE BEEN VERY NICE TO ME OUT HERE. I AM COMING IN RIGHT AWAY. TAKE IT EASY. LET ME BE THE FIRST ONE TO APPROACH YOU. I AM YOUR HUSBAND. SINCERELY, CHARLIE PARKER.

I was in deep shock as the telegrams, some of them strangely dispassionate, kept arriving, each one opening the wound even more. It took three days for Bird to return. When he arrived, he took the situation in hand with his marvelous strength. I had withdrawn into my grief, and my mother had been the fortress. When Bird walked in the door, she collapsed, weeping, into his arms. From that moment on, he took care of us all through the nightmare of Pree's funeral. American funerals are obscene: an open coffin so that loved ones, or anyone, can view the body. At Frank Campbell's funeral home, they whispered something to Bird and kept us waiting in the hall. When they finally ushered us in to view Pree,

I noticed that her nails and hair had continued to grow after her death and I was hysterical. I found out later why they had kept us waiting: Pree's mouth had reopened and they had been working their cosmetic miracle. Bird and I agreed that we didn't want a preacher mouthing hypocritical platitudes over her coffin. However, the people at Campbell's insisted that a nonsectarian minister be allowed to say a brief word. We decided to have Pree buried in the same cemetery as my father. (Only years later did I realize that the plots were in separate sections. Asking directions to Pree's grave, I was told it couldn't be where I said it was because that was where they put "the colored folk." My father was in the Jewish section.)

The day of the funeral, Bird was terribly ill with his ulcer. He was trying to hold me together, finalize the arrangements, and be host to the friends and relatives who came. He kept excusing himself to go and throw up in the toilet. The minister pontificated more than the few minutes we had agreed to. Bird sensed my anguish and held my arm so tightly that I knew that it was himself he was trying to control. At Pree's grave, I wanted to throw myself on top of her. Bird, who had been fulfilling his role of providing me with the strength of his support, took my arm to lead me away. When I pulled back, he felt rejected. Things went badly from then on.

Baird was still a baby, and I had gone through the abortion and the death of Pree that spring. New York was becoming the horror that it is now, and summers were particularly depressing. Bird decided we would take a house on Cape Cod for a month. We rented an old house with a private beach. We had Georgia, our maid, to take care of Kim and Baird. We wanted to spend some time alone as a family, to keep this time pure. However, one day Rudy Williams and his strung-out friends sniffed us out. Bird kept them on the beach, well away from the house and family. I was sure they had come bearing gifts. I was nervous and fearful. Bird had been taking massive doses of codeine, supposedly for his ulcer, although I knew it was to keep his habit at bay. When Bird came up from the beach, he forgot his shoes. He was carrying a struggling, wounded seagull in his arms. I never realized what big birds they were until I had one in my house! Bird was acting strangely. He went into the bathroom and I heard water running. Long sojourns in the bathroom usually meant trouble, so I banged on the door and asked what he was doing. He called out and said he needed my help. When I opened the door, he had blood running down his face from cuts where he had shaved off all his hair.

"God! You're so weird. Why did you do that?"

"Ah, Puddin', I had to. I had sand fleas in my hair." When he went back to retrieve his shoes, they had been washed away by the tide. Bird was shoeless and hairless for his gig in Boston the next day. He looked so weird that I refused to go with him. Then I starting thinking about all the wonderful music I was missing, so I took a bus to join him. He was playing a crowded, hot, tacky dance and I needn't have worried. No one thought his appearance was unusual; they figured Bird had embraced a new religion. Dick Twardzick drove us back to the Cape that morning. We spent the day on the beach with him and his old lady. He died shortly after. He was a gentle soul.

During that vacation, Bird and I had another bad scene in which even Georgia the maid got involved. Bird and I were screaming at each other. Bird, who was full of pills and whisky, had become abusive. When Georgia tried to intervene on my behalf, Bird informed her that I was not white, that I was a Jew. He screamed that everybody knew that Jews were black. He then snatched Baird from his crib, wrapped him in blankets, and announced that he was taking his son back to New York. It was four A.M. and I knew there was no way he could leave Cape Cod. Still, I was worried about Baird so I followed them. Baird walked to the nearest house, woke the people, and asked to use their phone to call a cab. I managed to calm him down and to talk him back to our house. But the idyll was spoiled. That summer was hard for both of us. I spent many nights with my mother.

When autumn came, I was looking for an escape. A girlfriend, who had moved to the small town of New Hope, Pennsylvania, invited me to visit. It was so different from the city. I fell in love with it immediately. I understood that, for my sanity, I must move away from the ugliness of the East Village.

Not long after my return to New York, Bird came home from an out-of-town gig a day late, very high and in an ugly mood. An hour after he got home, he asked me to pay the cabdriver, who was waiting outside. Bird had left his suitcase in the cab and, of course, the cabbie had split. Next, Bird said that he had made a will leaving everything to me and that it had been in the suitcase. He was acting strangely and his hostility then turned on me. I was frightened and unable to cope. Kim looked terrified. I ran out into the street and found two policemen who agreed to go back to the house with me. I wanted to get the children and a few things without any trouble from Bird. But Bird acted rationally with the police. He told them he had to work at Birdland that night, and they suggested he get a few hours sleep before the gig. When I left with the children, I knew we could return home after Bird had left for work. When we came back home, I was too uneasy to sleep, even though all the doors were locked. It was around four A.M. when Bird returned from the gig. He knocked on the door. When I didn't answer, he rang the bell and called out to me. I said that I was afraid to let him come in. Bird answered that he wouldn't bother me, that he just wanted to get a few things he needed. He just sounded tired and sad, so I unlocked our door. Then I quickly ran up to the first-floor entrance to the building and out to the street. I waited there for what seemed like hours, wanting to see what he would do before I cautiously opened the door. There wasn't a sound inside. I walked quietly down our long hall, still hearing nothing. I found Bird in the bathroom. He had swallowed iodine. There were open bottles of aspirin and other pills in the sink. My reaction was cold: "That was stupid. Now I'll just have to call an ambulance." As I was calling Bellevue, Bird wandered to the corner as if he didn't know what to do next. The ambulance arrived at the same time as the *Daily News* press car, and Bird was photographed in his long Bermudas being helped into it. Later, I called the hospital. They assured me that Bird was all right. Then I went to sleep, knowing that Bird was in someone else's capable hands.

I went to visit Bird the next day. He was in an end-of-the-line ward for alcoholics too indigent for the tender ministrations of private drying-out sanitoriums. He was yellow and smelled of paraldehyde. Dressed in institutional pajamas and robe, he looked pitiful and lost. But he tried to be cheerful. He told me that he had agreed to write five tunes for Charles Colin, who was publishing a saxophone book. Bird had been offered five hundred dollars, which would give Colin only the publishing rights. Colin promised me a mink coat if I could persuade Bird to turn over all ownership of the music. But it was no use listening to Colin's promises. He never paid Bird another penny for his composer royalties, and, if Bird had changed his mind, Colin would never have given me a mink coat. But then, a mink wouldn't have looked good with my jeans either. During my visits, I waited in the visitors' hall among the shuffling derelicts while Bird sought quiet sanctuary in the toilet to write the tunes. I delivered them to Colin.

One day, when I arrived at visiting hour, Bird already had two visitors. The young man, who had brought his badly painted religious canvases, was only an appendage to Sherry Martinelli, who called herself "The

Needle Lady." Sherry spoke about Ezra Pound, whom she had also visited, insisting that he wasn't insane, and citing the political motives behind his incarceration in St. Elizabeth's Asylum in Washington. She was convinced that Bird shouldn't be in Bellevue. On the contrary, I felt that being there might be his only salvation. I knew where the freedom of the streets was leading, and I was powerless to halt his rush towards death. At least here he was receiving both medical and psychiatric help, and he was unable to booze. Paraldehyde was the only drug he had access to, and he was eating regular meals.

I spoke with one of the psychiatrists who was sympathetic when he learned who Bird was. He promised to have Bird transferred to a medical ward where it wouldn't be so oppressive. He said that he would make sure that Bird would have some sort of treatment. I was very anxious to see him stay at Bellevue and very hopeful that he would be helped. On a subsequent visit, I was called into the head psychiatrist's office, and told that Bellevue had no facilities for such treatment. If I couldn't make arrangements for private care, Bird would be transferred to the state asylum. That was where Bud Powell's brain had been permanently damaged by shock treatments. When I pleaded that Bird was a very special creative man, I was briskly asked, "Madam, do you want a musician or a husband?" To explain that they were interchangeable was hopeless. This man had seen too many derelicts and his heart was cold. Uninvolved, he went on talking about Bird: "He's paranoid. He's a manic-depressive. If it were up to me, I'd shock him." I think much of the responsibility for Bird's death must lie on this man and his attitude. He told me to wait outside while he spoke with Bird. In five minutes, Bird came out of the office smiling. He had conned the shrink. He was being sent home. It was then that I knew it was all over. My efforts to find someone to subsidize hospitalization for Bird in a good sanitarium were all to no avail. Norman Granz refused any help. I called Bird's agent and pleaded with him. It was in their interests to have Bird on the street and recording.

While Bird was in Bellevue, I had found a small house in New Hope, Pennsylvania. It was this town he called home in his remaining months. Although he didn't spend a lot of time there because he was on the road or in New York, he often took the train to Trenton, very much the commuter in his vicuña coat and sneakers. Bird basked in his role as commuter. He enjoyed playing roles which he thought were part of the square, normal world. At the station in Trenton, he would come upstairs, newspaper under his arm, looking not quite like the other commuters, although he tried. I would meet him at the station in my funny 1937 Chevy, and he would disapprovingly wipe dust off the dashboard and tell me how important it was to keep a car clean. I think that during the brief period before his death, he most nearly reached his standard of middle-class living.

At home in New Hope, Bird mostly caught up on the sleep he wasn't getting while away. He had long ago exhausted his prescription for codeine and he would make long trips to distant drugstores to try to con some more. He never drank at home during that time, and was sweet and gentle with the children and me. Then, just before Christmas, he started drinking again. I had gone to New York to pick him up. We met in Penn Station as planned, but he was drunk and nasty. Although Bird had never harmed me, I was afraid of him when he was drunk. I didn't want the children's Christmas spoiled, so I ran away from him. I hid behind the pillars, sobbing. After that, I didn't see him for a month. Then one night, Bird drove up to our house in a new Ford Victoria. Baird was in New York having tests for a celiac condition. He was staying with my mother. When Bird saw the empty crib, he cried, "Tell me, Chan. My son is dead too!" I tried to reassure him, but he was irrational, and I couldn't get through. I think that, by then, he was out of touch with reality much of the time. The thought that he could show up at any time, in any condition, now that he had a car, filled me with panic. By now, it was difficult for me to be objective and not emotional. The next day, I found another house in Lumberville. I didn't tell Bird where we were living. The last communication I had from him was a letter forwarded from my mother. In the letter, Bird wrote that he would never harm me, and that it wasn't necessary to know where I was, just how I was.

I rented a checkroom concession in a dinner club in Trenton and tried to make a new start. One night at the club, a wave of longing for Bird swept over me, and I wrote a letter to him which I sent in care of his agency. I wrote that I had a premonition of his death, if not as a man, as a musician. On my way home that night, I stopped at a phone booth and called Birdland where he was working. They told me he was through, but it was only two A.M. and I knew he played until four. I didn't find out until it was too late that Bird had worked that night with Max, Mingus, and Bud, a volatile group. They had a scene on the stand, and Bud walked off. Bird went to the microphone and began calling, "Bud. Bud Powell. Come back here, Bud Powell." In retrospect, I realize that Bird was playing a word game. But Mingus put down his bass and told the embarrassed audience that this had nothing to do with jazz. When Mingus saw Bird later on the street, Bird was crying. He told Mingus, "It's all right. I won't be around much longer to bother anyone." Bird had once written a note to me:

> One breath in
> One breath out
> Domaine of the body
> Oh, where is thy release?

He was dead a week later.

The day after Bird died, a pigeon flew into Charlie's Tavern and roosted there for a week. No efforts could dislodge it. That freaked out a lot of people.

When I came home from work depressed, my mother, who was visiting me, thought I might have heard about Bird's death, and asked what was the matter. She wouldn't tell me until she was sure it was true. The doctors had said the body was that of a fifty-five-year-old man, and Bird was only thirty-four. Mother was afraid that I would be upset, would drive immediately to New York, and that I might have an accident. She awoke me the next morning with the news. It was raining. We put the children into the car, and drove to her apartment in New York. My uncle Lloyd went to Bellevue, identified Bird's body and had it sent to Campbell's Funeral Home where Pree had lain a year before. I'd have to manage this funeral alone. I was in shock and didn't know where to turn. I had thirty dollars. I called Norman Granz for advice and help. He didn't return my call, but had someone else call and ask for Chan Richardson. This was a slap in the face which clearly defined my position. I think his offer was three hundred dollars to bury Bird. Next, I went to Bird's agency, where I picked up my letter, which Bird had never received. I told them Bird's feelings about funerals. They insisted that he was a public figure and couldn't be put into the ground without pomp and circumstance.

Bird had given me instructions concerning his possible death when he was in Bellevue, and once on the way to the airport in bad weather. "Don't let them give me any benefit concerts and don't let them bury me in Kansas City." When I first saw Bird's body at Campbell's, it was no longer bloated and he looked young again. I slumped and might have fainted, but I felt him supporting me and I knew then that he would never leave me. He would haunt me forever as he had promised.

Then Doris showed up with her bigamous Mexican marriage certificate, which gave her the right to claim Bird's body and have it taken to a funeral parlor in Harlem, where billboards announced the upcoming funerals. (Why do they call them parlors?) She promised that if I didn't cause trouble and allowed Bird to be buried in Kansas City against his wishes, she would have him dug up after his mother Addie's death and be placed in the two-grave plot with Pree. She bought a new pinstripe suit for Bird and had a large crucifix placed at his head. I knew I could have nothing to do with planning the travesty that this burial had become. I was told a car would pick me up and bring me to Adam Clayton Powell's church, where the spectacle was to be held. It was raining again the day of the funeral. My brother Jimmy and Tony and Fran Scott accompanied me. I waited in the car an interminable length of time while seating arrangements were worked out. It wasn't easy with two widows. As mother of Bird's children, I was to play the role of the official widow, while Doris, who held the legal power, took a back seat. In the church, I looked around at the people who gather for any celebrity's funeral, and I wondered who was to blame for the death of Bird. Certainly Bird himself, and me. But I accused the unfeeling doctors and all the cab drivers who wouldn't pick him up because he was black. I accused the club owners, the record executives and the agents, bookers and managers who had exploited him. I accused the critics who didn't understand his music and the public that rejected it. This was a genocide of the spirit.

All Harlem had turned out: pimps, pushers, whores in their finery mingled with fans, and the businessmen who had had a vested interest in Bird when he was alive and looked forward to bigger profits now that he was dead. Adam Clayton Powell being a senator in Washington was replaced by the Most Reverend Licorice, who conducted the service. The coffin was surrounded by huge floral displays and my little daisy bouquet looked lost and innocent in that exotic garden. An organist played "The Lost Chord." (Bird never lost a chord in his life!) Reverend Licorice pontificated on what a fine man Charlie Bird had been. It was surreal. After the interminable service, there was another long wait in an alcove where Mingus mumbled insanely in my ear that it wasn't Bird in the coffin. Later, I realized what he meant. Then the coffin was clumsily carried past me by a sweating Teddy Reig, a distraught Leonard Feather, and others whose faces I didn't recognize. As they walked down the steps, someone stumbled and the coffin almost fell. It was placed in a hearse to be taken to Kansas City. I stood on the church steps shivering in the rain, saying goodbye as photogra-

phers and news cameras recorded my grief. I watched the man I had
loved for so many years being carried away from me on a long journey
to a place he hated and another long ceremony. Bird was on his way back
to Kansas City.

Forces were at work to organize a super-duper showbiz benefit for
Bird, bringing together the strangest crew yet. Hadn't Bird implored
me not to let them give him any benefit concerts? The organizers of
this humiliating and impractical scheme were Mary Lou Williams, Nat
Hentoff, Lennie Tristano, Mingus, and Maley Bartholomew Dufty. It
was to take place at Carnegie Hall. They forgot, or mostly didn't forget, to invite me. Fran Scott reminded them and I sat in her box. I
hadn't wanted to go, but I felt I had no choice since the proceeds were
supposed to go to Bird's two sons. They were using Baird's name to
raise money, and I was an unwilling pawn in the hands of forces I was
unable to stop. The show brought together a group of the oddest bed-
fellows yet. It opened with Bird's "Now's the Time" coming over the
loudspeakers in the darkened hall, and it closed with Sammy Davis Jr.
"doing his thang." That's all I remember about it. I wondered what those
misguided people could be thinking about, raising money for a two-year-
old's college fund when I didn't have the money to feed him the next day.
There was one practical lady there that night who didn't even know me,
but she realized that Bird had left me with no insurance or bank account.
Gerry Mulligan's wife took up a collection backstage and put the cash in
my hand. I had survived the funeral that I'd had no hand in, a benefit that
I hadn't wanted, and now I was free to return to New Hope with my grief,
to mourn in privacy.

My mother used to say that Bird bewitched me; in a way, it did
seem as if a spell had been cast over all of us. Time and distance were
suspended, and all events took on a dreamlike unreality . . . the good
dreams and the nightmares . . . and death was our houseguest. Bird had
a preoccupation with death, perhaps stemming from his father's murder.
Death was a lover whom Bird wooed constantly. It was ever-present in
Pree. In a macabre way, he even tried to connect it to me when he told me
I had the "stench of death" about me. This so distressed me that I repeated it to his psychiatrist, who felt that Bird was talking about himself.
Through all Bird's violence, his courtship of death turned inward upon
himself. I could do nothing, except hold on, drag my feet, and pull
him back towards life. All the time I was hoping to postpone the inevitable. I held on until I had to let go, lest I be pulled over the brink

into the darkness with him. Nothing he ever did overshadowed his love for me. But I always knew that even if he wore out my love, he would have his own way. In the letter I had mailed to him on the night he died, I had expressed my feelings in the following poem:

My love shrieks
Defying death
Cursing the waste
Of what might have been
Yet can never be.
For all my soul
Was not enough
To drain the poison
And leave the pure, unstained growth
Of man and talent.
I sucked the venom
From the wounds
Till my own life's blood
Became infected with imagined wrongs
And unfulfilled destinies
Admitting defeat
I made my stand
Then turned aside to convalesce
My strength returned with moral
Right and Sanity.
Why then, in the silences,
Does that pitifully weak voice rally,
Cry out in agony for release
And demand remembrance of failure?

Most of the correspondence I have from Bird, like the following two poems he wrote me, is a plea for understanding.

To my pretty little spouse
With headlights shining at me
Oh, shy one . . .
Please know me.
Why should pain wander so freely?
Absence of you is distorting me
Let me call you for something that isn't there

But still exists, away, lonely,
Put not astray.

A Portrait on Political Affairs

To play is to live and vice-a-versa
Play to live and vice-a-versa
Live play is vice perverse
Live verse is play.
To shun is to run
Running is shunning
But to shun running
Is shining shunning of running
Here is the day so long awaited
Sterile of the results contemplated
Unrest is whole and desire is nil
Yet here lies a soul that awaits you still.
Searching eternally for a dawning
a thought as the only incentive
knowing all the while there's bound to be.

That which one doesn't understand can become frightening, and the awesome mystery of Bird always frightened me. My mother used to say that Bird was a psychopathic liar and that I believed everything he told me. I did.

When I remembered the thin, unbloated body of the man I had loved with all my heart for thirteen years, with whom I had shared the birth of two children and the death of one, I could understand why Mingus rejected this body and cried "fraud." Bird had a power which carried on beyond death. Bird was a conservative man who believed in conservation. But that was part of his paradoxical nature because he overdid so many things. The air that Pres and Ben and the past school of saxophonists breathed out with their sound, Bird put into his horn. And that is what came out of the bell . . . a big, pure, wide sound. He didn't waste time, space, and effort with his fingers. They hugged the keys. That gave him his rapid execution.

Bird didn't believe in cluttering his heart, but his mind was cluttered with trivia: the dichotomy. Now my mind, too, is awash with millions of minutes of trivia: I hear him telling me, "You mustn't ever leave old Pop.

He loves you. Old Pop would die for you. Think how badly you would feel if I died and you had wasted these precious minutes." I see him in the bathtub or shower with the ever-present Camel in a cigarette holder. He was the only man I ever knew who smoked under the shower. I see his sweet walrus body. I see him with his poor swollen outsized hands trembling as he clumsily unhooked my bra. I see him asleep on the toilet. I see him walking around Birdland dressed as neatly as a Sunday boy. I see him laying soft and velvety on the bed, or sitting in a chair watching TV. I see the kids climbing all over him, Kim with her eyes bright and face flushed, a little awed by this strange giant who loved her. I see him in Cape Cod laughing, his hair full of the sand that Kim and Georgia had thrown. But most of all, I see him watching me with love in his eyes. "Thou wast not born for death, immortal Bird."

After Bird's death, I found it difficult to give away any of his possessions. I've never been able to hold back anything, and always felt I should share almost anything I had to give. But Bird was always able to keep his personal self private. The displays he put on were always because of the circumstances and not because of his feelings or thoughts. He never let the world intrude into our home. I had been haughty and proud because Bird had kept me invulnerable. Bird had been a battering ram between the world and me. There had been no situation he couldn't handle and I had always been safe and protected with him. He had never let any evil touch me. Now I was alone and I had never learned to cope. "That's dirty. That has nothing to do with you," were his answers to all the questions which might better have prepared me for a life without him. Consequently, when he died, I was an infant among the wolves. And they were voracious. One of the few kindnesses came from the Baroness Nica in whose apartment Bird died. She saved for me his horn, his car, and the few clothes in his suitcase. I had Baird. I thought I had Bird's name, but that was soon taken away, along with his body and my position as his wife.

7. PRELUDE

After the funeral, I returned to New Hope, unemployed. Because of all the publicity surrounding the funeral, the owner of the chic restaurant in Trenton where I had rented the checkroom decided it wouldn't do to have a white woman who had been living with a black man working in her posh club. I hadn't fit in anyway: my short hair, my clothes. I was just too different . . . weird they called it. The gig had been sad and lonely. The checkroom was cavernous, and after the dinner crowd left, things were quiet enough to allow me a few puffs now and then. Although the owner tried to foster an ambiance of quiet respectability, she looked as hard as Ma Barker and there were a lot of mafia types around the club. She was also a shrew who had made life so miserable for her husband, he had locked himself in a room and drunk himself to death. I wondered how fast you had to drink to die before you passed out. In my twenties I had been a rebel. Now I learned that to exist, one must conform. I had no identity. I was no one. I wasn't even Bird's widow, although I had lost my job for being close enough.

There was a lull in my life aside from that awful void of knowing Bird was no longer there with his love and protection. At the beginning, Bird said I was so young, it scared him: he described me wearing a blue suit on a ladder while painting my ceiling. As for an ending, there never could be one. But the memories came rushing back: It was 52d Street, I was around eighteen, bebop was new. I was alone in New York, life was a ball, and Bird was something I had never known. But somehow, life didn't swing anymore. All the things I had dug in my twenties seemed too strenuous now.

March was weeping cold tears for me from a freaky sky full of silent snow. New Hope was a white world. A million times a day I said his name aloud. He was never out of my thoughts. Spring had not yet come. For me, spring would never come again. One night, lost and lonely as a frightened child, I walked across a bridge. I began to run, but suddenly stopped, struck by the beauty of New Hope by moonlight. The yearning washed over me like a thick warm flood, and I cried, "Bird," and wept bitter tears for my lost love. Driving Bird's car brought him nearer to me. I would run from my house when the grief got too heavy, get into that car, and speed across back roads, not caring if I died, and feeling that if I did, the choice would be Bird's. I almost hoped some demonic ghost would spin the car out of my control and Bird would be waiting for me. I would park in the woods and release some of my anguish with tears. Driving that car was a religious experience. The radio was haunted because every time I turned it on, Bird would be playing. One night, a jazz DJ said he was dedicating the next song to "All the gals out there whose guys have gone. And Bird, Bird." I thought I must be imagining those whispered "Birds," but he played one of Bird's records and I knew he had been talking to me.

I found a job as waitress in a coffeehouse on the canal. The work was easy and I liked the patrons. Mel, the owner, wasn't overly enthusiastic about working hard, so he closed every day at five P.M. I made a deal with him: I would pay him rent and keep the place open after he closed. I only had one menu a night, but I had quality food. The menu was more imaginative than the hamburgers the regular patrons were used to. I served cheese and fruit, and Droste cocoa, and soon Mel's regulars were complaining about his food. Mel and I parted.

To be intimate with another man, especially a musician, seemed an invasion of Bird's privacy and dignity. I was still Bird's woman and wanted no other role or involvement. Bird's death, which took away my identity, left me wild, feeling ugly, in a quarantine, and reckless. But not reckless enough. Many young men came courting, mostly out of curiosity or in the hope of touching Bird through me. When I met a musician, I was on my guard. Did he know who I was? When was he going to drop a line about Bird? I was relieved to be mistakenly called Jan. Homosexuals were safe and I began hanging out a bit with the New Hope coterie. I lived in a constant state of suppressed hysteria and did a lot of aimless running around. I still couldn't face New York. When the urge to hear music became strong, I'd drive to the Blue Note in Philadelphia. One night, just after Clifford Brown's death, when I walked in and looked up at the sweat on Max Roach's beautiful face, I felt like it was Christmas. Max and I smiled at each other, although we were both grieving. He thanked me for smiling. Another time, Gerry Mulligan took me to a bar in Trenton where he played for me . . . but Gerry always liked to play anywhere, on any occasion. I wanted to be sure I was still a woman, but he observed protocol, as I did.

That summer, I was invited to be official widow at the Newport Jazz Festival dedicated to Bird. Zoot Sims and I went to see the Vanderbilt estate, The Breakers. Overwhelmed by the extravagance of it, I told Zoot that if it belonged to me, I would ball him on the front lawn. At a friend's house, I met an older man. A well-known actor, Victor was in a show at the Bucks County Playhouse. I was intrigued because he had scared me to shivers as a child when I had seen him in the villainous role of Injun Joe. We left the house at the same time and, in the garden, he tenderly kissed me. It was a kiss that was neither groping, intense, nor overpassionate. It was the kiss of an older man who intuited that I was a sleepwalker, and he offered it as therapy. I could respond or not; there was no involvement to threaten me, just my lonely need. Slowly, he brought me back to life, coaxing naturally, as a physician giving first aid to a comatose patient. If he hadn't been there at that moment, I might have frozen forever in the role of Bird's widow.

I was trying to support myself and the children by running weekly jazz concerts at a club, upriver at Point Pleasant. All the musicians rallied to my aid and came to work for me for token fees. Most of the Philadelphia DJs were generous with air plugs. I had the added pleasure of being able to hear music under ideal circumstances. The Modern Jazz Quartet, Max Roach and Clifford Brown, Jay and Kai, Lee Konitz, Herbie Mann, Tony Scott and The Six all gave concerts for me. No one could follow Bird in my life, though, and no one tried to. They knew he was a hard act to follow. After the concerts, the musicians would come to my house for a drink and, if they were stouthearted, a swim. I was living in Lumberville next to a canal by Tohickon Creek and the Delaware River. When the mist hung low on the surface of the water, I was tempted to believe there might be strange creatures lurking beneath the surface, waiting to pull someone under.

August of '55 brought Hurricane Diane and it rained for two days. The river was rising and Tohickon Creek had become a torrent. When I went to bed, the radio was carrying flood warnings and a good part of our land bordering on the creek had been washed away. By morning, the river had become indistinguishable from the canal, which was ominously creeping onto our front lawn. Before leaving the house, my mother insisted that the children eat a nourishing breakfast. I grabbed the horns, some of Bird's music, his scrapbooks, leashes for the dogs, and, on the advise of my mother, some candles. I threw everything in the car, admonishing my mother, the two kids, and three dogs to hurry. As we left the house, pieces of timber from washed-out houses upriver floated by with rats clinging to them. We were the last car to cross the small bridge over the creek. We lost our brakes as we drove through the four feet of water covering the road.

That night we had dinner at the church which had been set up as an emergency station. While my mother and the kids slept on cots at the high school, I went back to Lumberville with a lantern and rifle to protect our belongings from looters. No looters could have come within a half mile of our house which had water past the second floor. The only looters were the gawkers from Trenton who arrived the next day to scavenge the state-protected rhododendrons. The army also arrived, dispensing blankets, fresh water, and protection. I took a rowboat, ducking under the electric wires, to go back and see if the rumors that our house was floating downriver were true. The house was still standing, precariously hanging over Tohickon Creek. At the same time, I managed to rescue our cat from the attic of our neighbor's house.

The next two weeks were spent with our kind neighbor, Jack Hobson, who had always come to my rescue in times of need. Of course, everything in our old house was covered with two feet of vile-smelling mud. I washed off my records. Volunteer help, Mennonites and even local businessmen, arrived from as far as a hundred miles away. I remember one good soul who patiently turned over every shovelful of slime so I could search for nonreplaceable keepsakes. (More than twenty years later, when Kim and her husband rented that same house, it still smelled of mud.)

The Red Cross moved in. My case was handled by Mr. Neiswander, a pharmacist from Detroit who seemed to be fascinated and a bit titillated by my lifestyle. That is the only reason to explain how I came out of the flood in better condition than before it: Mr. Neiswander, courtesy of the Red Cross, set us up in a new house with new furniture, paid three months' rent, and gave me food vouchers and a ton of coal. He was accused of favoritism in my case, and transferred, but not before every shabby thing I had lost was replaced with a new item of my choosing, except the stereo: even though I let him know I could skip the sewing machine, he said he sympathized, but there was no way the Red Cross could cover a stereo. It seemed as if fate had washed away my old life and given me a brand new start.

All I needed was a job. One of my neighbors who had a construction firm offered me a job selling shingles in Perryville, Maryland. I was to work on commissions and could choose my own days and hours. When I said that I didn't know anything about selling shingles, he said there would be no problems and was vague about the job. Then he cautioned me not to discuss it with anyone. The following weekend I drove to Perryville and checked into the motel where my expenses were paid. My job consisted of choosing a random house and telling the owners it had been selected for a before and after advertising campaign. We would completely reshingle it at a reduced cost. It was an old scam, but I was no good as a con man. After three weeks, I'd made only one commission.

Being alone with too much time on my hands was not good for me. I spent a lot of time around the motel pool or watching the sea in Havre De Grace across the bridge. I found myself calling Bird's name; I was alone, frightened and wanting him so badly I could taste his saltiness. Even knowing he was irrevocably lost to me, how could I accept this? How could I think of other men sharing the intimacy that only he had known? How could I give myself so completely ever again? Who could understand my shy reticence? Who would love me as he did? Who could have his warmth and tenderness? Who could be all things to me? I dwelled on the empty spaces in my life; how, when I lost Pree, I lost my heart, and how, when Bird died, I lost my soul. Grief never lessens in intensity; in time, it simply becomes less demanding. . . . At sunset, the sea seemed to whisper to me: "Never forget. Follow the fishermen restlessly walking up and down the shore, reeling in their lines, and remember. Listen to the sound of a million tinkling pieces of glass clinking gently together as the soft wind sends wavelets to lap on pretty pebbles, and remember. The sunset is behind you, and so is the world you hunger for so badly that you ache." Was this what Bird was thinking of when he spoke of the place near Marseilles where the earth drops off, where the sea is the bluest blue, and the sunset is a red ball dropping into the sea? But no, here the sun sets behind you. Come back, Bird. How bittersweet to adore you. I need you. I want you. I need to be secure in your love again. I'll die too. There is no more music.

I wasn't cut out for the construction business, so I decided to return to the restaurant business. I opened a place in New Hope that I called "Bird's Nest." I sublet my house to Fran and Tony Scott, and moved into the two small rooms above the restaurant for the winter. "Bird's Nest" was cozy and warm with a fireplace. My old friend and neighbor, Jack Hobson, helped me redecorate the place. In addition, he supplied me with good beef, from the Black Angus cattle raised on the farm where he worked. I could cook, but I didn't know the first thing about purchasing. When a customer came in, I'd send the kids to the co-op to buy a loaf of bread and whatever was needed. I cooked in butter, used Pepperidge Farm bread and Droste chocolate. I had a soda fountain and an assortment of large apothecary jars of the candies I remembered from my childhood: red dollars, gummy and chewy, malted milk balls, yellow marshmallowy bananas with a flavor somehow reminiscent of gas stations, nigger babies, milk duds, red or black licorice whips, and jawbreakers whose layers changed color and flavor as they melted in your mouth. I tried to find as many of these penny candies as possible, and I sold them at cost. A few of the unmarried swingers ate dinner there every night. I fed musicians free and ran tabs for friends. I ran the place all alone in the winter when there were no tourists, but in the summer I had to become an employer. I hated it. No more leisurely espresso crowd; this was the grilled cheese/hamburger horde, and it was strictly business.

I escaped to New York whenever I could. I liked to stop by Charlie's Tavern. One night I ran into a friend I hadn't seen for a long time. "I haven't felt this good since I came in here," I confided. He replied, "When was that, fifteen years ago?" Charlie's Tavern was where I met Phil Woods. There were three good alto players after Bird died: Cannonball Adderley, Jackie McLean, and Phil. But Phil seemed to be Bird's most likely musical successor. (Although we had never met, Phil had caught my eye the previous summer: I couldn't stop my home movie camera from focusing on him while I was filming the band in Newport.) Now he bought me a drink and asked if I would meet him later. He told me he'd be the drunk in the back booth. We didn't connect that night at Charlie's Tavern, but Phil stayed in my thoughts. When he played in Philadelphia with Dizzy Gillespie's big band, I went to listen. Phil had a girl spending the week with him, but he was happy to see me. He left her sitting at a table and took me to the bar for a drink. I invited him to spend the weekend with me. When Phil came, he spent the afternoon raking leaves and fixing Baird's bike. He played his saxophone while I was cooking dinner. It was good and natural to have those sounds in the house again. After dinner, he carried his plates to the sink. He didn't jump on me. Clearly, this was a different kind of man. I was intrigued.

Phil had graduated from high school when he was only fifteen and had gone to New York to attend the Julliard School of Music. (He was still in school when the first of his two daughters was born.) When the liaison that produced his two daughters broke up, Phil was shattered. I couldn't understand why any woman would want to leave him. He was not aggressive. He was gentle and had a wonderful sense of humor. He was Irish, gregarious, full of fun and he liked to party. Still, I was sure that, with love and understanding, he wouldn't be the drunk in the back booth. One night I was listening to him play and wondering what I'd do if Bird walked in the door. At that exact moment, Phil interpolated, "I Love You." Since he was six years younger than me, I called him "Young Phil

Woods." When I worried about the day when I'd be fifty and he'd be forty-four, he'd reply, "You're my woman, Chan. I'll never leave you." But his middle-class parents must have been frantic for their son: They must have hoped that he was just sowing wild oats with a chorus girl. After all, I was not only older than he, I also had two children.

After an unsuccessful year in the restaurant business, I went back to dancing. I accepted an offer from a choreographer I had worked for to captain a line in Shrewsbury, Massachusetts. Phil's folks lived nearby, in Springfield. It seemed like a good opportunity for Phil to spend some time with them. We could be near each other and I could work. I hadn't danced in five years and it was hard work indeed. I was thirty-one, the oldest in a group of girls in their late teens, most of whom were on their first job. On opening night, my muscles were groaning. It took all my willpower to make my legs move. My dancing comeback was less than thrilling, because I was really too old.

Between shows, the boss came to the dressing room and asked if the chorus girls would join a large party of men at a ringside table for a drink. They were obviously regular customers. We were introduced to them, but most reverently to Al, who the other men called "The Champ." Their glasses were raised in tribute, as they sang the new words they had written to an old song in his honor. What was the best way to deal with this nest of small-time Shrewsbury mafia? Figuring that candor would be my best strategy, I explained to one of the least frightening lieutenants that these girls were a bunch of virgins. I hoped that this would keep the men at bay. It seemed to work, because, although we spent most nights between shows at their table, they never gave us any trouble. One night, "The Champ" even wiggled his cigar at Phil! In fact, Phil was picking me up after work to take me to meet his parents. Since I didn't have to work the next day, we planned to spend it in Springfield. At closing time, the drinks were lined up on the table. I was thirsty and I chug-a-lugged a few stingers before leaving. When the car pulled up at Phil's parents' house, I was drunk. I stepped out of the car and threw up. In spite of everything, his parents were gracious.

I felt that there was a promising basis for marriage with Phil: He was not only willing to follow Bird, but he had the strength to cope with all of the comparisons and antagonistic attitudes of black acquaintances who would resent that Bird's son had a white father, and to face the ultimate question of whether he was playing Bird's horn. In September, we decided to get married. But it was just a little more than a year since Bird's death, and I knew what the Ides of March would bring. That was to be the last test, so we set the date for the wedding: April Fool's Day, the first of April. Phil's parents were glad their son was marrying an older woman and settling down. His mother was more than willing to pass the reins to me. Finally, we were married on May 19th by Squire Delacy. The squire was the town barber, who also issued driver's licenses and even dog licenses. Between haircuts, he performed the wedding ceremony in front of his "God Bless Lindy" banner and his wife played the piano. Phil's best man was Hal Bach, my good friend and ex-lover. My mother babysat with Kim and Baird and provided the wedding feast . . . salami sandwiches and champagne. I wasn't feeling well and went to bed. Phil and Hal drank the champagne.

Our wedding had been delayed because, on the day we had originally planned to be married, Phil was driving my car to New Hope when he was stopped by a state trooper. The trooper immediately spotted a stemless pipe on the seat and further investigation disclosed an ounce of pot that Phil had bought to celebrate the nuptials. He was taken to the Jersey City lock-up. (Phil liked to say that his was the only time he ever managed to get off the New Jersey Turnpike without paying a toll.) He wasn't allowed to call me until late evening. By that time, it was so late that we had to wait until the next day to arrange bail. Phil was given two years suspended sentence with probation, but the FBI confiscated my car, saying it had been used to transport narcotics.

Even though Phil bought a baby-blue Buick convertible, I decided to try to get back my car: a '53 Raymond Loewy-designed Studebaker Commodore, the first American sports car. I had traded in Bird's green Ford Victoria for that car, and it broke my heart. Bird's car had been my refuge. I had driven it at sixty miles an hour on winding back roads to every wilderness spot I could find. I knew every dirt road in Bucks County so well that I could turn off the headlights at night and navigate by moonlight and instinct. However, I'd lent the Ford to Hal Bach and he had returned it with a cracked block: I really had no choice but to trade it in. I decided to file an appeal for my Studebaker. There had been a lot of criticism of the standard practice of the authorities keeping the cars from drug arrests and using them as unmarked police cars.

I've always believed in taking grievances to the head man, so I wrote a letter to Robert Anderson who was Ike's Secretary of the Treasury, telling him I was a poor widow with two small children . . . twang, twang, twang . . . and what a hardship it was for me without a car. Just because

I had been a good Samaritan who lent it to a friend . . . twang, twang, twang, etc. . . . I omitted saying that Phil had been on his way to marry me when he was arrested in my car. In fact, I also didn't mention the fact that we were now married and had another car. I got a reply from Bob himself, saying that he, personally, was looking into the matter.

Not long after I received the letter, a stranger appeared at the kitchen door, saying he was from the state narcotics bureau and had come to see me about my car. The timing couldn't have been worse! My letter had said I was a widow, and now I had a husband (who was in the living room getting high at that very moment), and a new car was in front of the house. I knew I should be doing some fast thinking, but I was stoned myself. Talking to the narc sent me into a panic, and I began babbling. When he asked about the new Buick, I told him I had rented it. He asked from whom and how much the monthly payments were. I gave the name of a nonexistent car dealer and made up the amount of my payments. Just then, Baird ran into the house and asked, "Where's Pop?" When the inspector asked who Pop was, I replied, "Oh, they call him Pop, and he calls them Poop." At this brilliant response, we both knew the farce was over. He asked to speak to Phil, who leveled with him. The nice narc said that if our local police chief gave a good report on us, we'd probably get the car back. Our chief was an old retired vice squad cop from Philadelphia who knew the score. He was more concerned with the local homosexuals debauching young boys than with an old head like me. We became a two-car family.

Point Pleasant, July 18, 1957

Yesterday a thrush knocked part of her nest down from the eaves near Baird's window. There was a small bird in it, too young to fly. This same awkward mother had already lost one of her newly hatched young, when it fell, unfeathered and scarcely formed, onto the ground below. In her anguish, had she never thought to check out how her neighbors constructed their nests? When I placed this second baby, frightened but alive, under the tree, she hovered over, flying frantically from limb to limb, calling cries of encouragement. At last, her baby tweeted piteously, clumsily fluttered its wings and flew with great effort a foot or two away. It clung precariously to a lily while its mother flew worms to its beak. "Eat, darling."

When I went to bed that night, it was still sitting there alone, abandoned and frightened. Having seen it fly a little, I hoped it would be safe until morning. Today, Kim found it dead, a gift from a sated cat. The mother sits in the tree calling her dead bird child. Yesterday Pree would have been six.

I wanted to give Phil a son. He was a father in every way to Kim and Baird and they adored him. He had two girls of his own and I thought the greatest gift I could give him would be a son. Two years after we were married, Gar was born. He was a beautiful blond baby, passive and serious.

> The family is all. All is the family:
> the roots, the truth, constant life renewal.
> Friendship satisfies the momentary need,
> fulfills transitory emptiness,
> the hole, the space.
> But the papa, the mama and the babies
> are as basic as a pride of lions
> or a family of baboons.
> Beyond all intellectual reasoning,
> instinctively, intuitively,
> the family builds a fire
> against wild beasts
> before their cave,
> and differ, not the slightest,
> from the family once removed . . .
> Neanderthal.

Kim had received Rudy the Rooster as an Easter present. He arrived as a chick and, since our cat Jazz never bothered him, he was on his way to roosterhood, tame and devoted. He would follow me around the yard, and even tried to follow me into the house, somehow managing to climb up the stairs when I went inside. One day, I glanced out of the window to see a squawking, thrashing Rudy being carried off by a stray cat who had been hanging around the barn. Screaming, I chased the cat through the blackberry brambles, but she eluded me in an impenetrable thicket of thorns. Poor Rudy! At this point he was beyond rescue and I had no eyes to view the remains. Another Bird gone. I sobbed all day, and when Phil came home, I demanded he board up all the possible entrances to the barn where the cat had been living. That evil animal appeared the next day and tried to obtain entry to her repossessed domain. She had a noticeable bulge and, not realizing it was Rudy, my hard heart melted. The poor thing had simply been trying to nourish her unborn kits. "Unboard the barn, Phil. That poor mother needs a home." We named this undomesticated creature "Jezebel." She was completely wild and Kim spent long hours trying to tame her, enticing her with choice morsels. Before long, Jezebel was indeed pregnant and soon gave birth to a litter of six savage kittens. Then she was pregnant again and again and . . . Jazz split, leaving us with his wild, thankless and numerous (twenty-four) family. The cats were in the trees, underfoot and in the cellar where they continued to breed more cats and more fleas. The house was becoming uninhabitable. When Quincy Jones asked us to join "Free and Easy" in Europe, we were relieved to have a reason to leave. The only problem was the disposal of the cats. The SPCA only kept animals for ten days. If they hadn't been adopted by then, they were put to sleep, as it's euphemistically called. We found the "Bide-A-Wee" in New York, which, for a small contribution, would care for an animal until a home was found for it. Every time Phil went to New York for a recording date, he would take whichever cats and kittens we could capture, a pocketful of five dollar bills and drive away with cats climbing all over him. At that time, Phil was working mainly in the studios, so that, by the time we had to leave for Europe, they had all been taken to New York. All, that is, except Big Daddy, the handsomest of all, who was last seen heading for the woods to restore the balance of nature.

Joseph Hiatt Jr. and Minerva
(front row), Uncle Alva,
Mina, Nell. Chan Parker
Archives. CPA

Mildred O'Violet Lankton, Glennwood, Iowa, 1905. CPA

My mother, about 1920. CPA

Mamie Brodis, my nurse. CPA

With my parents: I was then about three
years old. CPA

Johnny
Bothwell, my
first alto
saxophonist.
Photo X

Dave Tough.
DR

Kim, Bill
Heyer, and me.
Photo X

At the Club Iceland,
1947. Photo X

To Chris —
My only Darline
for ever, octsat
Charlie Park

Bird, about 1949. Photograph by Bill Gottlieb

Baird, Pree, Kim,
1953. CPA

Only extant painting by Bird:
his vision of Pree as an adult,
painted after her death, in
1954. CPA

Life was so sad after Pree's
death! CPA

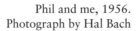

Recopying the orchestra-
tions of Quincy Jones,
1960. Buddy Catlett on
bass, Les Spann on guitar.
Photograph by Susanne
Schapowalow

My singing class at
Ramblerny, 1965. Photo X

Kim and Baird at the Bird's Nest,
1955. Photograph by Hal Bach

Phil and me, 1956.
Photograph by Hal Bach

Gar, 1959. CPA

The beginning of our life in Europe:
Aimée, Phil, Chan, Gar at
Kensington Gardens, London,
1968. Photograph *Jazz Magazine*

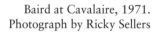

Baird at Cavalaire, 1971.
Photograph by Ricky Sellers

Phil, 1971. Photograph by Coleman Andrews

Kim and Chan on a
trip to Sweden, 1988.
Photograph by
Christer Landergren

Benjamin Alekzander
Sellers, son of Kim
and Ricky, at Champ-
motteux, 1985.
Photograph by Wivi-
Ann Hultin-Wells

David Ancker, my
musical guru. DR

Cannes, 1988, at the première of *Bird*. Clint
Eastwood and Chan in her trademark dress

Mildred at Champmotteux,
1989. CPA

Mildred in 1991, at the wedding of Gar and Georgann. Photograph by Alek Sellers

Champmotteux, 1988.
Photograph *Daily Mail*

Chan Parker. CPA

8. SCHERZO

"Free and Easy" was a remake of Harold Arlen's "St. Louis Woman."
The show was to tour Europe for a year and then open on Broadway,
starring Sammy Davis. Quincy Jones and Billy Byers arranged the music
and assembled an augmented big band which was part of the action on-
stage. The action took place in turn-of-the-century Storeyville and the
costumes and set depicted the sporting life. Phil flew ahead to Brussels for
rehearsals. I stayed behind to put the furniture in storage, sell the cars,
and close up the house. Two of the dogs went to a friend's kennel. The
logistics of the move were formidable: Gar would stay in the States with
my mother until Phil and I were settled in Paris for the long run of the
show. Our third dog, Turki, would stay with Gar. Kim and Baird would
go to school in Switzerland, Phil's steady salary for a year allowing this
extravagance. Somehow we were organized and ready to leave by the end
of November on the *Bremen,* the pride of the German Lloyd Line.

An Atlantic crossing in November can be rough. I get seasick in a
hammock! During the five-day crossing, I spent most of the time in bed. It
had been a mistake to cross on the German line, and when I later saw *Ship
of Fools,* I recognized some of the passengers. Our authoritarian steward
always burst into our cabin without knocking and terrorized us all. He
made up our berths with the kids still in them and ordered me to go on
deck to get some air. I'd stagger out weakly, breathe deeply, and run to the
nearest head. Our dining room steward, who was a special favorite of
Kim and Baird, was young and sympathetic. He couldn't believe the enormous amount of food the kids consumed and brought them leftovers from
all his tables. We found out later that Kim had worms. Baird just needed
the calories for the energy he was expending destroying the ship. As I
appeared for dinner only once, and briefly at that, the children had my
portion also.

Kim and Baird ran wild. I was aware of the havoc inflicted on
both passengers and crew, but I was confined to my sickbed. One
night as Baird was admiring himself in the mirror, the sink collapsed

under him. I called for help, and two beefy workmen answered. Sweating copiously and muttering angrily in German, they finally managed to sever the pipe connections. Two glorious waterspouts inundated the cabin and the workmen ran to get their heavy equipment. I surveyed the chaos from my bed, and complaints about my unchaperoned six-year-old came pouring in with the water. When the workmen returned, they decided to attack the pipes from behind. They threw all of our clothes out of the closet and then disappeared inside with brace and bit. As the ship pitched on, they began drilling through the closet wall into the bathroom to finally stem the flow.

On our last night at sea, we were all too excited to sleep. The kids finally drifted off around midnight, but they were soon awakened by the ship's alarm. The engines stopped. A deranged passenger, still wearing pajamas, had managed to get on deck, where he had climbed the rail, and gone overboard. The ship then circled for three hours, but he had vanished without a trace. We finally landed at Cherbourg where there was a dock strike, strikes being the normal state of affairs in France. The children and I took the boat train to the St. Lazare station in Paris. We had a four-hour layover before our departure for Amsterdam from another train station, the Gare du Nord. We discovered ham sandwiches, French style, and I sampled the Beaujolais of that year. Without sleep, the children were tired and cranky.

Our train reservations had been made on the boat. When we arrived at the station, eighteen pieces of luggage in hand, the man at the gate told us that our tickets were for the following day. We all cried. He was touched and let us board to take our chances of finding seats. We sat in the dining car. Phil met us in Amsterdam. What a relief it was to let him take the burden of luggage and kids. He took us to the Carleton Hotel, where he had rented a suite. Being accustomed to Holiday Inns, the kids and I couldn't believe the sumptuous marble bathroom with gold-plated fixtures, king-size towels and seven-foot bathtub. Phil ordered champagne. We gorged on room service.

We fell in love with Amsterdam: We loved the flower market, the church bells that rang every quarter hour, the good people of Holland riding their bicycles, the delicious milk, butter, and cookies. We were completely gassed by the city and its canals. Baird spent his days riding up and down the elevator with his new friend, the elevator boy. This was also my introduction to European theaters, which always seemed to have a cozy little bar tucked away somewhere. This is very conducive to missing a lot of action on stage.

The opening night of "Free and Easy" at the *Théâtre Carré* was a hit and miss affair. When the cast and band went into final rehearsals in Amsterdam, they still hadn't had a run-through of the show together. Because the musicians were also acting, they played the score without a conductor and had memorized all the music. Even if you knew your Storeyville history, the action of the play was total confusion. Bobby Breen, the director, was fired after the opening, and replaced by Donald Mckayle, the choreographer. Throughout the three-week run, the Dutch audiences never really understood the show.

After the Amsterdam run, the show opened in Brussels. The band checked into a very down-home boardinghouse out in the suburbs next to what was left of the world's fair. From the dormer window in the children's room, they could see the twinkling lights on the Atomium in the fair grounds. The food was superb to our American palates. My two voracious offspring immediately made friends in the kitchen and gorged themselves on chocolate mousse. Madame Williams, the owner, was motherly to all those who appreciated her French-style cooking. However, it was a long ride from the pension to the theater, and the swingers in the band eventually moved to an expensive hotel in town. We stayed on with Madame Williams, and had our transplanted Christmas celebration in the auberge. We bought a small tree which Kim and Baird decorated with the colored paper chains they made. I added the final touch with my jewelry: strings of pearls look very nice on a Christmas tree.

We all loved Porter Kilbert, the other alto player in the band. He carried Christmas with him every day and had a way with words:

"He was pissing on my head and telling me it was raining."

"She was so old she could tell time by the Rosetta Stone."

"Last night I was in the seamier section of town and I saw an alligator dressed in a kimono."

"I told her to come here . . . to throw a saddle on a rat, or ride a cockroach."

Porter had a good soul but a bad heart, for which he took enormous amounts of nitroglycerine. Phil had been his roommate before we arrived and worried that if Porter fell down, they would be blown to smithereens. Porter started the day with a glass of scotch and a Heinekin which Baird brought to his room every morning. He called Baird "my main man" and gave him a Swiss army knife for his birthday.

The kids needed a more formal education and they had already missed two months of school. So when the band left for dates in Utrecht and Rotterdam, the children and I boarded a night train to Switzerland where they had been enrolled at an expensive boarding school called Beau Soleil in Villars. Once again, Baird was too excited to sleep, and kept us awake. Baird was wigging out by the time we changed trains in Geneva for the breathtaking ride along Lake Leman. In Bex we took a funicular up the mountain. When we finally reached the school, the headmistress wondered if she would be able to cope with Baird. I assured her a good night's sleep would remedy everything, and left the children in her care. It cost us one hundred dollars a week, but the children learned to ski, skate, and keep their elbows off the table.

I took the train to Paris where I was to join Phil. On the train, I shared a compartment with Charlie Chaplin's secretary, who gave me an "inside scoop": Oona peeled grapes for Charlie! Phil and I took a room in a quiet hotel near the Eiffel Tower. France was in the throes of the Algerian War and, because plastic bombs were a daily occurrence, people were avoiding theaters and public places. The few who braved the bombs to come and see "Free and Easy" couldn't understand a word of the hip, black patois. Although morale was low among the cast, nothing could spoil the pleasure that Phil and I took in Paris. We both felt we had come home. However, we were tired of living in hotels and missed our family. Gar was now eight months old. We decided to send for my mother, Gar, and our dog Tuki. We would sublet an apartment in the suburb of Sceaux. We could bring off this coup by enrolling Kim and Baird in a French school, thereby saving one hundred dollars a week. Soon Phil was a commuter again.

Just after we were settled in the Paris suburbs, the producer's wife confirmed the rumor that the show was folding. "The party's over" was her quaint way of dropping the news. But for us, the party was just beginning, and we knew it. This was the best thing that could have happened; the band was free of a turkey and ready to shake up Europe. Quincy had one concert booked at the Olympia Theater in Paris and a weekend gig in Sweden. The band had been rehearsing every day and it was a bitch. We all had such faith in the band that it was enough to make all the musicians pass up free transportation home with the show and stay on in Europe to take a chance with Quincy. The Olympia concert was a sellout. At the concert, the producer of "Free and Easy" came backstage to hear the band and was stunned by the energy of seventeen musicians turned loose. After the triumph at the Olympia, Sweden was a success. That sewed it up and Quincy was able to book a long tour which lasted almost a year.

I tried to join the band on the road whenever it was possible. When they had a few days booked in Milan, Genoa, and Turin, I decided to take Kim and Baird to see Italy. As I went through customs with the children in

Milan, the agent pulled us aside until everyone on our flight had passed through. He then asked me what I was doing with these bambinos and whether I had permission to take them out of the country. The name on my passport was Woods, but the children had a separate passport in the name of Parker. I waved my wedding ring in his face and pointed two fingers in the air yelling (as if that would improve his English or my Italian), "Two, duo, two husbands!" By the time he agreed to let us into the country, the last airport bus had departed. We pulled up at Phil's hotel with a twenty-eight-dollar cab tab. The next day we piled into the band bus and merrily toured Italy.

Although she had come over with the show as a dancer, Jerri Gray had not returned to the States when the show folded. She had stayed on with the band as Ake Person's old lady. Ake was a Swedish trombone player, a blond Viking, and Jerri was small, black, hip, and funky. They adored each other, although Ake used to wonder why she said he was full of "sheet" one minute, and in the next sentence she would say he wasn't "sheet." Soon he mastered the 125th Street argot and was calling her his little black bitch. He even mastered the various nuances of *motherfucker*.

Julius Watkins, who played French horn, soon earned the nickname "Phantom" through his many disappearing acts. He invariably forgot his horn or mouthpiece, but he never forgot his flask of hot tea and spirits.

Later, when the band was in Spain, I wanted to join Phil, but our funds were too low to finance a ticket from Paris to Madrid. I went to the local Parisian rib joint, Haynes, where we were good customers. They agreed to cash a check drawn on our New Hope bank account. I made it out for the amount of the train fare with only a few francs to spare, knowing that Phil would meet me. I bought a ticket for the night train to Madrid, sent Phil a wire to let him know what time the train would arrive, bought a few goodies for the trip, and found an empty compartment where I made myself comfortable with our Maltese terrier, Tuki. The train finally left three hours late, due to a strike. I had no way to let Phil know about the delay, but I figured I'd deal with that when I arrived. The conductor came for my ticket and asked for Tuki's. A ticket for a dog? He cost ten percent of the regular fare! After paying for Tuki's ticket, I was left with only eight francs, but that would be enough for a phone call when I arrived in Madrid. During the night, a rough-looking man joined me in my solitary compartment. He sat opposite me and began speaking in French. Tuki, who barely weighed six pounds, snarled. This didn't discourage my suitor, who moved to the seat next to me and started doing some heavy breathing. Tuki, who seemed to understand where this cat was at, became more and more menacing. When I warned the man that Tuki was "très méchant," he left. So far, the trip was off to a bad start.

I finally dozed off, but I was awakened at dawn by someone banging on the window and motioning me off the train. What had happened while I was sleeping? I stumbled off the train, still half asleep, to learn that we were at the Spanish border in Hendaye, where Franco had accepted the unholy hand of Hitler. This was as far as the train was going. Since our train had left three hours late, we had missed the connecting train and the next one wasn't due until that evening. I joined the customs line with the Spaniards. They all looked rather poor, and the rich American with her dog was the target of some hostile stares. I remember that they ate dogs in Spain, and Tuki was a tender morsel. We were still eight hours from Madrid and I began to panic. Someone with a little English informed me that a deluxe train was due in ten minutes, at the cost of an additional eighty francs. I had the eight, but I was shy the zero. I went to the Cook's Tours office in the station and asked if they would call their Madrid branch to get the fare from Phil. However, it was Sunday, so their Madrid branch was closed. I asked the ticket seller if he would take a check on the Solebury National Bank. The what? The train pulled into the station in all its streamlined glory. As the conductor got off, I explained my predicament: small dog, small money, and no town in sight. He didn't speak English and only partly understood my distress. I offered him my watch. He shook his head in a definite "no." The passengers, more fortunate than I, boarded and the train prepared to pull out. As I stood there holding my little dog, a tear ran down my cheek. The conductor's hard heart melted and he motioned me aboard. I was sure everyone on the train knew my disgraced state, and Tuki and I made the journey like pariahs. Tuki had to stay in his basket and the heat was oppressive. The plains whizzing by were dusty and barren. The passengers who could pay were being served lunch and big, cold, frosty bottles of mineral water. The signs in the toilet read "Don't drink the water" in three languages. My thirst was enormous.

The train pulled into Madrid at four o'clock, one hour before Phil was due to meet us. I was escorted into an airless room, swarming with flies, and given a chair. Tuki badly needed to relieve himself, but the men in the room wouldn't let me out until they had my fare in hand. I called the hotel. Phil was out. I called back and asked to speak with anyone from the Quincy Jones orchestra. They were all at the bullfights. I must have sounded distressed, because the lady at the other end of the line asked if anything was the matter. I blurted out my problem and she sent a bellboy to ransom me. I went to the hotel to await my bloodthirsty torero who had fainted at the first picador. The band was in Madrid to do a television show. We spent the next ten days swimming in a chic pool, drinking sangria, and eating paella while Quincy was trying to raise the money to get us all out of town. He asked each musician how much he needed. It wasn't just an orchestra; we were a family.

Quincy's next tour was for Norman Granz with Nat King Cole. Baird and I went to the rehearsals with Phil. Norman cold-shouldered me during rehearsals although his entourage made a fuss over "little Bird." I never had to worry about Baird the year we spent in Europe. There was always someone ready to look after him and he had unusual independence and authority for such a young age. Since there were no available tickets for us to attend the first concert at the Olympia Theater in Paris, Baird and I were backstage. Baird wanted to see the concert from out front, so I told him to go and ask, saying who he was. Of course, there was a seat (second row center!) for Bird's son.

Norman had chartered a two-engine plane for the tour. It was so tiny that it was promptly christened the "Bumble Bee." On the day of departure from Paris, Phil and I were delayed by traffic and arrived late at Le Bourget airport. Norman didn't even glance at Phil. After five days of frosty silence, he turned to me and uttered laconically, "Hello, Chan." A few of the musicians went ape on that tour; the band was beginning to get the road jollies. Phil's passport expired during the tour, but he managed to cross several borders regardless.

The Granz tour was over and the band was on layover in Milan before starting another tour, this time in Yugoslavia. I rejoined the band once again in Milan. When Patti Bown, the pianist, returned to Milan after a few days in Paris, she asked me, "How's Baird?" with a strange look in her eyes. Unable to withhold the news, she told me that Baird had had a terrible accident. He had run through a plate glass door and cut his face. That was all she knew. I wanted to call my mother immediately, but there was no telephone in our apartment. I decided to take a plane to Paris, but there were no flights until the next day. I wanted to take the overnight train, but Phil didn't want me to spend a night alone in my agitated state. Finally, someone said that Quincy was still in Paris, and would know exactly what had happened. He was going to Trieste, where he would meet the band's train at midnight. If necessary, I could fly to Paris the next morning from Zagreb. When I saw Quincy, he played it cool since my mother had told him not to upset me. I finally dragged the story out of him. While Quincy's daughter Jolie and Baird were playing, they had run down the hill to our apartment building. Baird forgot that the glass door wasn't open, and slashed his chin. Poor Jolie was hysterical. Baird had lost a lot of blood, was taken to the hospital, stitched up and given raw horsemeat, which the French believe is good for the blood. He was fine now; there was nothing more I could do. He was in my mother's capable hands, so I continued on with Phil and the band. Phil and I were in a four-berth compartment with Tuki. Having learned my lesson during the Madrid trip, I was smuggling Tuki in an upper berth. Old Tuki snored like an adenoidal asthmatic. A well-dressed lady entered our compartment during the night. I'm sure she didn't close her eyes during the trip.

The band played in Zagreb and then made the trek to the hinterlands in a rickety chartered bus. The one-lane unpaved roads afforded a chilling view of a thousand-meter drop. There was no room to pass and fortunately we didn't meet anyone. We arrived at an old log bridge and all had to get out and walk across. It wouldn't have supported our weight, especially the trumpet section. Twelve hours later we arrived in Sarajevo and learned that the hot water in the hotel had been turned off at seven o'clock. On the trip to Banja Luka we added a passenger. One of the trumpet players had picked her up. We needed her help to translate for us, though she never admitted she spoke Yugoslavian. She claimed she was a German movie star. She made the entire trip with us with just the clothes on her back. That's funk. The band played a concert in Tuzla, a backwater town where they had never seen a black person. Jerri Gray was mobbed by curious hill people touching her skin to see if the black rubbed off. They were fascinated by her and she was in danger of being crushed by the circle they formed around her. She distributed the contents of her purse. I know there were women in the mob who had never seen a lipstick.

We said good-bye to our bus in Tuzla and continued to Belgrade by a third-class, narrow-gauge, wooden-seat train. The ride seemed interminable and our unwashed bodies blended into the general funk. We were cheered by the thought that the next day we'd be in a modern hotel in the biggest city and could luxuriate in a hot bath, our first since leaving Zagreb. A woman from the cultural ministry met us at the station. It was difficult to make pleasantries when my poor American body was desperate for a hot bath. I inquired as to the conveniences in the hotel where we had reservations and received a tirade about the suffering and bombing Yugoslavia had endured during World War II. At the hotel, Jerri and I elbowed each other so as to be the first at the check-in desk. She outflanked me and copped the last room with a bath. It was the first time on the tour I lost my cool. At that moment, in my funky desperation, I hated her. She quickly regained my friendship when she invited me to use her bath.

Quincy realized how hard the trip had been and grooved everyone when he engaged a private railroad car on the Orient Express for our return to France, where the band had one date to do in Bordeaux before returning to Paris. I hadn't been able to find any varient of Tampax in Yugoslavia. What did those women use? When the train pulled out I knew I was in for a difficult trip. The next evening, we had a three-hour layover in Venice. It was late in the evening when we arrived and all the drugstores were closed. Adding insult to injury, we were penniless and I stood at the dock waving good-bye to the wealthier members of the band as they departed on a gondola ride, their colorful gondoliers singing "Santa Lucia." I turned to Phil and cried in a fit of vindictive despair, "I haven't even got a Tampax!" I stormed back to the train and when my sweet husband reappeared, he was carrying a peace offering . . . a small souvenir gondola. We had another short layover in Milan. Phil and I were eating dinner in the station when we heard an announcement which we thought was for the departure of our train. I grabbed Tuki, and Phil and I made a dash to the platform after a slow-moving train. Phil could have made it, but Tuki and I couldn't keep up. For a brief moment, Phil seemed to be debating whether to leave the band or me. It would have been a disaster had we caught that train because it was the wrong one and all our belongings, including our passports, were in our compartment. While we were in Bordeaux, we tried the bullfights again, but we left before the first bull was mutilated. Everyone was tired and edgy after Yugoslavia, and I was down with a bug. Shortly before leaving Bordeaux for Paris, I was asleep in our room. Phil, not wishing to disturb me, took the tickets from my wallet, laying it on the bed. He let me sleep until five minutes before we had to leave to catch the train. In my haste, I forgot the wallet with all our capital, a twenty-dollar bill, and irreplaceable photos on the bed. Then, as we boarded the train, Quincy's wife, who was pregnant, began to miscarry. Life is hard on the road.

The band had a long lay-off when we got back to Paris. Phil and Clark Terry got a gig with Oscar Pettiford at a Paris club, "Le Chat qui Pèche." Once again, Phil was a commuter, traveling home to Sceaux each night after work. Being off the road gave us a chance to be at home, "chez nous," with the family again. Gar was just beginning to walk and Baird was learning street French.

When summer came, the band was to play a lengthy tour of Swedish folk parks, traveling by chartered bus. I decided to go along. I sent for Baird after the first few gigs because Quincy's daughter Jolie was on the tour. Baird's liberal education was furthered after spending six weeks on a bus with seventeen greasy wild men. During the tour, we flew to Cannes for a previously booked weekend. The chic Palm Beach Casino where the band was playing wouldn't let the wives in. Unfortunately, the customers hated the music. My mother, Kim, and Gar flew from Paris to join us in Cannes for a well-deserved weekend vacation. We checked into a groovy pension called the "Mai Fleuri." During our first lunch at the pension, we were served something tasty and cold. We ate our fill, and then learned that this was only the first course, and five more followed! Baird broke the house record by finishing with seven yogurts. When it was time to return to Sweden, we didn't have enough money to pay for our room and board, so we had to leave my mother and the children as collateral. They had a forced Riviera vacation . . . the hardships they had to endure!

As the Swedish tour drew to a close, the time had come for the band to leave Europe and go home to the States. I flew back to Paris to arrange the hippest farewell party in history. Barclay Records was footing the bill for the party and all stops were out. We hired Bud Powell, Pierre Michelot, and Kenny Clarke to supply the music. During the evening, Kansas Fields, Kenny "Pancho" Hagood, and Alice Coltrane, who was still Alice McLeod at the time, sat in. There was an open bar and everyone's favorite potion was served. The champagne was flowing and the caterers had arranged a marvelous buffet. The evening was festive and "Le Tout Paris" attended.

For the return trip, the band had reservations on the SS *United States*. I had been trying to earn some of our family's transportation money by helping Quincy with publicity and doing most of the copying of the bands arrangements. I asked Hodges, the road manager, if he had a ticket for Tuki. Glancing at his list, he stopped mid-way and read to the bottom: Mildred Berg, Kim Parker, Baird Parker, Phil Woods, Chan Woods, Gar Woods, Dog Woods. I had become pregnant on an upper berth on the way to Sweden, and my homing instincts were pointing west. I wanted a proper kitchen and a house with a porch. The return crossing was rough, but worse than that were the bad vibes that the band was subjected to. Europeans idolize artists; Americans revile them. In addition, the racism the band had escaped in Europe again became evident.

We landed in New York during a hurricane and a narcotics bust. Phil's folks, who had come to meet us, had to wait while U.S. Customs went through our suitcases and boxes with minute attention. We had accumulated an enormous amount of possessions during our stay in Paris. I had brought all the herbs from my kitchen, and they were sent off to be analyzed. Also, I had imprudently stitched an ounce of Paris green pot into the lining of my jacket. When they told me to join a few members of the band in the customs office, I knew they were on to bigger and better things. Most of the band had bought new Selmers in Paris and had expected to get some heat about them, but this was about a lot more than a few saxophones.

I quickly asked if I could take Kim to the toilet. We were accompanied by a policewoman. I couldn't believe that she let me go into a booth and lock the door. I ripped out the stitches as fast and as quietly as my trembling hands could function. I was sure my pounding heart would cover the noise. I opened the envelope, emptied it and watched the toilet turn green. Everything was cool so far, but how could I get rid of the pipe in my pocket? I spied two holes in the wall where a fixture had been removed. Breaking the pipe in half, I put the stem in one hole and the bowl into the other. It seemed as though an eternity had passed. I couldn't arouse my watchdog's suspicions any longer by rummaging through my purse for papers, roaches or whatever else might lurk at the bottom. I flushed the toilet and went out to face the matron. I thought she surely would know what I had been doing in there, and that a secret camera must have recorded my criminal activities. But she was looking at herself in the mirror and I was home free.

I rejoined my fellow prisoners. Phil was pale, and we did some serious eyeball talking. He understood my visual message. We were escorted back on ship: Phil and a few of the musicians were taken to one stateroom, and I was taken to another with our lady trombone player, Melba Liston, my mother, Gar, who had soiled his diaper, and even a girl who had come to meet her boyfriend. The matron told us all to strip. My mother, furious, began a tirade. It was certainly true that in all the countries we had traveled through, we had never been subjected to the humiliation imposed by our own country. When we were finally released four hours later, we stood in a downpour searching for a nonexistent cab, thinking, "Welcome home."

Retrospectively, would I change anything if I could? Throughout the tour, my needs at that period of my life were fulfilled. Although I may have been a sap at times, I wouldn't change a thing.

PART II
DA CAPO

9. CHACONNE

As much as I loved Europe and traveling with Quincy's band, when I became pregnant with Aimée, I covered our walls in Sceaux with photos of country houses, back porches, and canned preserves. I had a nesting instinct and wanted to settle into a bucolic American dream. We rented an old Victorian house bordering the Delaware River in Point Pleasant, Pennsylvania. Kim and Baird returned to more orthodox schooling, and our last daughter, Aimée, was born.

Phil had returned to Europe for a short tour with Quincy, and when he came back, he was offered a weekend gig by Freddi Redd, who had a dude ranch connection. The deal wasn't unusual . . . not much bread, but bring your old lady and spend a groovy weekend. We decided to go for it. We were ogled by the other guests as we were shown to our less-than-elegant quarters. Sunday morning things started looking up when we were invited on a trail ride. I had ridden often in school and really dug it. But it was the first time for Phil, and he wasn't too choked up about horses. Being a beginner, he was given the slowest and oldest horse in the stable. The only thing he had to fear from this old nag was death snatching her from under him. Her name was Champagne, but she didn't froth; she just drooled a bit in her senility. As we left the stable, Phil and I were riding together. Phil began to drop farther and farther behind. Being far too gentle and kindhearted to kick the horse in the ribs, he couldn't seem to make old Champagne move. Knowing nothing about the function of the reins, which dangled loosely in his hands, he gave her the further advantage of stopping at every choice blade of grass. The wrangler leading the trail ride kept yelling over his shoulder at Phil to keep up. I was finding it difficult to keep Phil's slow pace, and was soon riding ahead with the wrangler. This only added to Phil's frustration. He was making a poor showing for his old lady and now she was riding off into the sunset with some damn cowboy! Once too often, our leader leaned back and yelled at Phil, "If you can't keep up, get off and walk!" This struck Phil as a good idea. He dismounted and, leaving Champagne for the wrangler to handle, stomped off in the direction of the ranch. On the way back, we passed ahead of him. As we rode into the stable, Freddi Redd saw Be-Bop Cowboy Phil's horse, being led in. He was sure that Phil had been thrown and was laying out yonder somewhere, in need of medical attention. My old dude appeared around the bend. He was steaming and remained incommunicado until we were back in Point Pleasant!

Phil got a call to join Benny Goodman for a State Department tour in Russia. (Wouldn't you just know that America would send the King?) It was the first time the U.S. had sent jazz to the U.S.S.R. and, although some of America's best musicians were in the band, Benny was playing his 1930s book. It was a rough tour at best and working with the King was an experience musicians spoke about in whispers. The Russians were sure the band was padded with CIA men. On their return, the band was met at the airport by some men from Radio Liberty who asked them to record an album of songs by Russian jazzmen. Phil had become friendly with a Russian alto player, and Radio Liberty had kindly offered to send him reeds and a mouthpiece in Phil's name. In spite of disclosures about Radio Liberty and the CIA reading all mail going to Russia, Phil corresponded with the alto player for several years, and we worried about him.

There was an area in-river which the state of Pennsylvania had decided to flood into an artificial lake as part of a flood-control program. The state had already bought most of the houses, which they were renting on indeterminate leases. Many of the houses in that area were prerevolutionary, and we always felt it was curious to sacrifice them for society's need to improve its environment. We were able to rent a beautiful old stone house at a ridiculously low amount. Our last born, Aimée, was a toddler, and this was an ideal place to raise our four children. The house had a well-fitted large kitchen with a closed-in porch, an upstairs porch, and another porch which circled two sides of the house. The one-acre lawn ended in two stands of gigantic blue spruce.

Autumn, 1962

Kellers Church

Friends ask me, "What do you do all day in that little town two miles outside of Elephant?" What do I do all day?

Well, Gar and I watch the chicken hawk as it swoops and slowly banks, totem-like, tipping its wings back and forth like a small boy straddling a fence.

Or I watch the tulip tree grow. It has doubled its height in the year we've lived here. Isn't that what children do in their first year?

Or I look at the colors, brilliant in their purity: prime green grass, Gar's ball like a big, round lemon, and Aimée proudly pointing at each brilliant colored tulip. The elm, by the stream, is surely a female in its roundness and quiet strength. The willow is as introverted as an esthete.

Or I listen to the metallic static-like sounds of the wasps, busy on their long autumn journey, or the sudden excitement of a covey of pheasants rising from the thistles and blackberries in the field behind our house, their wings thrashing, and coarse cries signaling their haste. It's hunting season.

Or I watch the dogs and cats asleep and unaware in the noon torpor.

I show Aimée the clouds, a praying mantis or a flower. I listen to the kids in Baird's boat with helmets and toy rifles fording what great river?

Or I watch Kim, a self-conscious newly-become woman, walking down the road lost in thoughts of football and alma mater.

Or I just look at the old stone bridge resembling a petit Pont Neuf straddling, not the Seine, but a creek called Tohickon. I can almost hear the wooden stagecoach wheels and the hoofbeats of the horses of bygone days, bearing apprehensive travelers who worry about reaching the next inn before nightfall.

At night, I watch from my bed, as the rising moon silvers the windows and turns our blue room white. I watch Tuki grow old, sadly and fearfully. What an empty space he will leave in my life. I shall never again go to bed without looking for my little dog to carry upstairs.

After we moved to Solebury, Al Haig came to play a gig with Phil at the Bucks County Playhouse Inn. It was a rowdy Saturday night crowd, requesting "When the Saints . . .," and so forth. We invited Al to spend the night at our house. As the evening progressed, he became hostile and, at one point, picked up our poor twelve-year-old dog Tuki and started rocking him back and forth. My protesting only made him angrier and he began muttering about pampered little dogs. I decided to go to bed, thinking that Al would be more sober in the morning, and his gentle, well-mannered self again. As I picked up Tuki to take him upstairs with me, Al got off one last sarcastic remark, "Poor little arthritic dog!"

The next morning I awakened to Al snarling at Baird under our window, "Yeah, I knew your old man." (In fact, Al had been Bird's pianist for many years.) Baird had pointed out my cooking stash and Al had polished off all the small bottles of cognac, rum, sherry and other wines, and bourbon: he was bombed. I was going to New Hope on a shopping chore. Al said he would like to accompany me. He thought he had detected amorous overtures from the middle-aged lady who ran the inn where they had played the night before. He wanted to go pay a call on the fair lady whom he would hit on for some bread. Al insisted on driving! I needn't have worried as he drove slowly and carefully, coming to a complete stop at every dirt road leading into our route. However, he had misread the friendliness of the innkeeper, so his visit was to no avail. When we reached home again. Al decided to go swimming in the small, uninviting muddy lake in the state park bordering our property. Al fortified himself with several quarts of beer purchased illegally from our local bootlegger. In defiance of state laws, or any other, he was soon floating serenely on his back, chug-a-lugging from the large brown bottles. As the level of the last bottle went down, so did Al. He temporarily disappeared beneath the water leaving only the trace of his up-ended bottle. Al, who was feeling expansive, decided to spend another night as our guest. To my relief, Phil had a gig in New York City that night and insisted that Al leave with him. When they pulled away, Al was telling Phil what a lucky guy he was: nice family, groovy wife, lovely home. . . . During the sixty-mile ride, Al insisted on refreshment stops, and by the time Phil dropped him off in New York, Al's hostility had returned. His parting words were, "You're a jive motherfucker!"

Dave Lambert was a very special friend whose visits delighted everyone in the family as he made no distinction between adult and child. While we were living in our gingerbread house on the river, Dave decided one evening that we needed a boat. He immediately fashioned a very good one from our canvas hammock. True, it was a rude affair, blunted at prow and stern, resembling a scow, but it was seaworthy. On subsequent visits he improved it with caulking and made other refinements. On one visit, he appeared with a war surplus inflatable raft from a Japanese aircraft. Our fleet was growing. In his small kitchenette in Greenwich Village, he embarked on his most ambitious undertaking. For the small stream bordering Keller's Church, Dave built a fine blue rowboat and named it Baird, with bold brass letters on the stern. On the day he brought it in a rented convertible, we had the grand launching. Phil and Dave made the trial run. The stream, which normally reached a depth of one foot, had been swollen by melting snow and had become a raging torrent. It was moving fast and the course was made more difficult by large rocks under the surface. Dave at the helm was barking out orders at his crew, one unsalty bebopper who neither understood nor appreciated his officious manner. Dave, who was serious about his responsibility for the safety of all hands, was becoming annoyed at the landlubber. Harsh words were exchanged and Phil stood up, further imperilling the small craft shooting the rapids. Dave yelled, "Sit down! You don't know shit about boating!" They made it back to shore and by evening all hard feelings were forgotten.

On his next visit, Dave decided we needed a proper dock for our craft, and disappeared in the direction of the creek. He located a small cove which, once dredged of boulders, would serve nicely. Three hours later, I was dispatched to see how Dave was doing. He had stripped down to his jeans which were rolled knee high. He was thigh high in the brook, bent over a large rock which was resisting all his efforts to dislodge it from the creek bed. Dave's face was crimson from the effort and the rest of him was white and water-shrunk. Fearing apoplexy or a stroke, I tried to get him to rest. But Dave acted like a pro and persevered until we had our docking area.

When the state finally completed the dredging, we had to move to a landlocked house in Solebury. Two of our boats had already gone downstream in a flash flood. The one remaining boat would have to be beached. Dave took Baird for one last run on the canal in New Hope. More than one tourist turned for a second look at the sight of Dave at the helm, his beard floating in the breeze. When he returned to the house, Dave worked the rest of the day rigging up a marvelous contraption in the cellar which enabled the boat to be suspended from the beams. Both boat and berth survive today.

Aside from being one-third of the marvelous innovative Lambert, Hendricks, Ross Trio, Dave was a master of many skills. He had been a tree surgeon and held a card in the bricklayers union. He enjoyed working with his hands. On one visit, he showed up with a chain saw to dispatch a dead tree in our yard. Dave was the first flower child, and called himself "the world's oldest bebopper," a title I often challenged.

Holidays were never complete without Dave. He always showed up at Christmas and Thanksgiving. Sometimes he came with a pretty girl who always fit in, but mostly, he came alone. He enjoyed himself with the children as much as he did with us. One Christmas evening, our pestky neighbor who owned a mill down the road decided to bore us with her company. Dave cut short her visit by ignoring her, sitting on the floor with Baird and organizing a contest to see who could blow loudest on two very shrill whistles. For our last Christmas in Keller's Church, another third of the trio, my friend Annie, was supposed to drive out with Dave. Annie, who was trying hard to get her life together at that period of her life, didn't show up, and Dave finally drove out alone. Around noon, Annie called to say she would take the train. But this was impossible because the drive from our house to the station was a two-hour round trip and there was a foot of snow on the roads. For the rest of the day, I worried about Annie, alone in the city on Christmas. On our last Christmas day with Dave, we were awakened at dawn by pebbles thrown at our bedroom window. Dave was below with his Christmas present of six Lambert, Hendricks, Ross charts he had brought for me to use at Ramblerny, a summer arts school where Phil and I were teaching music.

> Crepuscule inverted
> Pebble sound on dormer window
> Slanting eaves above
> Dave below
> Christmas morn.

The following autumn, Dave was killed on a highway while helping a stranger change a flat tire. At our Thanksgiving table that year, everyone was very aware of Dave's presence, despite his absence. We laid a place setting for him, and in the years since, he has remained a part of our special family times.

We bought our first house in rural Solebury Township, not far from New Hope in Bucks County. It was an old white frame house on an acre of land. We had a large kitchen, room for the Steinway concert grand we bought, three bedrooms, and an alcove I collaged for Aimée. The only thing lacking was a fireplace. I loved that house. We bought a Ford convertible.

Phil and I had begun teaching at Ramblerny. This performing arts camp had José Limon in charge of the ballet department. Joyce Trisler was head of modern dance. There were also drama and art departments. It was a marvelous experience for the kids who attended. Phil and I were sympathetic to all their problems, both musical and personal, and we had soon acquired a larger family. Two of Phil's more promising students were Richie Cole and Mike Brecker. Our own kids took full advantage of all the classes. After a few seasons playing trumpet in the junior band, Gar told us, "I've gotten so used to jazz that I find it difficult to play 'Old MacDonald' straight." Phil, in charge of the music department, had as guest lecturers Elvin Jones, Gary McFarland, Manny Albam, and Chris Swansen. All our friends, including Morgana King, donated their time and gave concerts for the kids. Some of those concerts would have been sellouts at Carnegie Hall. Phil and I spent every waking minute at the camp, which was just down the road from our new house. The disappointment when the school closed in 1967 was one of the reasons we left America the following year.

December 1966

Solebury

Our house lies in the valley of a gentle rise and catches the least trace of wind. In the winter, the wind sings down the hill . . . really sings . . . so that I go through the rooms looking for a radio left on or a child playing pranks.

Five is the Christmas age. Aimée is so excited, so happy and full of secrets that she hugs me.

Gar hints that his hobby is books. He says, "Oh boy! I can't wait till Christmas. That's why I'd like to be a child forever." But then, he's very emotional.

Our Christmas tree is six feet, six inches high, the star is eighteen inches, but the ceiling measures just seven feet, three inches . . . Would you believe a hole in the ceiling? It will be a lovely Christmas even though we have little money.

Christmas has always been our favorite holiday. Aimée summed up our feeling perfectly in a poem:

The leaves are gone, the bugs are gone,
Hot chocolate is starting again.
Gar and I are waiting impatiently for Christmas.
We are waiting for Santa Claus to come.
It is magic at morning.
You come down by the Christmas tree
And plug in a plug and there you are!
Lights of every color
Blue, green, red, white, yellow and many others.
It takes you an hour to look at.
Our tree is decorated.
And usually you hear angel chimes.

It started snowing on Christmas eve and we had an old-fashioned blizzard. Our Christmas tree was groaning with presents which spilled out over the whole room: a four-seat toboggan, a guitar for Baird, and Aimée's first two-wheel bike. We went to bed with the wind howling and snow-drifts piling up. From our bedroom window the only thing that broke the blackness of the night was our neighbor's window lighting up a small space in the distance and silhouetting their tall pine tree.

The next day, I was lighting incense when my terry-cloth dress suddenly went up in flames. It was spontaneous combustion induced by a lint conflagration. Ablaze, I threw myself on the rug yelling, "Help, Phil, I'm on fire!" I thrashed around a lot, Kim flailed at me and Phil stripped me naked. When Kim's fiancé, Ricky, called, Kim told him laconically, "We just extinguished Mommy." In the heat of the moment, Phil looked at me disapprovingly and chastened, "Chan, you're carrying your smoking too far." Kim told me, "You're the only mother I know who has gone up like a Roman candle the day after Christmas and has been struck twice by lightning!" But it was a lovely Christmas.

I'll never forget the first time lightning struck me: I was holding the wire screen door ajar and standing on the rain-soaked kitchen floor in Point Pleasant. I was barefoot and pregnant with Gar. Lightning struck a tree across the road and rebounded up my arm. It still hurt a few hours later. I had a fright but remained otherwise unscathed. A pregnant cow, however, was struck and killed in Solebury during that same storm. The second time I was struck by lightning was in an open shed at Ramblerny. I had gone up there to rehearse with two of my students. Lightning ran up an uninsulated wire on the hill just as one of the girls, Holly Near, was switching on the light. It passed through her, I felt it on my legs, and it burned the leg of the girl on my other side. I'd been the filling for a lightning sandwich. That was the summer that Tadd Dameron died, and the lightning became almost supernatural. Although I had never met Tadd's wife Mia, I had written her a letter about the gentleness of Tadd and our friendship. Some time later, I was at my desk when Tadd came to mind, and I went to the piano to hunt for some music he had given me. Lightning struck nearby and hissed along the wire to put out the light on the desk I had just vacated. In that split second, the phone rang. It was Mia.

I dearly love the autumn. Phil had cut the long grass, which I burned one evening with the help of Aimée and Gar, the arsonist. Finally the smoke drove my little firebug away and I was able to convince Aimée of the dire pulmonary dangers which lurked in the night. I sat down, and looked up at the willow. The crickets and katydids sang, the T.V. was a distant hum appeasing the lulled children with the N.B.C. preview week cartoon on Judy's takeoff on Oz. With the fire at last contained and rising to an Indian signal period, I again looked across the road to Farmer Brown's field. At seven thirty it was past dusk already and almost dark, turning the fields and trees to olive and charcoal greens. I said silently to myself, "Remember this minute: the fields, the foreshortening of the spruce in the light, the willow and the lilac bushes that rise to the barricade of trees that separate us from Meeting House Road. The blue spruce dresses for winter in ice blue pantalettes and ruffles trimmed with pine cones, while the other trees undress." As I lay in the hammock, I saw the tracing of their nude limbs looking black against a cobalt sky.
There was a shrub with square branches which turned red in the fall and grew small orange berries. The sparrows had made many babies that spring. Every night at dusk they would begin a terrible clamor, skittering between the holly on the trellis and their nests in the maple tree to take away the bits of bread I threw out for them, pieces of bread dangling sloppily out of their beaks. Little piggies. I felt immortal and ageless. I had seen the children and the bulbs I had nurtured burst into bloom and I knew that I would endure. I felt a timelessness, a foreverness, no pattern of days, but a flowing.

I have a bank account of memories such as these. Could I ever say goodby to the seasons?

My cousin Toni was dead at twenty-one. Quiet, sensitive, gentle and lovely, she had Irish blue eyes and long, soft black hair. As a baby, one of her legs had been severely burned, when her drunken grandparents had passed out, leaving her against a hot radiator. Over the years, she had had twenty skin grafts on her burned leg, and was in constant pain from the unhealed scars on the bottom of her feet where they had taken the skin for the grafts. She lived on pain pills, and was facing another graft at the time of her death. Her impossible dream was to become a ballet dancer. She had been raised by foster parents and nuns. The nuns had made her cover her budding breasts with a bra, even in sleep. She only trusted cats, dogs, and children. She had told me about a secret place in the cellar of her building that she had prepared for her cat to give birth undisturbed. On June eighth, she crawled into that secret place in the cellar, took all her pain pills, and died alone. She was found a week later when the janitor noticed the odor. The cruel and wasteful thing was that many people could have offered her life and love.

The very religious are dry like butterfly wings or old parchment. Religious music is as dry as an old oboe reed or a violin bow in need of resin. Lutes and organs wheeze like ancient asthmatics croaking out parables.

Kim had been keeping company with a nice boy since high school. Ricky Sellers, whose family was everything we were not, had grown up in one house in Bucks County having security and a calm, normal life. Kim envied that just as he envied the exposure to art and life which Kim had experienced. He was an idealist and had a straight-ahead vision of life. He planned to go into world government and he was brilliant, steady, and logical. After Ricky and Kim graduated from high school in New Hope, he entered Wesleyan University in Middletown, Connecticut, and Kim got a full scholarship to Hofstra University in Hempstead, New York, where she majored in drama. They couldn't bear the separation and Ricky was spending his weekends with Kim instead of his studies. His family agreed they might as well get married so that Ricky could settle down to his studies.

When Kim showed me the guest list for the wedding, I realized it was becoming a huge, formal affair. On our side of the family, there were only four invitations: my mother, my brother Jimmy, and our closest friends, Chris and Meg Swansen. But even after eliminating everyone possible on the groom's side, there were still close to one hundred relatives and close friends. How was I going to feed all these people? Kim's reply was, "Tea sandwiches." It sounded ghastly! What the fuck were tea sandwiches? I finally said I'd compromise and have a caterer prepare 200 tea sandwiches. I'd make up a batch of my special sangria and that would be that.

On the night before the wedding, we were having dinner with Kim's roommate from Hofstra, who was to be the maid of honor. Kim, having last minute nerves, began criticizing the way I felt about formalities. Most children rebel against their parent's conformity, but Kim had always been ashamed of our Bohemian way of life and her weird mother. Looking me straight in the eye, Kim spat out, "I hope you intend to at least wear a dress!" Now she was worried that we would make a poor showing in front of Ricky's conventional family. I had no intention of showing up at her wedding in jeans, but I retorted, "For me, tea sandwiches are enough of a compromise!" Phil added, "Don't talk to my wife that way." Kim fled to her room in tears and her bewildered roommate finished her dinner with us in embarrassed silence. The next morning, I told Kim I had no intention of attending her wedding and she had better ask Ricky's mother to handle the sangria. I was in the garden when Ricky appeared with a shame-faced Kim and asked me to please come to their wedding. The ceremony was only two hours away. I relented and put on a silk dress. The wedding was to take place at Ramblerny, where all the kids had decorated the lovely old theater with garlands of roses. Gar played "Here Comes the Bride" on guitar and a sweet old justice of the peace repeated the vows. Kim wore a mini gown . . . so much for tradition. Suitably pelted with rice, the newlyweds drove off in a borrowed white Cadillac convertible with old shoes dangling from the rear fender. At our house, Ricky and Kim changed clothes, and returned to Ramblerny to join us in the pool. After graduating from Wesleyan, Ricky ultimately became radicalized and disillusioned with mainstream America. He and Kim bought thirty acres in Maine where they homesteaded for two years.

I was becoming increasingly aware of the problems in American life at every level. I noticed that there were no black faces in the illustrations in Aimée's textbooks at school. I raised a fuss about that. When Baird joined the Boy Scouts, he was told that he needed a letter from his minister. Of course, we had no minister, so Baird was excluded. I was called to school for a meeting with Baird's teacher, a light-skinned Negro named Mr. Hickerson. (This same Mr. Hickerson would eventually meet his death while collecting rents on his apartment houses in Trenton. Rumor had it that he was murdered by the KKK.) Mr. Hickerson often slapped the students, so Baird both feared and hated him. It was recommended that both Baird and I have psychiatric therapy. I was enrolled in a group led by Dr. Cavetta, which met once a week. I found it difficult to relate to the group, an odd assortment of young waitresses, mechanics, and supermarket workers. I was bored by their problems, which I thought could be easily solved with a bit of intelligence. I could only talk about politics, Vietnam, and the miserable state of life in America. "There you go again, disliking people with your closed mind," one woman remarked to me, explaining it was a shame there were no more minstrel shows because she had enjoyed them so much. They had been such good entertainment and no intelligent Negro had ever objected to them. I replied that I must know a lot of dumb Negroes. She said vacuously, "There's good and bad in every kind." Dr. Cavetta said that I was a strong person with a closed mind, a rebel and self-outcast from society. If all the inequities of the world were corrected, he said, I would have a breakdown.

I wanted to live in a society that was not racist, but when I tried to think of where such a place might be, I drew a blank. Now it seemed my need to protest injustice had become neurotic. Maybe so. But could the small-minded people around me tell me where to go to get out of this world? How to adjust to a society in which so many were rejected? An oppressive society always harms the oppressor because the minority is strengthened. The young white people in America rejected society as it was, after seeing young black militants reject integration. Of course they did. Who wants to integrate with corruption? Cuba, China, and the Communist countries which were supposedly free of racism had authoritarian governments which I could never accept. Brazil, the multicolored nation, was a dictatorship. America was so corrupt that it was dying from dry rot. I hoped the puritan money-making ethic was on the way out.

By rejecting values I felt to be immoral, was I a monster producing disturbed children? I understood that children suffer from unconventional parents, but I felt it was worth the price for them not to grow up to be unthinking carbon copies. After a month of this therapy, it was concluded that Baird's difficulties stemmed from me keeping Bird alive and the resulting confusion over having two fathers. Bird lives!

Gar wrote the following letter to Bobby Kennedy:

February 1968, Solebury Pa.
  Dear Senator Kennedy,

My family and I will be voting for you. Are you going to run? I am
very upset about how our country is wrong. I am eight years old.
My family and I admire you and we all admired your brother.

My father was the soloist on "The Kennedy Dreams." Your mother,
Rose, wrote a nice letter to Oliver Nelson. Have you heard "The
Kennedy Dream"? Its a wonderful record. Everybody who made it,
made it with love.

Sincerely,

Garth Woods

P.S. I hope you run.

It was becoming more and more difficult for me to live with the American involvement in Vietnam. The brutal events we witnessed in our
living room on television seven nights a week were marking our children. We watched a suspected Viet Cong leader being marched down
the street and coldly shot in the head. That was teaching reality to our
six-year-old son, although I would have preferred to shelter him from
such brutality. The U.S. had wiped out a town with our bombs and an
American major said, "Sometimes it becomes necessary to destroy a city
in order to save it." I decided that if we were to live in America, I would
have to try my best to change it. Phil didn't know how to handle a wife
who cried every night after the evening news and he was less than thrilled
at the thought of being married to a politically involved woman. Even
though Phil was apolitical and naive about Vietnam, he was disturbed to
see me becoming so obsessed with politics, so he tried arguing with me,
repeating the official line. I knew he was wrong, but I needed more information to be able to refute him. As I read Bernard Fall on Vietnam, I
learned the history of that beleaguered country. When our forces dug in at
the Khe Sahn, I was amazed at the stupidity of the military mind: deliber-
ately placing themselves in the same exact position, making the same
documented mistakes as the French. I wondered if Johnson would have
the same grace as the French artillery commander who shot himself during that debacle. We razed the culture and history of Hue, and we were
dug in at Dien Bien Phu. After the Viet Cong began controlling the cities,
the American draft laws were modified to include graduate students who

had previously been exempt from conscription. Senile General Hershey's reply to inquiries regarding the intellectual gap this would produce was that students didn't need such advanced education: "After all, Thomas Edison didn't go past the eighth grade."

It had taken me forty-two years to realize how schizoid America was. We had become a nation divorced from reality, believing in our own greatness, generosity and morality while producing mass murderers, drug addicts and homeless, despairing people. Although we were trying to police the world, we were unable to recognize our own lawlessness. "Ask not what your country can do for you, but what you can do for your country." I had never thought of asking my country to do anything for me.

After Kennedy was killed, the only thing I could do for my country was to leave it. I had been yearning to return to France since the "Free and Easy" tour, but Phil had become established in the New York recording studios, had become one of their most called upon musicians, and he was making a good living. However, I understood his musical frustration. The American dream was beginning to seem plastic and empty. Phil was still drinking and sometimes not coming home. He knew he had a drinking problem and he wrestled mightily with it and, for the most part, had it under control. Our marriage had been good. Phil was faithful, loyal, and a marvelous father to our children. Aside from his family, his only interest was music. That was fine with me, as that had always been my interest also. Sometimes I found myself with responsibilities of running the house I would have preferred him to handle, a small inconvenience considering the stable life Phil had made for us all. Gradually, Phil and I came to feel that we were going through the gestures of a happily married American family. We were both ready to give up our secure but sterile life. To paraphrase: Some use mundane means to a mundane end. Isn't it better to use mundane means to a magical end? We missed Europe. I had been working a not-so-subtle campaign, telling the children about *pain au chocolat,* French cuisine and the beauty of *La Belle France.* But I had given up the thought of leaving. One morning, Phil asked me to call the travel agent and make a reservation. I hardly dared to ask, "For where?"

Phil had written letters to everyone he knew in Europe and to every club owner, booker, and agent. His first reply was from Ronnie Scott's club in London, offering four weeks at four hundred dollars a week. With this small one month of security, we bought one-way tickets for the family and took a chance. What a ballsy old man I had! It took great courage for Phil to leave the security of the studios. Phil was in search of himself as an artist, an impossible quest in the anti-cultural climate of America.

We found someone who would rent our house for the summer. We weren't thinking beyond the four weeks at Ronnie Scott's. Phil was determined to make it playing jazz. Our friends from the Quincy tour, Ake Persson and Jerri Gray, were living in Berlin and Phil could probably have found work with the German radio. But he'd been a studio musician for the past eight years and didn't really want to become a radio musician in Europe. He figured he'd have a year to work jazz gigs before the novelty of being American wore off and he became local. We hoped that during our month in England he'd be able to line up enough work so that we could live simply and frugally. Holland was the cheapest country to live in and we planned to settle there. We put our valuables in the attic and dragged down our twenty-eight pieces of tacky luggage. We packed a huge crate which we christened the "goody box" with everyone's most precious belongings. Phil put in a lot of score paper and his football, my recipe books followed, and the children's games were next.

When we boarded the plane, Phil was carrying his briefcase, full of arrangements he hoped to sell, and his sax. I had his clarinet and hand luggage. Aimée insisted on carrying her snare drum and Gar had his trumpet and guitar. Everyone asked if we were a family band. Our baggage was incredibly overweight. Somehow, we managed to get through without a hitch. We only had one-way tickets and eighty dollars in cash. It was an auspicious start on our new adventure.

10. MODULATION

We were overjoyed at being in such a civilized city. It was incredible to be in London and to follow on television the burning and looting in America that spring of '68. Our feelings that we had escaped the holocaust just in time were only reinforced by the scenes of smoke rising over the White House and machine guns on the Capitol steps. It looked like Germany in the thirties. We were unable to forget the racism: Martin Luther King was assassinated.

Soon after our arrival in London, we found a charming, quiet family hotel in Kensington and spent a lot of time by the Serpentine in Hyde Park. The house on our corner had a plaque indicating that Sir James Barrie had once lived there. Aimée went into the garden in search of Peter Pan. The children were amazed when a bobby looked down at Aimée and said, "'Ello Luv." We felt wonderfully alive and optimistic. We did all the things that tourists do. We went to Hampstead Heath fair. We visited Christopher Wren's Kensington Palace, Kenwood House, and Dickens' House. History that went back that far sent my young American mind reeling. In England, I began to develop a feeling of historical continuity.

We renewed our friendship with Annie Ross and Jon Hendricks, who were both living in London. Annie gave a party for Aimée's seventh birthday. Georgie Fame replaced Dave Lambert as they sang "Happy Birthday" in trio. As we discussed the situation in the States, Jon started telling us about his army days in World War II. He had gone AWOL and spent V-Day in a square in Lyons shouting, "Allons enfants." At that time he had already been AWOL longer than most American servicemen had been in Europe. When he was finally caught, he was put in the stockade and sentenced to be hanged. He pleaded extenuating circumstances: a race riot in his company. His sentence was changed to fourteen months hard labor. Jon told us the trustees were so brutal that once one of the men was shot twelve times by three different pistols. Eventually Jon was made a clerk and he had to write the reports when prisoners were shipped out of the prison. One day there were only forty-five live bodies instead of forty-six. . . .

Not knowing that the Blue Note in Paris had closed, Phil had written a letter asking for work. Simone Ginbre had seen the letter and got three weeks for Phil at the Cameleon. Simone had been a jazz singer before she married Jean-Louis who was the editor of *Lui* and *Jazz Magazine*. Jean-Louis, who played bass, was a fan of Phil's and wanted to do a cover story for *Jazz Magazine*. They had come to England for the interview and Phil asked Simone if she would handle his bookings. She agreed to follow up on the answers Phil had received to his letters.

We were trying to be prudent with our money, and had found a house in Amsterdam. The children and I would go there when Phil left to play at the Cameleon in Paris. However, when the time came, the house was still occupied. Phil decided that we might as well all go to Paris together. We checked into the Hotel du Levant on the Rue de la Harpe. I became more and more excited. As we drove through the city, I thought, "I'll never leave Paris. Here, I'm me: no hang-ups, no inhibitions, nothing up tight. It is so beautiful and I'm happy just being here."

Jean-Louis and Simone regaled us. They took us to dinner at the Trois Frères on Avenue Georges V. Jean-Louis, who was an epicure, chose a perfect wine and feted our arrival with a bottle of champagne. (A strawberry tart cost five francs, quite expensive back then.) After dinner, he drove us around the l'Arc de Triomphe three times as we all applauded. We stopped for coffee and cognac on the Champs Elysées. I'd forgotten how perfect the coffee was. Afterwards, we went to the Living Room to hear Art Simmons. Phil signed the guest book, "I'm glad to be home." So was I. We ended the evening at the Cameleon listening to Cecil Payne.

Paris was a magic place for us where miracles could happen. The streets were alive with everything and anything imaginable: St. Nicholas playing accordion and singing in a fine baritone on Rue de la Harpe, a gypsy family with their goat and baboon performing on the Rue St. Severin, and even someone playing a washboard to accompany the blues played by a harmonica on Rue St. André des Arts. I walked in a gentle rain with my nose deep in a May Day bouquet of lilies of the valley, smiling and thinking how lucky I was, "*C'est vraiment la bonne chance.*"

Simone had put together a rhythm section for Phil's opening at the Cameleon. This was the group which became The European Rhythm Machine and would win the *Downbeat* award as best new group. George Grunz, Henri Texier, and Daniel Humair were the best European musicians at that time and Phil was very pleased with his made-to-order band. We decided to cancel Holland and try our luck in France. Simone and Jean-Louis became our good close friends and gave us all their help and support in getting located.

Our hotel was on a small cater-cornered street which dissected the Boul' Mich and the Boulevard St. Germain in the student quarter. Night and day, we had front row seats on the greatest theater in the world, but we didn't know we would be on the scene of history unfolding. We came out of the St. Michel Metro station one evening and saw police vans and about twenty policemen standing quietly. At the corner, we saw around one hundred young people blocking traffic on the Boulevard St. Germain. At that moment, the scene was frozen and looked like a movie still. Cars were strangely quiet. There was no honking. When we reached our hotel, we heard the muffled explosions of tear gas canisters. The students began rocking cars. That night, we ate dinner in a restaurant across from our hotel and then walked up Boulevard St. Germain looking for ice cream cones for the children's dessert. Groups of CRS (the blue nasties) protected by riot helmets and shields were charging small groups of students who would retreat and then regroup. It seemed like a game until one of the riot police trampled my toes and another nearly knocked Aimée down while pursuing a bloodied student. "Get those kids off the street!" they yelled at us. It was no game. The events of May 1968 which would topple de Gaulle had begun. The Latin quarter was no place to be at this time with two small children. With the help of the Ginibres we found a sublet in a residence in the Paris suburbs in Bougival.

La grève . . . all Paris was on strike: transportation, banks, post office, factories . . . tout . . . eight million people acting together. We were in the middle of a revolution. We had left a disintegrating America to arrive in England in time for Enoch Powell's racist ravings, which had seriously shaken the Heath-Wilson government. We came to France and de Gaulle was tottering. All France was paralyzed. Nothing moved on the Seine. The barges blockaded all traffic and no one worked the locks in Bougival. All the ports were closed. The airports at Orly and Le Bourget were closed. There was no exit or entrance to the city. We were under siege. The Odeon was occupied by students and Jean-Louis Barrault. There was no phone service, no mail, no buses or metros or railroads running. Garbage piled up in front of the Opera. Banks were closed and there was a run on food at the stores and talk of hoarding. But the cafés were open and swinging.

People were *tranquille* and cool. We were well provisioned and relatively secure in Bougival. *Vive les anarchistes!* Baird and our dog Snoopy caught the last flight to land in France. Now we were six.

Our concierge didn't like children, dogs, or Americans (not necessarily in that order). All children were to be in their apartments by dark, dogs must be leashed at all times, and no one should be free. One night when Phil was playing in Germany, the kids had taken Snoopy downstairs on her required leash. The phone rang. It was Henri calling to tell me that de Gaulle had gone to ask for the support of the army and that things might take a turn for the worse. If the army refused, actual shooting and full-scale revolution would begin. I told him I wasn't afraid and reassured him that we were cool. When I hung up, I heard the sounds of unrestrained glee from the grounds below. I looked out the window. A prevailing spirit must have been in the air, because the children had let the dog loose. In unaccustomed, joyous freedom, Snoopy was chasing a small, black spaniel through the well-kept grass and flower beds. The kids from all the buildings were caught up in the excitement and shouting encouragement. The concierge was choleric, waving his arms and yelling, but no one was intimidated that evening! I yelled out the window, *"Vive la liberté!"* Finally, de Gaulle allowed fuel to be brought into Paris on a Friday. He knew his Frenchmen well: everyone filled their gas tank and left for "le weekend." The revolution was over.

June 6, 1968

Bougival

Bobby Kennedy died this morning of an assassin's bullets. To me, at this moment, the birds swaying precariously on the ends of the tiniest boughs are more precious than all life which has become corrupt. The world is ugly, futile and senseless. Nature is hard but mankind is cruel. Phil called from Yugoslavia. He said people had lit candles in doorways and placed flowers next to Bobby's picture. He had gotten out of his cab and joined them and wept with them in the rain. He dedicated "And When We're Young" to Kennedy. When he was asked to make a short statement for television, he held up his horn and said, "I speak many languages with this."

I fell ill with a virus.

I was almost forty-three years old. I found a grey hair in my bangs and felt ugly. But I didn't feel old. Goddamn bodies that betray while the mind and legs are still twenty-five. Nothing had changed, except my old face. I constantly wondered if my clothes were too young, my husband too young, my children too young. Was I ludicrous? Silently, I pleaded, "Tell me I'm lovely, Phil." I wanted to wear a mask. It felt strange to see young people with whom I might have much in common, and realize that I was not of their generation and they would be uneasy with me. My eyes looked old, but what they saw was young. My nose delighted in odors. My taste buds enjoyed new foods. My mind, though somewhat disillusioned was never jaded. But I looked in the mirror and hated my image.

I wondered what Phil and I shared besides our children and music, our insecurities and needs. What were our inner thoughts? What did he know of me or I of him? Surely he had similar thoughts that he couldn't share with me. He neither probed nor revealed. There were too many subjects we couldn't touch upon. I had a silent scream that sounded in my ears like a railroad train.

June 27, 1968

Bougival

Good morning, world! Bon matin, Bougival, city of impressionists. After misplacing four days somewhere in a lung-induced fever, at 4:30 this morning, the birds were calling me to come outside. Snoopy and I went to watch the sun come up over the locks. We walked for an hour and picked wild flowers as we listened to the lazy snug-a-bed barge roosters yawning cock-a-doodle-doo, cocorico. The legacy of the men who painted here, Monet, Renoir, Pissarro, is present in the landscape. This morning I truly feel their continuance and a life-force of renewal. The roadsides are a blanket of red tissue paper poppies, deep blue thistle and yellow buttercups. The well-pruned cherry trees are so heavy with fruit that their boughs touch the ground. Who prunes all the trees in France? Peonies and roses are in bloom. Iris and lilies are so thick that they are in danger of exterminating themselves and each other.

Across the Seine, the perfectly pruned trees march in formation up the hill past the neo-renaissance Greek temple, past the waterworks built by Louis XIV to bring the Seine to Marly, up to the tip-top where a white, almost hidden, villa peeks out just far enough to spy on the Seine below. The light here is marvelous, as usual. In St. Germain-en-Laye one day a sudden storm turned part of the sky dark grey while the sun still shone. The old white buildings with their grey slate roofs took on a new face, and I saw what Utrillo painted. I thought of the photograph of Bobby Kennedy lying on the floor, looking in extremis like his brother John. Perhaps at the end, he had become his brother. Maybe that was what kept old Joe and Rose going. Through all of this, perhaps, in their Catholicism, they believed there was no death, but simply a transmission, a passing-on, from one to another.

I know that Bobby and John would have some choice words for the turn of events, and the choice of the presidential candidates: Gene, who would be but can't. Now L.B.J. has turned it over to H.H.H. who can't make it without Ted: Hube the cube who shouldn't but will and wants Ted to pull him in as John took L.B.J. who later refused Bobby who gave his life for L.B.J.'s resignation! The Republicans have asked another loser, Rocky, to run. It's Abbott and Costello's "Who's on First?"

There is an old barge tied up. It is full of water and in danger of being swamped. Last night I saw it from the window and the moon-light made the Seine dance around it. I love you, France.

Bougival lies between Paris and the army base to the west. On July 14th, Bastille Day, we were awakened early in the morning by a frightening thunder. We rushed to the window and saw tanks, half-trucks, troop carriers, and vehicles carrying monstrous rockets which looked like predatory sharks swimming past on the cobblestone road. That morning, they had a two-fold mission: apparently, to parade the glory of France down the Champs-Elysées, but more important, to show the leftwingers that the army was behind de Gaulle with all its military power.

The ugly khaki monsters made a dreadful roar as they passed and I realized how inured the Europeans were to war. I shivered in the July heat, as I thought of conversations with our French friends and neighbors which often included references to World War II. One elderly lady used to make bicycle trips from Paris to Normandy in search of fresh vegetables and eggs for her children. Another lady told of being chastised by a German soldier because he saw her small child give a piece of chewing gum to his dog. To hear people speak casually of the occupation and to watch the army roll down the same roads twenty-five years later, made one wonder at the naive Americans playing at war in Vietnam. To most Americans, the war was something served up between other violent events shown in the Huntley-Brinkley report on television. At this point, most Americans viewed the longest war in their country's history as TV serial, with time to attend to one's comforts during the commercial breaks.

Before leaving America, we had taken our Ford Galaxie convertible with stereo and all the American gizmos to our friendly Mort's Sports Car dealer. He arranged for a trade-in and ordered a tiny new Fiat to be delivered to us in Amsterdam, where we intended to live. He gave us a bill of sale for the Fiat and $50 change. It took us three months to track the new car down, and we were only successful because Simone, who spoke Italian, came to our rescue. Phil had picked it up on the way home after one of his gigs in Germany. It was the first time in thirty years that I have driven with a stick shift. I started taking it for test runs in Bougival to do my grocery shopping. Aside from this, I had no experience whatsoever driving in Europe.

Phil had left for a long Scandinavian tour ending with two weeks at the Montmartre club in Copenhagen and a radio broadcast in Holland. The kids and I decided to drive to Denmark to join him for these two dates. I packed the necessary provisions for a long journey: peanut butter, jelly, soda for the kids; bread, cheese, a few bottles of bordeaux for me; and dog food, water and anti-chuck-up pills for Snoopy who got car sick. We left Paris at 6:30 in the morning. We took small back roads and enjoyed the beautiful French countryside. We stopped on a dirt road in Belgium for a picnic with some nosey cows, and crossed into Germany in the late afternoon, where we encountered rampant bureaucracy. The border police insisted we purchase an identifying decal for the car to show what country we were residing in. But I didn't see why the policeman said we should buy an "E." The car had temporary Italian plates, but we were Americans residing in France, although the wine, cheese, kids, and dog (they couldn't see the peanut butter) may have misled them. We were willing to do whatever they said was necessary. Baird jumped out of the car in a downpour and returned with a big "E," but a few minutes later he had to go back and buy an "I." The policeman had said "Eee," but he meant "Aye" in the foreign pronunciation of the alphabet! For the rest of the trip, every car we passed with Italian plates greeted us with an enthusiastic "Buongiorno!" We continued our journey through Cologne and stopped for the night in Leverkusan, the city of Bayer aspirin.

The next morning, we began hours of autobahn driving. I was dismayed by a big Mercedes tailgating us, flashing their headlights. This seemed rather bad form when the car involved was an un-broken-in Fiat trying to pass a truck on a steep grade. After the *laisser-faire* of the French, the brusque attitude in Germany was strange and rude. In the mountains, the sky turned black and there was torrential rain. We pulled over until visibility improved. The sun came out just past Lubeck. We had our first view of the North Sea and the Hansel-and-Gretel thatched-roof cottages. It was six in the evening when we arrived at the Puttgarden ferry to Denmark, where we had a two-hour wait for the next one. By the time we reached Danish customs it was dark. We hoped there would be no further delays, as we didn't know what hotel Phil was staying in, and the club closed at one.

When we went through the customs gate, we were told to pull over. We were kept waiting until all the cars from the ferry were cleared. Then they told us no dogs could enter Denmark. They were adamant, even though Snoopy had just had all the necessary shots. They sent for a vet to examine Snoopy. After paying thirteen dollars to the vet, who did no more than glance at Snoopy, we were informed that our only option to leaving Denmark on the next ferry was to put Snoopy in quarantine the next morning, and leave her there during our stay. We finally got on our way, and reached the Montmartre just as the last set ended. We received a warm welcome from Herluf, the owner, Kenny Drew, and Dexter Gordon, whom I hadn't seen since 52d Street. Many hugs and kisses awaited us from a happy Phil, and we bedded down in Herluf's beautiful apartment, which he kindly turned over to us for our visit. Nice people, the Danes.

The next morning, to the children's delight, we discovered the "walking street." Then it was time to incarcerate Snoopy. We had been told she would have excellent care, that she would be kept in hospital conditions. However, all the caged dogs set up a fearful noise which caused Snoopy to tremble. This was more like a prison than a hospital. Holding back our tears, we promised Snoopy that we'd visit her every day. But when we made good our promise the next day, Snoopy wasn't the same dog we had kissed goodby just twenty-four hours earlier. She was wet, drugged, and frantic. She had tried to dig through the concrete, so her paws were bleeding. She had also tried to bite through the bars of the cage. Despite the fact that she had been given a tranquilizer, she went wild when she saw us, clawing and even biting Aimée. I put my head on her cage and sobbed. We knew we would have to take Snoopy and leave Denmark. After much red tape, a man brought poor, dear Snoopy and attached her by a long rope to the inside of our car, sealing it with a piece of lead. "We'll notify the border," he warned, "so you'd better leave Denmark immediately." Our two lovely weeks in Denmark had come to an end in just one day. We left Phil with tears running down his face, and all of us sobbing. We drove straight to the border. The custom's man didn't even glance at Snoopy, and when we asked if we could free her, he told us to cut her loose on the ferry. The children had combed Snoopy as best they could, but she still smelled terrible. After spending one day in Germany to have the car checked, we drove without a stop until we reached the friendlier border of Holland. We spent two lonely weeks waiting for Phil in Hilversum.

None of us was happy in our Bougival apartment, since we had been used to living in our own house with a large yard where children and animals could run free. Through an ad in the *Herald Tribune,* we were fortunate to find a small carriage house with a yard to rent in the congenial Parisian suburb of le Vesinet. Aimée and Gar were enrolled in the International School in neighboring St. Germain-en-Laye and they rapidly learned to speak flawless French. Baird, who was older, attended the nearby English School. We became a bilingual family in Le Vesinet, transplanted, but happy and at home. One evening Aimée's five-minute dissertation in beautiful French was brutally interrupted by Baird yelling, "The porcupines are here." My response was, "Is there anything for them to eat?" Phil, having had too many bad experiences with hungry strays, growled, "What is this shit?" Gar ordered Aimée not to step on the porcupine. "Don't step on the porcupine?" Phil mused in wonder. Sometimes our household was a surrealist happening.

Phil and his European Rhythm Machine were quickly becoming the most popular group in Europe. Phil was playing with a new freedom and joy, and sounded marvelous. Simone was getting him all the best gigs and he was working steadily, doing what he'd always dreamed of. It was true that an artist is respected in Europe. Phil was making more money, playing jazz only, than he had ever made in the studios in New York. He had recorded a few albums with his group. "Alive and Well," his first album, was to be issued in America by Bob Thiele. Guy LeClerq, the French photographer, had been hired to take the photos for the cover. Guy wanted to shoot in the Rue Lepic, the most famous street market in Paris on the steep hill between Pigalle and the Sacré Coeur. Kim and Ricky were visiting us at the time, and Kim decided to tag along with us. It had been too cloudy to shoot in color, but, as soon as we arrived, the sun broke through and shone down on Phil in his blue velvet jacket. He looked handsome although somewhat out of place in his formal attire and carrying his sax. There was even an accordion player on Rue Lepic and it seemed to us that we had wandered into a René Clair movie set. It was lovely. We walked up the street, pausing at an occasional pushcart. Traffic was backed up and the market people were having a ball. Tough butchers yelling in patois acted as if there was nothing extraordinary in having a dandy with a saxophone, accompanied by a weird entourage, posing with lemons on Rue Lepic. Phil posed, his horn resting on a fine bunch of leeks, the saleswoman, attired in a blue orlon *tablier* and carpet slippers, beaming because her leeks had been chosen for posterity. We continued on up to the Place du Tertre, everyone's favorite postcard. Phil posed at a café, luckily deserted by tourists, and in front of a Balinese statue near a blue house. A plaque nearby proclaimed that this was the restaurant patronized by Suzanne Valadon and her son Maurice Utrillo from 1919 to 1935 . . . a long meal even by French standards! Another house bore a plaque dated 1347! On a narrow street, the barred window of a funky ground-floor pad was open, and a magnificent black cat was sitting on the sill eating its lunch. Guy scrawled "Phil Woods" on the wall in chalk, and Phil posed. The concierge was leaning out of her window, as concierges do. From the look in her eye, the old crone was no doubt thinking about what a good-looking young man Phil was. Paris was too much.

When Phil had a few gigs near Marseilles, we drove down to that Eden. Leaving Lyons, we drove south through the wine country where the earth is covered with well-tended and well-pruned vines, heavy with lush grapes. Provence at sunset is a pink marvel: villages of stone houses perched on cliffs, the cypress and cedar trees black silhouettes. Ancient Roman fortresses have arrow shaped slits cut into the rocks of the natural ramparts, and an old church is the focal point of each medieval village. My first glimpse of the Mediterranean was a red horizon made by the setting sun, the sea reflected black and bright pink. The Camargue lies in the delta formed where the Rhone divides as it rushes to merge with the sea. The ground is partially covered by the flood tides. We drove, unable to turn back, on a narrow rutted path, no more than a finger of land surrounded by water where, we later learned, tourists were regularly rescued after being caught by a sudden change of tide. That trip was an experience I wouldn't have missed.

The first formal meal we had in a French home was an invitation for lunch in a doctor's villa, high above the Mediterranean in Bandol. As clean plates and glasses were placed before us at each of the numerous courses, I blew my savoir faire and anxiously inquired, "Who does the dishes?" Slices of cold ham served with a local rosé wine opened the meal, followed by sole and another delicious fish, unknown to me. Both had been fished fresh from the sea below us that morning and the lemons garnishing the fish grew in the garden. Next we had asparagus vinaigrette. Red wine was served with the roast lamb. A salad course with local celery was, of course, followed by the cheese board. The first strawberries of the season, to make a wish on, were presented with a bucket of chantilly cream, accompanied by champagne. After coffee, there was a choice of cognac, armagnac, or Napoleon Mandarine from Corsica. I chose the latter and discovered a new taste. As we left the house, I was presented with a single yellow rose and an armful of mimosa from the old doctor's garden. The fragrance of the mimosa haunts me still.

The sun was shining. A black cloud scooted by and on one side of the window it was raining. The road on the left remained dry. There are many rainbows in France.

Baird made a painting of hell: all red and gold swirls. I ventured that it looked Byzantine which drove him to the dictionary. Gar was reading Allen Ginsburg's "Vortex." Things were normal at our house.

As Courcelles becomes Batignolles

Looming in the distance

That improbable confection

That Sacre Coeur

Looking more like a pleasure palace

For a rich man's darling

Than a place of pilgrimage.

It had been foggy and the lights turned everything into an Impressionist painting. How natural that Impressionism was born in Paris.

Perhaps the attraction I'd always felt for that school of painting explained my love for Paris.

During the Christmas season, Paris was lovely at night . . . all lights and Christmas trees. The Conciergerie was ablaze with floodlights. It was a thrill every time I saw it. I'd never become blasé.

11. OSTINATO

Gar was asked to play the role of the Genesis Apple in Duke Ellington's Sacred Concert. The first performance was to be in the Cathedral of Saint Sulpice in Paris. Suddenly thrown into the midst of the ageless professionalism of Duke's band with the Swingle Singers, Gar became acutely aware of the implications of performing on the altar of a great cathedral before television cameras and a live audience. Gar understood, for the first time, what he would have to face and began to have doubts. My nine-year-old son had a headache and a stomachache, and began to regret the chore he had taken on. During the performance, the mike went dead in the middle of Gar's speech. Duke came up to him and gently told him to start over again. It went well, and Gar, who was relieved when it was all over, hung around the dressing room signing autographs.

Gar and I went to his second gig, in Lille, by train. We checked into the hotel where the band was staying and rode the legendary bus to the cathedral. All the cats had their special seating arrangement and we observed protocol by respectfully asking which seats were unclaimed. One of the musicians asked me if, before he died, Bird had told me any secrets about playing. After the gig, we had supper with Rufus Jones and that sweet gentleman, Russell Procope. As we left the next morning, the roadie was pleading "Moving out," but the bus sat outside only half filled.

A few days before Gar's last concert, Phil left Le Vesinet for Italy to play some concerts at the Roman amphitheater in Carthage. After Carthage, Phil and his "Machine" made headlines at a pop festival in Palermo: "Phil Woods, Conquistador." The fact that Arthur Brown had exposed himself, causing a grand Italian riot, was of little interest. The impact of the music was overwhelming, causing thirty-thousand people to chant: "Phil Woods." A white jazz group at a pop festival had caused a miracle!

It was gig time in the Roman ruins for the men in our family. For Gar, the grand climax would be his last concert with Duke in the amphitheater in Orange. This amphitheater, which existed before Christ and was erected by Caesar Augustus, is the most beautiful and best preserved Roman antiquity in the world. The acoustics are a marvel (when the mistral wind isn't blowing) and it seats thousands. The day before Gar and I were to leave for Orange, he came down with the mumps. Trouper that he was, he decided that the show must go on. Although we had decided to delay our trip until the last possible moment, Gar woke me up early the next morning and said he felt fine.

When we arrived in Avignon, it was full of tourists and hippies. Gar and I visited the Museum Lapadaire, containing artifacts from centuries before Christ. We started chatting with the dry old concierge of the museum. He wondered why the hippies were begging rides on the roads and said that if he wanted to make a journey, he would wait until he had the money to purchase a ticket. I tried, in vain, to explain that money wasn't important in the culture of the young hippies. Picasso's last exhibit was at the magnificent Palais des Papes, built in 1334. Three hundred oils and drawings, all done in 1969, were exhibited in the Salon de la Grande Audience. To be in that room filled with Picasso's joyous riot of color was thrilling. That prolific master had spent one year painting several large canvasses a day. Preoccupied with his waning sexual prowess, that "dirty old man" had produced a splendor of pornography.

That afternoon, we had lunch in a neighborhood bistro. Gar and I had both become vegetarians, and the menu choices presented some problems. I explained this to the sympathetic owner, who had the waiter bring us the largest plate of canned peas I ever saw. The French don't understand picky eaters. Phil was in Avignon to play a late afternoon concert in the Cloître des Célestins . . . one of the best concerts I ever heard.

Phil was still feeling triumphant about Palermo. He played his ass off! He and the Machine were brimming with self-confidence, which showed in the masterly way they played that day. The day before Gar's concert, we drove through the countryside of Chateauneuf-du-Pape, stopping for lunch at an impeccable two-star restaurant in Vaison-la-Romaine, a town which had been the capital of the Celtic tribes in 4000 B.C. Finally, it was the night of Gar's last concert with Duke. Everything was perfect despite the mistral wind from the north which roared in the microphones and sent the music flying around the stage. It was good to see Baby Lawrence, who danced in that concert. I was happy to see him looking so healthy and straight after all those years in limbo. After the concert, Duke told Gar, "Well done!" and gave Phil, Gar, and me four kisses each. As we checked out of our small hotel too drive back to Paris, I was touched by the parting gesture of our waitress, who gave me a necklace.

We decided to go back to Paris the long way, through the Ardeche region. This lovely countryside has remained unchanged since the mountains first spewed out the lava which created it.

La Chaise Dieu ("The Chair of God") is situated one thousand meters high in the old volcanic mountains in Auvergne. We arrived in the evening, tired after our day's ride from Orange. La Chaise Dieu is famed for its fourteenth-century abbey. The town was full of curio shops selling religious artifacts and liquor made by the monks. We found a homey-looking hotel and checked into a clean, comfortable room with a bay window which opened onto the mountains and sky. We were still finishing our dinner in the dining room when, at precisely nine-fifteen, everyone left. We had noticed a small fair in town and thought perhaps some sort of entertainment was to begin. Gar asked the waitress why everyone had suddenly departed. Perplexed, she looked at him and answered, "Because they have finished eating." So much for logic. After dinner, we walked through town to the fair, which consisted of one "dodge-em" and many shooting galleries. Phil embroidered a story for Gar: "This town only pretends to cater to tourists. In reality, all the townspeople are involved in a plot and the bullets in the galleries are live, picking off passing tourists, who are robbed and never seen again. This is the real industry of La Chaise Dieu and the abbey is simply a come-on to lure unsuspecting innocents into its dark passages." We found a small park and looked up at a sky awash with stars; it was so clear we could see two of Jupiter's moons. Then, like children who thrill to the chills of a ghost story, we braved the long dark passageways of the abbey, which connect all the streets in town. We chanted the monk's song. (No, not Thelonious, but the one from "The King and I.") Phil turned a corner ahead of Gar and me. He had disappeared into the darkness. Gar and I tremulously began to search for him. As we entered a dark room off the passageway, we were still spooked by Phil's story. There he was, sitting on a stone bench in a wall recess smoking a joint. This assured us of the normality of our situation. Compared to the shooting gallery, it was calm and peaceful there. We sat for a long time, talking about life. Later, we learned that we had been in the Hall of Penitents. Since that night, whenever I hear male voices chanting, I remember the closeness we felt in the "chair of god," for it wasn't always so easy for Phil and Gar to touch. We walked back to the hotel through the now-quiet streets. From our beds we had a spaceship view of the sky and we fell asleep, feeling peaceful and content.

Before leaving La Chaise Dieu, we bought a three-legged stool from a local craftsman. We had just put it into the car and were getting ready to leave for the final trek to Paris when the chambermaid from the hotel rushed up and said we had forgotten something. Gar and I went back to the hotel and were confronted by the proprietress of the hotel who had seemingly gone berserk. The choleric, buxom woman was brandishing a large kitchen knife, and she stepped in front of the door, barring it with her body. She screamed at us in outrage: Gar was a dirty child who had made peepee in her bed and ruined her mattress. If we didn't pay, she would call the gendarme! This seemed like much ado about a small peepee and I warned her to calm down before she had a heart attack. I asked her price to let us depart in peace, but she raged on about parents who traveled with their unhousebroken children. Gar was humiliated. I thought about two nights earlier when he had performed with Duke Ellington in a Roman amphitheater in front of five thousand people. But I thought it best to humor her. How could we expect justice in a small town where, no doubt, everyone was related and the gendarme was probably her brother? I remembered Phil's saga of the previous night, and deposited one hundred francs in her free hand. Gar stood mute before her, as she hurled abuse at him, continuing her tirade. She finally stepped aside and let us through the door, but her shrill voice followed us down the street. Although our grand adventure had been considerably dampened, a leisurely lunch somewhat restored our spirits before we arrived back home.

As I walked the many acres of the grounds of the palace at Versailles, I wondered how long they would remain unvandalized if this were America. To enjoy freely the domaine created for the pleasure of the most powerful monarchs in history is truly a privilege. As I entered one of the parks, the flapping of a large bird's wings and the sound of small creatures scurrying on dry autumn leaves drew me to a small path. I walked a few yards and entered the stillness of a primeval forest. I had left behind the brightness of the day and the sounds of humanity. Only in a few places did the sun break through the tall trees, and I had the same sensation one experiences in the grandeur of a cathedral. I was completely alone and suddenly I felt uneasy. If I continued deeper into the forest, would I ever find my way back? I turned away from this "other" realm and took a few steps. But I was drawn back, for this place was infinitely more beautiful in its sixteenth-century solitude. I continued deeper and deeper into the forest. As I cautiously rounded a bend in the narrow footpath, I dissolved in laughter . . . to find a most civilized modern chair, thoughtfully provided for a body's repose and the soul's introspection. I politely sat and enjoyed a moment's respite. Pressing on, I went around another turn in the path and came upon an octagonal pool surrounded by marble benches. The amount of money required for the maintenance of such grandeur boggled my mind. The Grand Trianon is pink marble and surrounded by lavish gardens. Although it was the end of October, they were blooming in summertime glory. I peeked through the windows into the rooms which had housed Marie Antoinette and King Louis.

I spied a grand red desk where decisions of great consequence had surely been pondered. Sitting beside it was a color TV. The dressing room had a most un-seventeenth-century telephone. Workers were putting up a red canopy and laying a red carpet at the entrance. I didn't know it was being readied for a state visit by Brezhnev and that he would sleep in the queen's bed. When I saw that bed through the window, I had wondered how she could fit into such a short bed. I have since learned that people then slept almost upright, propped up by pillows. Still, that doesn't explain accommodations for Brezhnev, who would be arriving the following day. There was a number of men ambling about, more than likely security men. Later I realized they may have been checking me out as a potential bomb planter.

In the French language, everything is either masculine (*le*) or feminine (*la*). All the words for violence are feminine. The word for war and even for shit is feminine. I'll go along with almost anything that the French want to endow with gender. I'll say *la grève*, although a strike seems a most masculine thing. I'll even concede that hair has gone masculine, but I can't bring myself to say *le camembert*. To me, it will always be feminine. I love hoodlums being called *voyoux* and cheats being called *tricheurs*, masculine cheats that is; feminine ones are *tricheuses*. These are two of the first words to be added to the French vocabulary of an American child. This doesn't make me question the honesty of children as much as the frankness of adults. There is an established formality in France that I find very civilized. No one feels he must be friendly immediately. It's *de rigueur* to add *madame* or *monsieur* to almost every sentence. There are formal and informal forms of "you." I feel embarrassed and gauche when a "*tu*" slips out to a stranger, or a "*vous*" to a child.

I've found that the way to get around French bureaucracy is to be very feminine. This ploy will melt the hardest heart of the meanest Gauloise-smoking petty official. I even persuaded the head detective of the Vesinet police headquarters to write a letter for me to the traffic court in Marseilles. On second thought, femininity is a universal value: in America it's Woman and Motherhood, in Latin countries it's sexual regardless of age, but in Scandinavia it doesn't exist. Couldn't a woman be a hero? Is she necessarily a heroine?

I had been criticized for not being a submissive French wife, because I needed the car to drive the children to school. In France, the man kept the car. Baird was constantly harassed by the police who thought he was Algerian. He had been arrested for playing his guitar under the Pont Neuf (the oldest bridge in Paris) and had had a trial. He had been arrested while still in the English School on suspicion of stealing a car. He was arrested for stealing two pieces of candy from the Prisunic. The police *commissaire* was becoming an acquaintance.

Nothing had changed since the night in 1968 when we saw Nguyen Cao Ky's brother-in-law shoot a prisoner in the head, except that in France I called the children to translate the detail from the nightly news. If the Vietnamese incident was the reason I could no longer live in America in good conscience, that sickness has festered and spread in the intervening years until it seemed the whole world was going mad. Although I admired some revolutionaries for their ideals, I found it difficult to understand giving one's life to overthrow a bad system, only to have it replaced by another. If people are corrupt, they desire only personal gain. If they are idealists, most wish to impose their ideals on the majority. If someone would help humanity, first see to the children, for they are the future, and see that a neighbor is not in need. Then propose reforms, rather than legislate them. The revolutionary assassin who drank blood from a victim's wounds does not share my ideals.

April in Paris. The chestnuts were in blossom with their waxen candelabra and the cherry trees were already in their prime. The flowers overflowed onto the streets. In my small circle of a garden, the pansies, tulips and hyacinths bloomed. We were one growing month ahead of America.

The pace of the market quickened. I bought honey, still in the comb, cut from a large white block. The olive man was selling dates, nuts,

115

figs, apricots, four varieties of raisins and as many different kinds of olives. I turned away from the chickens, plucked except for their limp heads with beady eyes, hanging by their withered feet along with the corpses of pheasant, quail, pigeons, and little wrens. The inevitable rabbits were skinned, except for their furry paws. (Were they left on to bring good luck? Certainly not for the rabbit!) The poor creatures had been split in half with their livers exposed. It was not easy to be a vegetarian in France.

In April, the Pinder Cirque came to Le Vesinet. April is the month Aimée is one year older. It's March that's cruel, T.S. April in Paris is "douce."

Better to feel deeply and be wrong, than to allow life to buffet one hither and yon.

Better to participate than to withdraw.

Better to die violently than to expire with a whine.

Better to exist in a maelstrom that a vacuum.

Better to be mad than senile.

Better to hate than ignore.

Better to scream than be silent.

Better to be stung than ignored.

Baird asked me, "What do you expect: to graduate? twelve teflon pans?" Yeh. I hope to end up with at least twelve teflon pans!

After dinner one night, I went upstairs. I was having trouble breathing, so I opened the windows for oxygen, and lay down on the bed. I felt I was dying, but had no fear. My only concern was that one of the children would discover my dead body. I seemed to be having an "out of body" experience: I realized that I was eternal and would live forever through my children and the people I had touched. I would simply be leaving my body: this flesh, this meat which had nothing to do with my spirit. Phil came upstairs and I told him what was happening to me. He was very disturbed, even though I tried to reassure him that it felt natural to me, and that he must be strong for the children. But when he said he couldn't live without me, I knew I couldn't die. (Fucking sense of responsibility!)

He insisted that I come along with him to Lugano the next day. He was going there to record with an international band in the villa of a wealthy Swiss magnate. The estate was magnificent, perched high in the mountains, overlooking the lake. The first night, they threw an extravagant party. I related my strange experience of the night before to Dexter Gordon, who explained that it must have been *petite mort* and assured me that he, too, had experienced it. Later on, I began to get that strange feeling again and asked Phil to take me back to the hotel. There was no transportation, but he took me out to the carpark and pleaded with me once more not to die. Death seemed so friendly and natural to me, but I couldn't make him understand. Two musicians appeared. They were returning in an open jeep which they had strung with bells. Phil asked them to take us back to the hotel. As we rode down the winding mountain, the Indian bells they had strung were singing and promising me nirvana.

12. Alto Ego

Phil never drank at home during a gig. When he was working the studios in America, he often drank after the date and would spend the night in New York. I understood his frustration with the music he had to play in order to support us. He would come home the next day sober and full of remorse. I didn't realize the dangerous pattern we were falling into. I always scorned our friends who married square chicks and had to sneak down to the cellar to get high. A marriage should mean sharing everything, but now this was happening to us. Phil couldn't handle whiskey and became aggressive, hostile, boring, and less of a man when he drank. I'd heard enough Bird stories and I didn't want to hear Phil's friends laughingly recount what an ass he had made of himself. Phil was hiding the part of himself that was intolerable to me, and I was being forced into the role of mother, policeman, and flogger.

All my life, I've admired strong independent women: Isak Dinesen, Edith Sitwell, Marjorie Rawlings, Arletty, Annie Dillard, Oriana Fallaci, Anaïs Nin, Gertie and Alice. Now I found myself in a role I couldn't tolerate. Still, our marriage had been functioning for fifteen years, and although it had this structural weakness, the good times made up for it. I knew Phil had a strong love and need for his family.

In Europe there were no musical frustrations. Every gig was played without compromise. Phil had won the *Downbeat* poll as best saxophonist and his group won the new star poll. His album had been nominated for a Grammy award and he was nominated as best soloist. When Phil returned to America for two triumphant tours with his band, he received the recognition that had been withheld before. He returned on his own terms as an artist. He was earning $1,000 and more for each concert.

Life seemed rosy, but Phil couldn't sustain it. He began fucking up on gigs. This was a new phase in his alcoholism. Before, he had been able to remain in control, but now he was running out of places to which he could return. The world was closing in on him. Simone was having trouble booking him as his reputation rapidly spread. Phil attributed this to his becoming "local." Now, when he came home he was often still drunk, defiant and ugly. I didn't know how to handle it and would threaten to leave him. The following day, there would be tears, remorse, and promises, but I kept waiting for the other shoe to drop. Phil was going through physical changes also. Forty isn't old, but it's old for a saxophone player, and Phil wasn't holding anything back in his playing. After a concert, I was always fearful to see how thin, pale, and drawn he looked.

At the end of August 1971, we took our first vacation in Cavalaire on the Riviera. Kim and Ricky came for an extended visit and my mother was in France on her annual summer vacation. The eight of us rented a house close to the sea for three weeks. For all of us, it was a paradise. Everything, including the weather, was perfect. We passed the days swimming, sunning, and eating long family lunches under the lime tree in our yard. Kim and Ricky fell in love with France and we went looking for land to buy.

Phil had been commissioned to write some arrangements for a big band in Marseilles. One day, he and Baird left for Marseilles, intending to return that same evening. They showed up late the following night. Phil was drunk, and Baird, who was sixteen and without a driver's license, had driven home along the dangerous mountain road. Phil was garrulous and expansive. I went to bed, hoping he would do the same. But he wanted to stir things up. He came into the bedroom to tell me he was going for a long swim in the ocean. When an hour passed and he hadn't returned, I began to worry. I went to the beach in search of him. I walked up and down the beach in the black starless night, calling his name. There was no reply. I even tried to find his footprints in the sand. Certain that he had drowned himself, I drove to town and found the police station closed for the night. My frantic pounding on the door roused a sleepy, unbuttoned gendarme. I blurted out my fears that my drunken husband had done himself in. The policeman assured me that I would probably find my husband at home. At any rate, the police could do nothing before daybreak. I drove back to the house and woke up Kim. We drove to the beach again, this time taking Snoopy to sniff for Phil. Kim spied Phil hiding behind a tree at the edge of the road. I was furious. This seemed more like a replay of my life with Bird. Phil had crossed a line and I knew he had no more control over his demons. I went back to bed. Phil came in, gleeful at having caused so much fuss, reciting in a very bad Irish accent, "Would ye buy me song for a penny? A penny for a song." The next day, he wouldn't get out of bed. We all went down to the beach, but Phil was too hungover to face us. At lunchtime, I brought him coffee, but he still wouldn't come out of the bedroom. He was terribly ashamed. Late that afternoon he joined us on the beach, presented his apologies to all, and made a vow never to drink again. His misery and uncontrollable compulsions upset us all, and our remaining vacation days were subdued by the awareness of an unresolved problem.

Kim and Ricky wanted to stay in France. Ricky had a small inheritance and Baird had finally received the Bird benefit money. We decided to pool our funds and buy a house with some land big enough for the whole family to live in happily ever after. There was no doubt that Phil and I wouldn't stay together forever. Somehow, he would manage to work out this problem which was killing everything he held dear. He knew he had to regain control or lose all the success he had worked so hard to attain for so many years. Ricky went back to the States to arrange a transfer of his money and Phil went to Copenhagen for a gig.

While they were gone, Kim and I found *the house*. It was in the small village of Champmotteux. An old farmhouse, it had no plumbing and only the rudiments of electricity, but it had a field for a garden large enough to feed us all, an orchard with pear and plum trees. It also included a few farm buildings, a stable, a small house, and a large barn, which were grouped with the main farmhouse into the enormous garret, a *grenier* with natural exposed stone walls under the roof supported by the high vault formed by the original old rough-hewn wooden beams, I knew that this was *our house*. This garret would become our bedroom. It would be like sleeping in an inverted ship. The small house would be perfect for Baird. Kim and Ricky would convert the barn for themselves. We could live in the country, yet Champmotteux was only an hour's drive from Paris. Kim and I called Ricky and Phil. The farm was a bargain at $8,000 and they said to go ahead.

I was so anxious for Phil to like the house. The day after he returned from Copenhagen, I drove him to see it. I got lost and we drove around for hours. When we finally arrived in Champmotteux, Phil was sure I had been exaggerating when I told him it was just an hour from Paris. As we walked through the rusted gate and he saw the gaping hole in the barn roof, he exclaimed, "Oh, Chan, what have you done?" The three tiny downstairs rooms painted a dreary grey, pink, and brown did nothing further to enchant him. After seeing the garret, he came down the stairs and started making exploratory taps on the walls. I knew then that he was caught up in my dream. Soon afterwards, we signed the papers.

While I held down the fort in Le Vesinet as Gar and Aimée finished out the school year, Phil, Baird, Ricky, and Kim spent every available minute fixing up the house: They opened up the downstairs into one large room and built one huge stone fireplace to replace the two small corner ones. Another wall was knocked down revealing an old, rustic, handcrafted winding staircase. They installed electricity and plumbing, and a bathroom. Ceilings were knocked down to expose the original beams; windows and doors were put into the *grenier*. Phil installed a floor in the stable and connected it to the house. This was to be his studio. Baird put the small house in shape for himself. Kim and Ricky added a second floor to their barn.

Phil had always loved working with his hands. But even though remodeling our house was fulfilling, he was using this time away from me to drink. That pattern was becoming more deeply established. For the second time, he lost his wedding ring . . . this time permanently. After we moved into our dream house, every gig precipitated a crisis. He had come home from one gig crying, "Don't send me out there again, Chan. I'm not Charlie Parker!" In Europe, every jazz fan knows his jazz history, and Phil was under heavy pressure. Phil's music was constantly referred to as "Parkerian," and everyone knew that he was the alto player who had married Bird's widow. I felt deeply for him and what he must be going through. Finally, a one-night gig in Berlin became the pretext for a five-day drunk. I was frantic with worry, not knowing where Phil was or what had happened to him. When he finally showed up, he was in bad shape. Phil realized how close to the edge he had come, and decided he needed therapy. We decided to sell our house in New Hope so that he could take a year off. That way he could get himself together without any financial pressure. Phil wanted to try California, and I agreed. Five days before Christmas in 1972, we left our new French farmhouse for America.

California was a disaster. Phil's music met with hostility and the only gigs offered him were back in the studios. It was as if the past six years of his career had never existed. We rented a track house with a swimming pool in Canoga Park. The owners sold us their furniture, which was as ugly as the house. But it would just be for a year. It had cost us all the money from the sale of our house in New Hope to set up our new household in California. The schools were a waste of time for the children who had come from the demanding French educational system.

Everyone had told me that in California we could live purely, but everything there seemed as natural and pure as BHA-preserved food. We hated California life. I was afraid to touch anything in California because I was constantly being shocked. Alec Waugh once wrote about the electric shocks he had received in America. Perhaps the static electricity was the result of America being laid wall-to-wall. Gar kept asking, "What are we doing here?" I asked myself the same question one day while sitting in a parking lot surrounded by the deep fat smells from the ever-present taco take-out, Chinese take-out, McDonald's take-out, and Kentucky Fried Chicken take-out. The longer we stayed in California, the more we seemed to be eating take-out food on paper plates. I seldom went swimming in the pool. But when dinner was over and I had finished washing the dishes in our small, hot kitchen, I would submerge myself, fully-clothed, in the cool water of the pool. I was becoming a person I didn't know. Gar's graduation summons up words and images of machine-knit, overly drycleaned white orlon cardigans; upwardly mobile, silver-mink-stoled, badly wigged women; red-necked, sideburned, slicked-back, collared men; double-knit, Instamatic, skinny, cancer-tanned blonds; and 146 out-of-tune choruses of "Pomp and Circumstance."

Phil was drinking and staying out nights more than ever. Now there wasn't even remorse. We were running out of money, and by July we were down to get-away money. I missed France terribly and felt trapped. Phil was rehearsing a very good group and wanted to record with them before leaving California. I suggested that I take the kids back to France in August, enter them in school again, and open the house. Phil could make his recording and join us in six weeks at the most.

Gar flew to New York where he joined my mother to accompany her to France for the summer. Aimée and I left Los Angeles on August second. Somehow, we all managed to arrive at Orly at exactly the same minute! Baird, who had come to meet us, drove us home to Champmotteux. There were a few things he had neglected to take care of, such as having the electricity turned on and retrieving the keys from our neighbor. But nothing could dampen our joy at being back in France. Baird had remembered the important things: bread and cheese, a bottle of wine from the cellar, and a bottle of "homegrown" from the attic. We feasted by candlelight and caught up on each other's news. Only Phil was missing, and he would be home in France before long.

France is so incredibly beautiful. It's hard: there are none of the American conveniences and a lot of red tape and hassles. It closes every August, the month our Fiat always needs attention. The earth, which is full of thistles, nettles, and thorns, is heavy with clay and is back-breaking to hoe. "Champmotteux" means clod of mud, but it is the most fertile region in the world. I groaned over the Camembert and found a *marchand* of wine who had not only an excellent, fruity *vin ordinaire,* but also Beaujolais at a dollar a bottle. In Champmotteux, everyone was so polite, chatting about the weather as they emerged from behind their walls and iron gates to buy long loaves of crusty French bread from the baker who passed every day in a van.

The next few weeks were devoted to getting the house and car back in shape. The grounds were a jungle. I kept busy and time flew by. Phil was staying with friends. I wrote him:

Darling,

Do you remember when we were building the house and I had spent the night here with you? We only had candlelight and you made me sit halfway up the stairs to dig the room? We have the loveliest house in the world. If I were passing by and looked in the windows, I'd have to knock on the door. Today Monsieur Poiget took Aimée, her friend Christine and me to shop in Maisse. The piece for our brakes, the shoe, I think, got lost by train between here and Paris, of course, it being the month of August. We went to the bank. They were pleased to see me I think. We had a discussion on the dollar . . . a thumb down gesture accompanied by a quick blowing out of the lips with a subdued raspberry, or Bronx cheer, depending on your heritage. "Il monte" slowly, "je crois." *Famy* being closed (it's August), we went to the spiffed-up, *Entree Libre,* old grocery store where I grabbed one of everything while Aimée and Christine made quick hits at the P.O., the pharmacy and the bakery. Then to the *boucherie* run by the drunken, angry butcher (or sullen if he's sober) and his fawning wife and cowed daughter. I hate that place. I overcame my distaste and copped a *rôti de veau* and some *escalopes de veau* (our first veal), and a steak. For Snoopy, Fido and Steaky: 2 "repas complets pour chiens," just like Gaines Burgers or Top Choice, a bit of Canoga Park in Maisse. Mr. Poiget told Aimée that I spoke French very well and he wishes he spoke English as well. He said, "You can't interrupt her. You just have to let her keep going and get it all out."

We spoke of the weather mostly, back to before the war and specifically of the snow in 1944. The fields are dry. The seasons have changed since the war. I asked him to apologize to Madame Poiget for me, as I had made him late for lunch. He was very patient with me, but looked a bit quietly annoyed, as you do, when I finally came out of the butcher's. He flew us up that great straight road home.

I weeded the garden around the courtyard. A lot of Mademoiselle Marie's flowers have come up. Mother put supports up for the honeysuckle and I cut down the junk tree by the studio. We watched three snails mating, and disturbed some very large spiders. The courtyard is slowly coming together. The back is going to be tough. It will take some sickle swinging. We're getting the orchard under control. The plums are abundant with trees near the fence I didn't know we had. I picked a plum yesterday and it tasted like sunshine, so I picked a dozen more. The iris have spread. I hacked down all the nettles under the grape vines which are heavy with fruit. There is a carpet of ivy underneath and wild asparagus growing.This evening was cool, more like French weather, because it's been so hot. After dinner, I put Grady Tate on the phonograph, went out into the yard and looked in the window. The fireplace is so beautiful I had to come in and climb halfway up the stairs to dig it better. The stone walls are singing. I know there was a reason we should have white drapes. We have so many red accents: the vase, the candle, the speakers, a lampshade, the Kremlin Tower and Kim and Baird's Tapioca poster.

Then I went outside again and looked through the other window at the shelves with our pottery and *bocaux*. It looked so warm and cozy inside I had to come upstairs and write this letter to share it with you.

I love you.

The few letters Phil wrote to me were filled with his frustration as he tried to sell the album, and the loneliness he was experiencing. I knew he was drinking. He replied to my concerned letters with bitterness. This was part of our pattern, so I continued believing that he was faithful to me, trying his best to wrap up his business and come home.

In September the children went back to school and the hunting season began. I began to have more time on my hands, and spent my days waiting. Although I had learned more tolerance for the hunters, by the end of September, I welcomed the peace and quiet of the nights. The nights balanced things a little, but the children's presence couldn't make me forget Phil's absence. Something was wrong, but I couldn't put my finger on it. Phil had two weeks work at the Half Note in New York, and left L.A. in our Fiat to make the cross-country trek. I didn't understand what it was that Phil had to prove in America. I never saw one redeeming aspect of competition. But it's so easy to get sucked into attitudes and so difficult to be objective about one's actions and desires. In spite of everything, I knew that Phil had to be acknowledged in America. Being the toast of Europe didn't mean a thing to him as long as he still hadn't made it in the States. I didn't completely understand, but I tried to dig his need and be patient.

I had decided the whole world was shitty: you had to find the sweetest smelling shit and find a way to keep from being immersed in it. For me, this was France. Not that it was shitfree, but it did have the prettiest sky, the purest land and the best-tasting food. France was a perpetual feast for the senses. Here, I was able to relax, surrounded by peasants and nonintellectuals. Between Paris and Champmotteux, no one knew I was Bird's widow. The drawback was being a foreigner, an outlander, an *étranger* and, therefore, a misfit. I was neither a village farmer nor a Parisian weekender, so I was beyond all local classification, and looked upon as a temporary resident in transit. On the other hand, we were artists and landowners. We had chosen to live in Champmotteux and, although we had left once, we had returned.

It was autumn. The sky, an ever-changing drama, allowed us to see the light Utrillo painted. The view from the window was Van Gogh. The linear tiled rooftops thrilled me. The cookbooks were being well used, bread was baking, the sweaters were unpacked and the logs stacked to dry. Flash, our cat, checked out warm nests, as did the field mice which were preparing winter homes in the cupboards. Snoopy moved from the tile floor to the rug in front of the fireplace where she lay snapping at delinquent flies. My French vocabulary was increasing. I learned, through necessity, the word for pipe (as in drainage). It cracked me up: it's *tuyau,* a masculine word pronounced like a queeny rhythm section on the Benny Goodman Twee-o, as opposed to the Gramercy *Cinq.* I picked up my neglected knitting, but the sun kept calling me out to prune the garden. The grapes hung heavy on the vines that autumn, ripening from green to red before turning a deep matte blue. I hacked away at the invading plum trees. (To each his own territory in the orchard.) Our hyacinth-colored grapes and plums made forty-six jars of jelly that year.

The harvesting began. Huge combines, looking like prehistoric monsters, tractors, trucks and even horse-drawn carts filled the fields and roads. The sugar beets were piled in mountains by the roadside and numbered according to their field, until they could be hauled away. Then the fields were almost bare, only the winter wheat showing green. In the spring, those sparse blades would be transformed: the wheat would wave in the wind like a cool, northern sea. But now, it was time for the crows to return to scavenge left-behind corn. A great change took place in this rural community. These country people, like the animals, lived much closer to the land, following the natural rhythm of the seasons. The modern urban dweller is a stranger to his environment. Perhaps this is the reason for neurosis and anxiety. People, like the fields, become fallow. In America, the most technically advanced society, there are no old-fashioned farmers left. The farmers are part of the business community. In France, the farmers mostly keep to the traditional way of doing things, the wise way. Being flexible and in harmony with nature, French farmers are in tune with life.

Each year after the harvest, there is a weekend celebration with fireworks and a band. Once a year, the world from beyond the fields comes to each small village in France. The first weekend in September, Champmotteux is ready for its two full days of celebration. A bright red pavilion is installed on the churchyard lawn. The sagging, old, dried-out spruce tree, donned with last year's faded crepe paper decorations, and the tree which has hung over the café all year long, is replaced by a fresh new green tree decorated in brightly colored streamers. The old tree lies in the road until the day of the final ceremony when it will be burned. On the first evening, a real, professional band from the city plays in the pavilion, bringing pop music and a discreet touch of rock and roll, disguised, but still adhering to the twelve bar blues. The townspeople, usually abed by ten o'clock, are serenaded through loudspeakers until three in the morning. The café, instead of closing at 8:00 P.M., is still roaring at 5:30 A.M. Cars are parked bumper to bumper from one end of town to the other, and there is much door slamming, horn honking, and calling back and forth. The French love affair with the automobile is displayed in the revving of motors and drag-race-style getaways. The excited children can't wait to set off their firecrackers. The next afternoon, cakes are sold door to door to help pay the band. The second night is the official fireworks, sanctioned by the mayor. The firetrucks from neighboring Maisse stand by and are often needed. After the fireworks, it's every man, woman, and child for him- or herself. Horns of any sort have been dragged down from closet shelves, although this year, one serious fellow started getting his chops together two days ahead of time. Firecrackers are set off by roving bands of kids, and Gerard, owner of the café and the biggest kid of all, drags out his cap gun. In the café, the bugle player struggles manfully to get through a tune. Anyone with a piece of metal and a mouthpiece contents himself with making any kind of sound, usually loud and painful to the ear. Snoopy panics and hides, shivering behind the oil burner. Last year, the mayor's dog ran away and took refuge behind my sink. It did my Yankee heart good to close the shutters, and, as my part in the celebration, put on Charles Ives's "Fourth of July" at top volume. I had a smile of satisfaction when "Columbia, Gem of the Ocean" in all its discordant cacophony overpowered the noise made by some local soul playing a bugle outside my window. One does what one can.

Living this life made me even more puzzled about what was happening to Phil. What could be keeping him away from his family so long? When was he coming home to Champmotteux? One night, the thunder rolled overhead and grumbled away to the north so loudly that it woke me. I closed my eyes again, but the lightning penetrated my closed eyes. I remained awake, watching the light show. Eventually, a gentle rain lulled me back to sleep.

PART III
ANDANTINO

13. CAESURA

I remembered the time when we were still working on the house in Champmotteux. One evening, while we were eating the dinner we had cooked in the fireplace after a hard day's work, a pair of swallows flew in and circled overhead. They must have decided that we were trustworthy, because they built their nest on the beams. Soon there was an egg in the nest: "Lenny" and "Lena," as we called them, had started a family. We were careful not to disturb them. But before the egg could hatch, I found Lena dead in the weeds. She must have been poisoned by the grain from the surrounding fields that had just been sprayed. Rather than bury her, I conceived an Indian funeral, placing the dead swallow on the highest wall in our yard. Within minutes, the sky was dark with other swallows which, like true Indian mourners, circled several times over Lena and then flew away. The egg in the nest remained unhatched, and Lenny disappeared. However, the following spring, two swallows circled over our courtyard, and then flew into Baird's house through a door which happened to be open. I'm sure it was Lenny, back with another Lena. The new mate seemed less than thrilled with the site of her new home. Lenny flew in and out of the house, and finally managed to persuade her to set up residence there. We were stuck with an open door for the summer. . . .

Phil's letters from the States remained loving and full of promises of his return to Champmotteux after the next gig. He often called when he was drunk, saying he would be home the next day, only to call back when he had sobered up to say he was committed to doing another gig. Too many people had been nice to him and he couldn't let them down! I felt that Phil's ambition and thirst were driving our marriage on the rocks.

Meanwhile, Phil had left L.A. to drive cross-country. The car broke down in Pennsylvania where Kim and Ricky were living. When they came to help Phil, they discovered that he wasn't travelling alone. He had two women with him. Kim now understood her stepfather's reasons for not returning to France, but she thought that Phil should explain them to me himself. Her silence assured that Phil's secret was well kept.

Kim and Ricky decided to spend Christmas with us in France. We were all surprised by a cable from Phil announcing his imminent arrival at Orly. At the airport, he gave me a cursory kiss, and handed me his horn and hand luggage while he went to pick up his baggage. Back home, Snoopy went wild. Gar embraced Phil strongly and Aimée hugged him for hours. Diplomatically, Kim and Ricky took the children out to do some last-minute shopping, leaving Phil and me alone. Phil spent the next few hours hooking up the stereo. Before dinner, the first night, he got out the carton in which he kept all of the things he took along when he went on the road. Sorting through the cold water washing powder and shampoo, he regaled us with jokes about how clean he was. After dinner, pleading jet lag, he went to sleep.

The next night, he got into my bed and serviced me quickly; in the morning, we snuggled, but he couldn't get it up. He insisted that his head was messed up, and denied having anyone else. When I asked him what he had done for sex during the past six months, he answered, "I jacked off!" He kept assuring me that worry about his drinking and career made him impotent. He told me how bad it had been, and that he had even called Alcoholics Anonymous. As long as he didn't drink, he would be cool. I believed him.

On Christmas Day, Phil made a recording of the family as we opened our presents. When we listened to the cassette, it was punctuated with lots of hearty "Ho ho ho's" from him. All of our presents were wrong. In addition to some underwear, I had decided to replace the wedding ring he had lost. He gave me a bath mat and some ugly, matronly pajamas. Baird's fiancée was there, although he had started seeing someone else and we all knew it. Kim and Ricky knew that Phil had someone else back in the States. We all spent Christmas lying to each other.

Phil had a round trip ticket, a 21–45-day excursion fare, which meant that he had to stay in France a minimum of twenty-one days. Phil said he had to return to the States to do an album, but he would be back in France in six weeks. I believed him. When the children pressed him for a definite date, I told them that Phil had a lot on his mind and that they shouldn't pressure him. During the time he spent in Champmotteux, he was busy every minute. He made all the necessary repairs on the house and showed Gar how to change the fuses. He asked me where I wanted the shelves put up in the studio. "But it's your studio," I protested. Kim and Ricky, who wanted to drive to Luxemburg via Switzerland before returning to America, left Champmotteux ahead of their planned stay. Phil had planned to leave a week after New Year's Day. However, when I returned from the market on January 2, he told me that he thought it best to leave the next day. He had changed his mind because he wanted to have a few days to rehearse before the recording date. I knew he was low on cash, and worried that he would need a few dollars to get into New York from the airport. He told me he had already phoned someone who would be meeting him.

Before leaving, Phil suggested that I sleep downstairs in the studio during the winter so we wouldn't have the expenses of heating the garret. We drove to Orly in a snowstorm. He told me to drive carefully on the way home. He kissed the kids goodby and said he'd see them soon. Then he walked out of our lives forever. Perhaps, anticipating my grief, the last thing he said to me was, "Write, Chan. Write about all the things you know."

> Write, he says.
> Write of things you know well.
> Write of comings and goings,
> Write of empty hearts and empty heads
> And empty pages and empty beds.

Trying to write has made me realize that I can't bullshit anyone anymore.

On January 20th, I felt unusually depressed. Suddenly, I realized that it was exactly one year and one month ago that we had decided it was to be "Phil's Year." I had to stop sorting through the broken pieces of my life. I had to throw away the shards and put away the glue. But every time I did, I found another piece and so I dragged them all out again and tried to fit them together. Still, there were missing pieces. The ides of March were coming, and I had to prepare myself to meet them alone for the first time. Pree was in my thoughts. I'd always felt so self-contained, but I didn't seem to be able to function without Phil. I had to be born again and start life anew. I was filled with wonder at the miracle of an orange crocus which had blossomed from a bulb I had planted in the autumn of '72, before our disastrous return to America. When I first came back to France from California, I used to enjoy being alone. For a short period of time, I had even thought that, perhaps, I was meant to be celibate. But I continually experienced so many wonders that I wanted to share with my man.

Now, I tried to find some small comfort in the earth around me. There were little yellow flowers on the winter jasmine in the garden, and the leaves had already appeared on the tree by the studio. I dared to hope that the early January thaw would continue, so that, somehow, this year, I would escape the cold and depression that, for me, had come to be synonymous with February and March.

I went into the studio and began to write. How things had changed from the time when I got my first gig dancing in show business. In those days, all a dancer had to do was fake a time step. If you knew what a *tour jeté* was, you were cool. Then along came Agnes de Mille with "Oklahoma!" The same thing had happened in writing. Since Allen Ginsburg, Ken Kesey, and William Burroughs, you couldn't jive anymore. Even Anaïs Nin was being published. I used to be a jazz girl. Had the music changed, or had I? I had always said that if anything ever happened to Phil, I might never be able to listen to music again. Now, I couldn't hear the music anymore. What the fuck! Does everything, including the human soul, have planned obsolescence built in? As each thing in my life broke down, the effort to patch it together again seemed overwhelming. So much cheating, scheming, twisting, and justifying were involved in maintaining the easy life that it was easier to do without and live life simply. I guessed every motherfucker sold out in the end. Youthful optimism, naiveté, and resilience were needed in order to keep bucking the inevitable tide. It had been a longer time than I could remember since I had felt love.

I was a warm woman. I needed romance, tenderness, and desire. I wanted life and growth. I loved the earth, green things, the sky, the clouds. I loved wisdom and innocence, friendship and love, discovery and antiquity, young people and old people, joy and sorrow. I felt like going to see a million old friends who would smile and wish me well. I wanted to break the record for long-distance running. I wanted to live in the present again. I wanted to be doing things, to have my days filled once more.

As it was, I spent my days hurrying time along. When I awoke, I willed the clock to move quickly to ten o'clock, so that I could get the mail. If there were no letters, I could pass the time until lunch with the *Herald Tribune*. Afternoons weren't easy. I created work for myself. I searched the house for clothes to be washed. How funny, to miss having Phil's clothes to wash. I made plans for gourmet dinners which I seldom got around to cooking, I read a little, tried to write a little, had a kir, and somehow the day would pass. But at night, I began thinking of time as being six hours earlier. I would start to wonder what Phil, in his time zone, was doing.

My letters to Phil remained unanswered. When Phil sent us money, it came without a message. I continued to be sure of his fidelity, concerned that he was on a bad binge. Finally, unable to stand it any longer, I called the friends in New Jersey where he was staying. It was early in the morning, so I was sure that Phil would still be home. Some heavy, frantic whispering went on, before I was told that Phil was no longer living there. I called Kim, who pleaded ignorance. Desperate, I called her again, and this time the truth finally came out. Kim burst into tears as she told me, "He has someone else. Oh, Mom, he wouldn't treat a dog this way!" However, I still couldn't believe that Phil would leave his family after seventeen years. I was laid so low that it took me two more years to realize that he could, and had.

Phil had said he was fighting for his life. One doesn't win a war by sacrificing one's allies. When a father walks out on his family, life naturally changes for the worse. A family divided, as ours was, is like a sick cell, incapable of normal growth, and forced to settle for less than its natural potential: We were abnormal. All our problems had multiplied. We could no longer function as a strong unit. We were like a cancerous cell.

Dinner times were the worst. The children, who were in school all day, didn't have to witness the extent of my grief. However, it was impossible for me to get through the evening meal with them without bursting into tears. Aimée still believed in the Hollywood ending and kept faith in her beloved daddy, but Gar was completely disillusioned. He was terribly worried about me and his schoolwork suffered. He had always been a good student and was two years ahead in school. That year, he was held back.

Marriage, as I'd known it until then, had been an agreement: the male assumed the financial responsibility and the female filled his needs in the home. I didn't dig the roles. I objected to being an unpaid maid, receiving bed and board and fulfilling sexual and social needs. Curse my parents, who assumed I'd meet a "sugar daddy" and have no need to make my own way. . . . Perhaps the women of their time could gain a dishonest advantage by fulfilling a role I was unable to believe in. There can never be an honest relationship between a man and a woman as long as economic and sexual advantages lie with the man.

Phil was balling another chick, but he was losing part of himself and I no longer cared. In spite of Phil's tendency to be dependent on a mother figure, I think he had been struggling all his life to free himself from maternal influence, and to mature. It's more difficult for a male to become an adult and free himself of the womb, since he is always seeking to return to one. Contrary to what we are taught, it is the woman who takes the man. He surrenders his seed. As the men are sorted out from the boys, all that are left are the women.

I knew who I was and I had always been honest in our relationship. I'd always been strong and sure of what was "the right way." I couldn't understand a man striving for anything less than perfection. Perhaps that is why I found myself alone. I'd always felt I was more like my father than my mother. My father had wanted a boy when I was born. He had given me his initials, "B. D." (and an expensive set of Lionel trains!). He told me that I would be a businesswoman, and that I should always be strong, wise, and brave. But I did wish I could have been financially independent, as everything seemed to be on the side of the one supplying the bread, rather than on the part of the exploited woman. However, any woman without an independent income or the ability to contribute financially to her well being cannot be happy in this money-oriented society. It was hard to be creative alone in my funky bachelor studio, housing the oil-burner. Phil had sent me only three small checks, along with his promise that he never broke a contract!

In that period of readjustment, reevaluation and reorganization it was amazing how classical music could evoke the past. Debussy's *Danse sacrée et danse profane* made me think of 52d Street, when Kim was a baby and being a harpist seemed to be a suitable ambition for a lady. Hearing *The Rite of Spring* brought back the memory of perfume burning and one small blue light in the room in the Piccadilly Hotel where I discovered love, and had my heart broken. In retrospect, I was grateful. Johnny had been gentle and wise, and he opened my world to Stravinsky. *Afternoon of a Faun* made me tell the children how lovely ballet is. I realized that, for me, most discovery lay in the past, whereas for my lucky children, it lay ahead. Listening, I felt again the excitement I used to feel everyday in the past, but which I occasionally felt now: I remembered the sheer joy of life and the wonder of beauty (which many people never feel), and the thrill of anticipating what is in the next room. That is the best high.

When death takes a husband from his loving family, the course of grief is clinically predictable: shock, disbelief, panic, anger, and finally the acceptance of the inevitable. Roar, rail, curse, bellow, holler as one may, nothing can reverse death. Eventually, one looks to the living and the wound finally heals. I thought our home had been a happy one. When Phil walked out of it, I went through all those emotional changes, except the final one. How could I accept what I didn't understand? Somehow, I was convinced that the whole situation was just a horrible misunderstanding. Phil hardly fit the pattern of a philanderer. He had been devoted to his family. I needed an answer, so I began writing him letters, three or four a day, mostly unmailed. I carried on a monologue.

It was like the summer after Bird's death and all the torch songs seemed to have been written for me. I knew I must move, yet I was unable to get past the gate. I felt frozen, suspended between two lives with no energy: I couldn't even find my glasses; the toilet flush came off in my hand; I watched the oil gauge go down. My copious tears seemed wasted. It couldn't be all about twelve bars of blues, could it?

The children convinced me that if we called Phil and apologized for whatever it was we had done, if we told him how much we loved him, he would come home. Aimée made the call. Sobbing, she begged him to come back to us. He asked her why. "Because we love you," she cried. Phil's reply was that he couldn't afford these phone calls. As sharp and cold as a dagger's steel, he thrust those words into Aimée's heart. There was nothing more to say. I could no longer be Phil's friend because I didn't like the way he treated his children. I couldn't stand to look at the pain in their faces. They were inconsolable. I was so glad it was time to close the shutters on the windows. Another day had ended and we had managed to get through it. What was time to children? They didn't understand. I couldn't just wait here alone and mourn. I had nothing, not even my impregnable ego. I had no more strength for my children. Now, it was they who tried to comfort me. I wanted to run away and hide. I no longer cared what happened. I was hysterical, unable to think. The pain unhinged me and I didn't know how to cope.

Phil finally called and told me that he loved someone else. I'd lost him. I felt so cold and alone. I was falling to pieces. I couldn't seem to pull myself together. The family was bleeding to death, but Phil didn't even offer to dress the wound. In fact, every time a scab started to form, he insistently picked it off. I felt soiled and used, the victim of an obscene act that Phil had committed. However, Phil complained bitterly that he was the victim, suffering from our critical questioning and our lack of self-control. I had expected an Ives symphony and all he came up with was a Strauss waltz.

What could be the source of Phil's pain? Why was he so tortured? Surely it couldn't be for the sake of his ego that he had sacrificed his family. I couldn't understand his suffering. Had he ever watched a child die? Had he ever stood by, helplessly, unable to prevent the death of a loved one? He had never looked on death, and never even lost a parent. Had he ever been part of an oppressed minority? Had he ever felt hunger or poverty? Had he ever had anyone turn their back on him? Had he ever felt sympathy for the victims of wars? Had he ever felt the need to fight injustice? Had he ever felt pity for the downtrodden? Had he ever loved humanity or even a flower? Had the world never recognized his genius? Phil must have needed something he had never experienced. He needed it so badly that he had to manufacture it himself, with self-inflicted pain, the missing sensation. But there was more to living than such thin-blooded self-indulgence. For years Phil had told me of his suffering, the pain he felt. This was his artistic right, which I accepted and tried to alleviate. But we never really narrowed it down or identified it. Surely, if he was now a craftsman, as he insisted, and not a creator, he couldn't continue calling it the pain of being an artist. I wanted to give it a name. Name your pain.

One day, a big red and yellow balloon almost landed in our field. The children and I heard the people in the gondola shouting. We watched as a big butane flame sent the balloon up into the sky once again. Gar took off after it on his motorbike and Snoopy barked, setting off all the other dogs in Champmotteux. Great excitement! We were alive!

On summer evenings, I opened the door and listened to Billie Holiday. In some small way, it felt so healthy and seemed to make up for her pain. She was in Champmotteux and her presence seemed fitting. Listening to all the music on 52d Street, I realized what a sensual feast those years had been. Christ! Jesus! God! I missed music. I missed that making of something important. I missed Lady. I missed Basie rehearsals and the experiments of Boyd Raeburn and George Handy. I missed my youth. What a glorious time it had been to be young. The old order died out with the war and the new order was free and had not yet gone wrong. I was born into an era of giants. This was the age of mediocrity. I had known greatness, and the fear of being a cliché was the horror of my life. I missed the time when people touched. I had become cold and sterile since I met Phil. He had sapped my strength and made me as bitter and as cynical as he was. I had wasted so much time exorcising this ghost. I felt cheated, as if my wedding ring had turned my finger green. All those years, I had excused his immaturity, excused the self-centered sentimentality, and waited for depth and feeling. The feeling had come through words, words of self-pity and drunken garrulousness. I had made a vow and I had seen it through. But I missed the music.

I felt young, yet I realized that I was forty-eight years old. The last time I had found myself alone, I was thirty-two. Being alone at this period of my life filled me with horrible insecurities. The chances for a new life dim with the years. My main preoccupation all my life had been that of wife and mother. My daily garb was jeans, and I didn't really know how to dress and I'd even forgotten the technique of make-up. My eyes were fading and the lines around my mouth had deepened. My neck was becoming crinkled and my skin looser. My body was shrinking as the juice of youth dried. In unguarded moments, I thought I perceived the inevitable specter of death. Had the fact that I was old reminded Phil of his own mortality? Surely an unexpected death, a youthful death, is best. We are taught to look away and ignore old age, and to hide from our ultimate fate.

Did he remember when he was twenty-five and I was thirty-two? He had promised he would cherish me and love me forever. I'm sure he spoke in passion and really meant it at the time. I had thought of the future: that when I was fifty, he would be only forty-three: his options would still be open, while mine would be pretty slim. I had such faith that Phil was a special man. That's probably what he had difficulty living up to. I'd had less than I thought, and one can't create a deeper capacity for love in a vessel without depth. I'm sorry I expected so much, and I should have been glad that he'd found someone who would settle for less. But he did whine a lot. If I had had one hundred cocksmen waiting in line at my door to worship me as supreme woman, I couldn't have done that to him. Were all his coins counterfeit? What would he have to spend in his old age? Would he think of his children growing up never really knowing who he was? Would he regret missing the miracle of their discoveries? What memories would he draw upon? Phil, who had always known that life and art should roar, had copped out with a whimper and a whine. Roar, motherfucker! Stop whining and roar! Perhaps he had forgotten how to. Did he really sell his song for a penny? I didn't feel cheated, for I couldn't have lost what never existed. I felt enriched because I had gained from the experience and by overcoming the pain. It was another penny for my piggy bank of life.

Although I was down to 103 pounds and my legs looked like a sora bird's, I was tan and my hair was a good length. I had been doing manual labor in the garden and trying to open myself to good vibes. I went up and down. My vision was fading and I could no longer drive at night. This limited my access to any excitement outside of rural Champmotteux. Sometimes I asked myself, "What's a nice girl from 52d Street doing in a farming village where she is looked on with suspicion because she is a foreigner, a woman alone with two children who speak to each other in another language?" Life is strange: I was basically content in Champmotteux; this was my nest. I wanted to stay here in my home and groove with my children.

Maybe I should have put an ad in the *Herald Tribune:* I am a widow with two children, but only have one dog now. I am part owner of an estate in France. In a few years my children will be grown and I shall be free to travel. I love music passionately and, since I haven't heard any live music in over a year, I miss it terribly. Celibacy has made me extra passionate, and abstemiousness had made me trim. I read a lot, write a lot, and think a lot. My intentions are serious because I am not, by nature, a frivolous woman. Although I am no longer young, I am fairly well preserved. I am seeking a companion with whom I can enjoy mutual pleasures, and share my life. I've experienced much sorrow, but I have been able to retain an optimistic outlook. I enjoy simple pleasures and don't covet wealth. I care deeply for children, old ladies, animals, flowers, and all growing things. On the other hand, I tend to be bossy and dogmatic, which may be a cover for insecurity and feelings of unworthiness. I've made many mistakes and will try not to make the same ones over again. I have the failing of holding too tightly to those I love. But I love deeply, so that can't be too bad, can it? I'm stubborn and tenacious, and I endure. I'm willful and sometimes destructive, but I try to curb those negative traits. I'm not able to handle boozers in a balanced way, because whiskey has caused me much sorrow and pain, but I'm trying to be more rational about that. Still, I know it's a failing and I don't handle it as well as another woman might. I daydream a lot and am apt to fantasize more than I should. I am gullible and trusting, and so I lack a strong sense of humor. Won't you tell me something about yourself? My life is very lonely now and letters help brighten the day. I know you are a busy person, but it would mean so much to me.

The psychological process of a psyche recovering from a devastating blow may be clinically interesting. However, it must be terribly boring to friends of someone who is as verbal as I am. I had run the gamut: The outrage—"he" will have some heavy dues to pay behind this shit. The self-flagellation—it was all my fault; I didn't give "him" what "he" needed. The pleading for another chance, which comes from the terror and helplessness of being alone. The bitterness and the woman scorned, the evil and the desire for revenge. The certainty that "he" must be deranged, or terribly ill, or in need. The pity for "him." The thoughts of martyrdom and pious sacrifice. And, in the end, the boredom and ennui, the resignation and relief. It was finished. It was too sordid and pathetic.

While I was trying to bury this husband, forces were at work to resuscitate the last one. It was a big Bird year in America.

14. LARGO

As I looked through the trees in my garden in Champmotteux, the wheat fields in the distance were like a sea of golden sunshine. A sudden storm turned the sky mauve and sent children and animals scurrying inside until a rainbow appeared, the overcast broke, and big, white clouds flew past, leaving a blue wash which deepened to azure.

The houses and buildings in Champmotteux have thick walls which reveal their age. The thicker the walls, the older the house. The walls of our house are one-half meter thick, and it dates back 150 to 200 years. The café is 75 years old; and our electrician Mr. Malechère's house is over 200 years old. Up the road, towards Boigneville, is the original site of Champmotteux. An underground finding was hastily covered up there: the skeletons of many women and children were found thrown together helter-skelter as if by a great cataclysm.

According to the last census, we had 139 souls in town, but on weekends and in summer, the town swelled with Parisians who owned "country houses." They arrived with small children and an aggressive desire to till the land and cultivate their small gardens. They brought with them the pace of the city, and life in Champmotteux quickened. The weekenders strolled past our house on the way to the café, and cars parked in a line which reached our house. Strange faces said, "Bonjour," and their children filled our house. Their days were full of projects, work to be done in the garden, bike rides to the pool in Maisse, horses to ride at the ranch. Records or TV played all day, and small bodies sprawled in every room. Bicycles piled up on the lawn and motorbikes filled our driveway. The natives were seen only when a food truck passed. The trucks came through town every day, selling meat, vegetables, fish, *charcuterie*, staples, bread, and even live rabbits. The pace picked up toward noon, when most people were preparing the big meal of the day. The baker, the most welcome vendor of all, came between twelve-thirty and one. If he was late, the small groups of gossiping villagers would begin to show signs of anxiety. The French must have fresh bread daily, and the people of Champmotteux were no exception.

Our small village made headlines in the French newspapers and TV in what became known as the other Don Camillo Affair. The church is central to Champmotteux, as in all old villages in France. "Our" priest, the terrifying Father Harry, or "*Monsieur le Curé,*" serviced several small towns in the area. The mayor of neighboring Boigneville stole the pulpit from the church in Champmotteux. When Father Harry told him to return it, the mayor refused. The priest went to the Procureur de la République in Corbeil. The affair finally reached the highest minister in Paris, who came all the way to Boigneville himself. The mayor was told to return the pulpit.

For the press, this resolved the problem. However, it had drawn attention not only to Champmotteux, but also to the priest. In character and person, he was heavy and menacing. He would move his large body slowly through town, impeded by a wooden leg and his long black cape. His face, red from wine, was rough and tormented. In truth, he was an Englishman, born in London. He was proud of his ability to speak several languages, but pretended to know only French with his parishioners, whom he privately scorned. One day, before the pulpit incident, he had deigned to exchange a few words with me, professing to be intellectually starved and cheated by his backwater parish. He told me, "These small villages are from the middle ages, and serve no purpose. They should be leveled." I protested that times were changing, and that this generation was different, to which he had replied angrily, "No, they are just as ignorant as their parents." He mocked the taciturn peasants, and stated they were an anachronism. My attempt at further conversation was rejected with "I usually ask the questions." Poor Father Harry! (He was one of the very few people Snoopy ever growled at.) By the time the Champmotteux church got its pulpit back, Father Harry had been sent to the booby hatch.

The church in Champmotteux was built around 1600 by Michel de l'Hôpital, a Protestant who was a peacemaker between the Catholics and Protestants during the Reformation. He lived in nearby Vignay and there are underground tunnels connecting the region for many kilometers. These are now being used by the farmers as drainage ditches. Although the tomb of Michel de l'Hôpital is in Champmotteux, it is empty. His body was removed during the religious wars, and completely disappeared during the French revolution.

So many times during those past ten months, when I missed having a man, I daydreamed that some stranger, somewhere in the world, would find his way to Champmotteux and fall madly in love with me. At the very least, I hoped the phone would ring and it would be someone from my past, newly arrived in Paris, who had waited for me all those years until I was free. Champmotteux looked like an MGM movie set for a World War II saga. I expected to see Van Johnson come sloughing out of the fields, freckled nose properly muddied, and blue eyes twinkling through the grime. He would knock at the door and, with an all-American grin, ask for a glass of water, ma'am. Intuitively, I'd know he was hungry and watch with pleasure as he wolfed down a gourmet meal and a fine old Bordeaux. He'd fall asleep on the couch and I'd cover him with an afghan. In the morning, he'd make his way through the fields to the front line. I thought it funny he never mentioned a bath. . . .

One day a helicopter passed over our courtyard. I was wearing shorts, a halter, and shades. I knew I didn't show my age from that height. Sure 'nuff, they made a circle and returned to hover overhead. In the open door of the copter, I could see a man digging me. They didn't land and they didn't return.

A few days later, not looking at all dap, I was returning from shopping in the car loaded with groceries. The man in a Mercedes in front of me pulled off the road. I passed him, and by the time I had reached Cely, he was tailgating. When we reached a narrow, wooded stretch of road, he began flashing his headlights. Thinking he wanted to pass, I slowed and moved over to give him room. He slowed and blinked his lights again. I threw up hands in the air, French style. He made a gesture and blinked again. I thought perhaps he was plainclothes fuzz, although that seemed unlikely in a Mercedes. Perhaps I had car trouble. I pulled off the road and stopped. He pulled up behind me and got out of his car. I was psyching myself to deal with what he might have on his mind, getting my French together for papers, insurance, tires, or whatever the problem might be.

He was young, nice looking, and well dressed. As he sauntered up to my car, he said something which I didn't understand. However, I knew it had nothing to do with papers or tires. I asked him what he had said, "*Comment?*" He leaned on my open window and, in a heavy-eyed manner, asked seductively if I was in a hurry, "*Etes-vous pressée?*" I groaned, threw the car into gear, hoping he wasn't attached to it in any way, and roared off. By the time I reached the next village, I was fantasizing: My god, it could have been "Last Tango in Paris." Or I could have asked him, "*Quel âge avez-vous?*" If he answered "thirty-two," I would have wiped him out by saying that next month I would be forty-nine. Or I could have leered, "Follow me," and seen how far he would have lasted. But I couldn't have outrun the Mercedes with my Fiat and, besides, I was nearly out of gas. Would he have paid for it? Would he have helped me unload my groceries first? What kind of freak was he?

A month later, the Concorde, carrying the Shah of Iran on a demonstration run, buzzed over our house. It made about fifteen low passes over Champmotteux. I tried to look very sexy.

Mr. Malechère, who is a crackerjack electrician, had managed to make my broken turntable operable, but only one track of the stereo was audible. I was still trying to find the lost channel where Jobim sings the missing lyric to "How Insensitive." I finally decided to tackle it myself. As I pulled it out of the wall cabinet, a large can fell open, and a treasure-trove of five home movie reels came tumbling out. They documented the complete saga of Champmotteux to L.A., Paris to New Hope and points west: the breakup of a marriage unfolding before my very eyes. Watching the films from my present perspective was very enlightening. In all the long shots, Phil was looking back over his shoulder, in annoyance, wife and kids following in purdah, as if we were insufferable bores. We weren't a family, we were an entourage. What a charade! What an awful relationship we had! How many wasted years! We hadn't had a loving marriage. We must have had some kind of silent agreement . . . arrangement. I hated it when I saw it with an uninvolved eye. Later, I found the stereo channel myself.

Phil had said, "Fuck George Wein. Fuck Charlie Parker, fuck his wife, his son and his horn."

I said, "Fuck the imitators. Fuck the blood-suckers. Fuck Los Angeles. Fuck self-destructive cats and hungry bitches. Fuck America and Nixon and red-neck republicans. Fuck the motherfuckers."

I continued:

Fuck the men who can't grow up.
Fuck the masochists who love their pain.
Fuck the fathers who deny their children.
Fuck the quitters and cop-outs.
Fuck the insensitive, indiscreet weaklings.
Fuck the whiners.
Fuck the live-negators.
Fuck the liars and the cheaters.
Fuck the inelegant and undignified.

Fuck the ones who cause pain and wallow in gutters.
Long live the children, the shouters and affirmers.
Long live the constructors, growers and givers.
Long live the laughers and smilers.
Long live the keepers of the earth.
Long live the watchers of the sky.
Long live the tenders of animals.

It was one full year since I had been alone and I felt very unmarried.

After all the heartbreak and pain, I was just terribly disappointed and let down. I had expected more. There are so few times in our lives when people are able to reach out and touch without preconceptions, prejudice, or role playing getting in between the actual touching of the essence of two people. I tried to remember the times we had touched. I thought of two instances when we had come close.

The night Phil took me halfway up the stairs, he was high and wanting to get higher. Perhaps that was his essence. But at that moment, I dug him . . . really dug him as a man, although I felt much less safe with him as a husband. Then there was the night we came down from the mountain in Lugano. Was I, perhaps unconsciously, trying to break the pattern? Flushed by his victory, he was certainly someone else: that man who walked to answer the door with a hard-on. I can't think of many other times we even came close to touching. I'm sure it must have been as lonely for him as it was for me. I hoped he had finally found out who he was and that he was living his truth. I had rediscovered myself and was trying to adjust to what my marriage had taught me.

Some people are drifters, others are settlers. I had a need for the land which he lacked. Some people need to compete. I had a piece of land and I didn't need to win the world. These were irreconcilable differences.

He was extravagant and went to the brink. I was thrifty and careful. I nurtured. He created. I abided. He was a zephyr. I held back. He didn't look where he was going. I needed tomorrow. He lived for today. I sipped slowly. He gulped.

Yet, I was clumsy and sloppy. He was careful of detail. I was thoughtless. He brooded. I was scatterbrained. He couldn't relate. I liked and needed people and a family. He needed self. I couldn't lie. He bent the truth. I would endure.

After swearing that I would never have one in the house again, I broke down and rented a television set. French popular culture leaves a lot to be desired and it was disillusioning. I much preferred the farmers or upper-class French to the bourgeoisie. The middle class seemed to think anything American was chic and this was rapidly ruining the charm of France with all the worst of America. It would be sad to see the two-hour lunch go.

One of the French TV programs showed Nixon's "Checkers Speech" from 1952. It was completely out of sync. He spoke about his little black and white spotted dog, his two little girls who loved animals as all children, and his wife, Pat, whom the camera picked up as a 1950s Hollywood starlet type. She looked at her man with adoration. When he got to the part about the simple, old, cloth coat, pressing his thumb and middle finger to the bridge of his nose with head bowed, we were shown the inauguration, replete with high-stepping, choreographed majorettes and the snappy military parade. The program continued, showing a series of Nixon stills: Nixon in candid, introspective poses, revealing the insecure manic-depressive. A few words followed about his strong mother and quick-tempered failure of a father. Films of his Marx-Brothers-Ruratania-comic-opera White House guard finished things off.

Why did our inaugurals look like something out of Hitler's Germany or a banana republic? I'd never seen a European inauguration with such an overabundance of uniforms and flags. The next candidate who would promise no more military parades would get my vote. Such preoccupation with flags and power in America was unhealthy.

There were incredible revelations about the CIA. We always knew about the corruption, the anarchy, the assassinations, Radio Liberty and General Gehlan. But when you were in the minority, you almost accepted the majority opinion: if you swam against the main stream, you were some kind of crank. I didn't understand why there should be such bewilderment that we supported dictators all over the world. The U.S. led the rank of fascist countries.

France used to be a pleasant country to live in despite the government, which every good Frenchman ignored anyway. Since they replaced their shoebox files and pencils with typewriters and IBM computers, they haven't been so easy to ignore. As a result, the population was faced with what we always knew. As a result, the people were becoming more up-tight and unpleasant.

There was anarchy all over the world except in America. It wasn't because we were so cool. Maybe we could bluff it through with enough files on our citizens, but I didn't see how other capitalist countries could survive this decade. The Third World, which had just become self-govern-ing, would begin the cycle anew. In Europe, the government had already lost control.

Kissinger had become the de Gaulle of America, with the power and inclination to do great evil. Reading about the coup d'etat in Portugal, I flashed on the CIA before coming to a paragraph which stated that a senior Portuguese officer had hinted at U.S. involvement, saying the Ameri-can ambassador had better leave after what had happened. I heard that he was being replaced. Did the U.S. government think that another cam-paign contributor would be any more acceptable? America had its shoulder against the door trying to stem the tide of freedom and justice.

From my bed at one end of the lofty garret, I looked through the long hall to the far side of Aimée's room, across the upturned hat in the vault in the garret, past beams which hold a myriad of objects: old milk cans; the goddess of good fortune. Kwan Yin, that Bird had given me (humph, she hadn't brought me much good fortune!); memorabilia from the Russian tour. The far wall was covered with Miro, Daniel Humair's paintings, posters, the RCA dog. Further on I saw a ladder, a jar of knitting needles, a lamp made from a Grand Marnier bottle. My gaze continued, uninter-rupted, beyond two doors and through the lacquered, collaged, womb-like hall and in across the threshold of Aimée's room. Here Mick Jagger and Miles Davis shared the scene with horse photos, decals with silly sayings that appealed to a thirteen-year-old's sense of humor, and shoes with stacked heels. On the right was Gar's room with his trains and the biggest library in the family . . . bilingual *plus*. To the left was the door to what Aimée and her friends thought was the hippest bathroom in the world. I as-sumed this was because of the Alice Cooper and Santana posters, the Picasso lithograph, the avocado plants, the handmade toilet paper holder and shelves, and the dark blue toilet seat. Our bathroom had *ambiance*.

Sometimes I felt that all the undirected, creative energy would make our house rise into the air. It was electric and I could feel it. We needed a focus again. We were three people in search of a center. I couldn't believe that someone out there wasn't in need of what we had to give.

Outside, the terra cotta tile roof had sprouted three fine bouquets of pink sedum. The swallows dipped and dived across the sky before dart-ing into Baird's house to feed their hungry family of five nestlings. William Burroughs wrote: "There is something almost pathetic in the fact that the bird remains forever the same. You grow old, your friends die or move to distant lands. Yet there in your garden or orchard are the birds of your boyhood, the same notes, the same calls, and, to all intents and purposes, the identical birds endowed with perennial youth."

I had a Ricard at the Deux Magots café in Paris after the movies. It was six P.M., rush hour, assignation hour . . . the city quickening . . . a Pontiac Fury, disproportionately important, fat tires speaking of American luxury, was on the corner holding up traffic . . . freaks, lovers, whores, tourists. I thought about giving up my American citizenship. I walked past the Café Flore as the sun broke through the grey sky and rain, light as mist, began to fall. An American playing guitar on the sidewalk sang "Here Comes the Sun." I hesitated but didn't want to interrupt. It was francs he was wanting, not conversation with a lonely old woman. Ah, but the wisdom and love I could have offered. Perhaps he was playing, caught in the spell of Hemingway or Henry Miller, and was as well connected.

Such a strange mixture was my son Gar: man and boy, American and French, conservative and humanist. A solitary loner, he could be gregarious and socially poised. He was a cynic, a thinker, a worrier, slow to give affection, yet capable of a great depth of feeling. On the walls of his room, finger-marked pictures of motorcycles hung with thumbtacks, along with a peace medal, an American flag, and a beer opener. Tangerine peels and mild-clouded glasses were strewn next to his library of classics in two languages.

Gar went to his first *boum* (French for what they used to call hop). He telephoned me the next morning and said to get the aspirin ready. I immediately flashed hangover. Aimée didn't reassure me when she said it was awfully hard not to drink at those affairs when everybody else did. She was quick to defend the faults of those she loved. I had my lecture all planned, but Gar was just exhausted from staying up until eleven-thirty after dancing all day from two P.M. After the *boum* there had been some streaking, and a few boys had gone to the cemetery to scare themselves. They all had a grand time. They had had four bottles of beer among thirty kids and Gar said he had had very little. They had consumed three kilos of cookies, three cakes, six bottles of apple juice, and about a thousand cigarettes. Gar didn't smoke. He was proud to tell his host's mother that there was no food he didn't like. He reiterated for the third time that I was truly forty-nine, nearer to fifty. When his friend's mother didn't believe it, he turned to me and said, "Well, your hair is still dark and your skin is good."

Gar got a summer job on a nearby farm. His first day at work, he drove the tractor all morning and forked hundred-pound bales of hay into the truck all afternoon. Every hour, they stopped for a drink. Gar demurred at the watered wine and on the next break was given orange juice. At the end of the day, all the workers were given a pastis. Gar soon learned to drink watered wine. The end of the first day, he had an aching back and his boss thoughtfully told him not to come in until the next afternoon. One day, he had to help unload a freight car full of fish manure. When he came home that evening, we made him throw his clothes out of the window into the courtyard. He loved working on the farm and continued to work there on all school holidays.

I felt as if I was just awakening from a long nightmare. I seemed to have lost a year. Who could have meant so much to me that they could steal a year from my memory? The past July I remembered watching Watergate in California. Soon, I drank steadily but moderately through the day . . . enough to allow me to function and hold the bitterness at bay, enough to blunt the sharp edges. It was a routine from which I seldom varied and it didn't seem accumulative, although some days were harder than others. I tried to discuss all of this with my mother one night during her annual visit. We had been bickering about everything from housework to the children:

"I didn't wash the bedroom windows."
"They don't need it."
"The bathroom didn't look dirty either, but you should have seen the dirt that came out of it!"
"Tell him not to read in that light."
"Why should I nag him too? You just told him twice."
"Well, somebody should tell him."
God?

I censored my sarcasm. But when it came to the casual way she called the Japanese "the Japs" and the Irish "the micks," I could no longer hold my tongue. For me all derogatory terms were the same. It was just as bad as talking about "the kikes," "the spics," "the wops," or "the niggers." I'd never learn to be tolerant of intolerance. I wondered whether my mother had become a WASP and lost her ability to relate. Perhaps only Jews and niggers could relate, as some kind of compensation! I was furious, and my mother, beside herself, retorted, "I hope I never say a f-f-fucking bad word like some . . ." and dissolved into tears. For the first time, my mother had said *the* word. That was, in itself, a victory. But I felt guilty and out of touch with her. Where was the mother who had pawned her diamond and emerald bracelet, a present from Daddy, so that I could go to summer stock? What had happened to the young widow who had been courted by the razor-blade heir, Bobby Gillette, in a spiffy Cord automobile? Had she forgotten the days when her lover was Jay Calhoun, a rumrunner during Prohibition who had become president of Cutty Sark Scotch, a real-life prototype of the Great Gatsby? Living with my mother back on 52d had never been difficult. Where was the music we had shared? She was an encyclopedia of songs. In fact, three generations had kept the flame alive: the music she passed on to me was present in my children. Besides, my mother was the only old lady I'd ever heard whistle, with tremolo, along with a John Coltrane chorus. Now, I needed her support more than ever, but she only responded with platitudes.

It was all bullshit and had nothing to do with real life. I dug how together my mother was for her age. But no one with sensitivity should have to endure the indignity that eventually crept up on all of us. Life was a bitter joke that ended with a fart, humankind's final comment. Human life was such a degrading, demeaning, disgusting affair, and I was weary of being compassionate, understanding, responsible, concerned.

Life with Phil had been a dead end. But I loved the alto sax. My world had always been in E-flat, except for one small detour into B-flat and my childhood in C. My childhood seemed another life. Did I ever live in Yonkers and go to dances? Had I really been "the Queen of 52d Street," desired by more men than I could handle? Why do people live past the time they are loved and desired . . . or is that purely an American phenomenon? Death was wooing me. I had to be sly and carry the secret lest I be found out and dissuaded. This was my problem alone, for death was a lover I welcomed. I knew I must not cause grief, but why should anyone deny me the relief I sought? I spent more hours in the garret, that inverted schooner that had become a cold, cavernous battleship. How could anyone believe in a god who had made such imperfect creatures? The pressure in my head was very intense at times, as if warning of the dark, evil thoughts which crept into my brain. Had other women ever carried on like this? I might have been in a Greek drama. The innocent people I knew seemed to be ostriches, hiding their heads in the sand, or seeking small pleasures where they could, hoping disaster would overlook them. I guess we all hide out.

I was so cold one day that I suddenly started crying and didn't realize why until I turned the upstairs radiators back on and lit a fire with our small remaining supply of wood. For the first time in my life, I was without small creature comforts. Although I knew I was still fortunate by world standards, I could better understand the bitterness most of the world feels towards those who enjoy warmth and food without thinking that it couldn't be the norm for everyone. How would the children and I get through our first Christmas alone? The ghost of Phil was haunting us; this was a dead man's Christmas. I was almost fifty. What would old age bring? I felt used. I was used.

Time, for me, had always been marked by Christmas. This was my half-century mark. By being forced to begin over again, I knew I could have another half-century. But what a strange Christmas that one was. When I brought in a log for the fire, the stars and moon were shining, making the barn and Baird's house glow. I even put on the Mormon Tabernacle Choir record of Christmas carols. I hoped that later Aimée and Gar would listen to Dylan Thomas' *A Child's Christmas in Wales* with me. But when the children came home from the café, they disappeared into the studio to watch TV, which drowned out the carols. There was nothing to do except take off the Christmas album and listen to the only truth in this family . . . Bird. I knew this land, this sky. They were mine. I knew it, it felt right to me and made me strong.

I had considered breaking our tradition by not waiting until Christmas day to open the presents. But tradition finally prevailed, as we waited until morning to open our humble presents covered in recycled market paper which had once wrapped our vegetables. Aimée and Gar were thoughtful in their selection of gifts that year. There were also presents from Phil for the children: a model for Gar, and stationery and a crewel kit for Aimée. (It was also cruel, because it wasn't her bag. Had Phil's daughters hated the presents I used to buy them?) The three of us went to Paris for lunch, then to a movie, and got through the day pretending it wasn't Christmas and we weren't alone.

Gar worked twelve hours over two days, sanding and painting so he could take me to the movies on my fiftieth birthday. But the twenty-five francs he was paid weren't enough, and, to salvage his ego, I wanted to make up the difference with part of our remaining three hundred francs. Fifty years seemed forever, and I wondered how we were going to make ends meet. We'd been eating beans, rice, and salad from the garden, but dogs are not vegetarians. I went outside and smoked half a joint in the garden, came inside, finished knitting a hat, and worked on a sweater to sell. Maybe Bird would swoop and there would be a surprise in the mail the next day.

Aimée had to have a tonsillectomy. I spoke with the hospital social worker to try to get a single-parent reduction of the fees. She kept probing and asking question after question, unconvinced that we had any financial difficulties. The longer we talked, the more humiliated I became. Finally, I spat forth, "My husband is an alcoholic. He was in this hospital for psychiatric treatment. He left us a year ago. He sends money when and if he can, and I just hope every month that I'll have the 128 francs to pay the mortgage. Both my children had operations here and I paid the full rate when I had a husband. If I could pay it now. I wouldn't ask for a reduction!"

This was our life: pathetic. Now it was my turn to be sick. Although she was still convalescing, Aimée had to cook dinner. I could be brave in the summer, but it was hard to be stouthearted in February without the money to heat the house. I promised myself I would never be cold again. Kim called. She was three months pregnant. She told me that I should come back to the States.

"You're foolish to hang onto the house," she said. "You'll have to keep putting money into it, and it will need a new roof."

"That's cheaper than a new house."

She kept insisting, "But the house will deteriorate in a year."

"We all deteriorate in a year."

I felt as flinty and hard as stone, and as dry. I'd been head of the house for more than a year with no husband to give me sympathy, comfort or tenderness. Aimée and Gar had been stoic and supportive. How sad our life had been since Phil left. I needed to make some sense out of the breakup of my marriage. I wanted to go home to my mother. My children needed a bit of luxury and they needed to see their father again. But I needed to carry my French life to my new world. I made a list of things to ship, of necessities and food for my soul: a few paintings, certain records and books which were old friends. I sublet the house; it would open its doors to strangers while we were in America. Soon the garret was full of half-packed boxes. I tried to prepare myself for culture shock.

In many ways, my life had expanded without Phil, rather than diminished. I'd almost forgotten who I was and had become *wife* in the worst sense of the word: holding on when there was nothing. I had come to be grateful that Phil had been strong enough to sever a less-than-fulfilling relationship. But he was wrong when he said I always was and always would be Chan Parker. Along with a new year, I'd crossed some kind of threshold and had come through the longest trauma of my life. I felt strong again, and I still loved life. Far from being ready to lie back, I was looking forward to the next chapter.

15. INVERSIONS

We found a place in the woods just outside of New Hope, Pennsylvania, on the top floor of a two-family house. Kim lent us an armchair and my mother found us a couch in a thrift shop. I found a chest of drawers in a yard sale. Refusing to become enslaved by too many possessions, we made a table by putting a board on the blue metal trunk we had brought from France, and put our mattresses directly on the floor. That was all we needed.

New Hope was so different from Champmotteux. The deer in the woods behind our house came close to our door. There was a lake across the road where Canadian geese wintered. As I walked across the bridge connecting New Hope and Lambertville in the drizzle, I remembered the many times I had crossed the footbridge to the Quai d'Orsay. Instead of the rococo Grand Palais or the *belle époque* Pont Alexandre III, I had a view of the autumn trees lining the banks of the far bend in the Delaware River. Other times, as soft as the Cher River, the water made me feel so peaceful that my imagination transformed Bowman's Tower into a Loire château. But one day, as Lambert, Hendricks, and Ross had predicted years earlier, the rain that fell carried strontium 90. Would the French government have informed me that I was strolling in radioactive mist?

I soon learned about the bounty of the American welfare system. Phil had told me to apply for food stamps; everybody did. My caseworker was sympathetic, and told me that I was also eligible for free prescription medicine. My medical card allowed me new glasses and free dental work. But I had to pay for this with petty humiliations at the supermarket. My grocery purchases always included a lot of imported cheeses, since we didn't eat meat. One check-out cashier snapped, "You could buy a weeks worth of meat for what that cheese cost!" I started to feel like a loser.

Had my Westchester background set me up as a willing victim? Could I have been more comfortable living by my own standards? Did I unconsciously play the role of victim by loving a black man? Hadn't Phil warned me himself that he was the drunk in the back booth? Hadn't I closed my eyes to his lack of emotional depth? Didn't I excuse his emotional abandonment of me years before his actual desertion? Hadn't I blamed even that on his alcoholism and artistic sensibilities? And now I had applied for government assistance and become the complete statistical victim.

One week, I reported to the welfare office and found my new caseworker was an obese, middle-aged, bleached blond who was packed like a sausage into a bright yellow, polyester pantsuit. She immediately attacked me, asking why I couldn't work. After I explained that my husband had left me, that I was a fifty-two-year-old woman with two children, she took a holier-than-thou attitude, "*My* husband left *me,* but *I'm* working!" she hissed.

When Phil and I were first married, I had found a job delivering phone books because we needed the small pittance it paid. I would leave in the morning with a Thermos of iced coffee for my assigned area, a Mennonite region which was completely new to me. Phil had been furious, and composed "The Children's Suite," some of his best music. Now, I went back to delivering phone books again, for one week at the minimum wage. Driving my newly purchased MG-B, wearing my Pucci blouse, I was delivering telephone directories to Congressmen Pete Kestemeyer and William Zeckendorf in order to pay my own phone bill. The supreme irony.

After working as a census enumerator for a few days at one dollar an hour, I heard about some jobs at the Bucks County Playhouse. They were being paid by the CETA program, which trained welfare people for future work. I drove thirty miles, filled out a form, received a number, and waited for an hour. Then I was called to a desk, and registered. Finally, I was called to the Playhouse for an interview and given a job as a prop person. The season would start in six weeks. Meanwhile, I had to work outside, in the hotdog stand. Even if I hadn't been a vegetarian, I would have been repelled by their practice of reheating the grey, swollen, leftover hotdogs for the next crowd. Although the director and the set designer, when they came to the stand for a snack, would ask if I wasn't overqualified for my job, my boss had nothing but criticism for me. Not only did he object to the way I dressed, he also told me, "I know the French drink wine with lunch, but don't bring it in here anymore." I asked him if I was too racy for him. After that, I had the French bread, brie, and jar of wine I brought to work everyday for lunch in my car. I thought of my house in France, the luxury I had known in Europe, and the cultural experiences of my past life. So I was trained by CETA, a government-sponsored program, for a job that the union would never permit me to hold. But when the season began, I enjoyed the work. My job was to find the needed props for the shows. The prestigious name of the Bucks County Playhouse gave me an entrée to all the local antique shops and art galleries, where I could borrow whatever I felt suited the set for the current play. It was like shopping without money. A bonus was the pleasure of mounting a new art exhibit each week in the lobby. I had a free hand, and that was fulfilling.

However, I wished I didn't know that the Shah of Iran was a corrupt dictator, kept in power by my government. I wished I didn't believe that the "influence" in Saudi Arabia was less corrupt, more honest and frank, than the Americans who went to Iran for the money and sent their children to American schools. They lived with suspicion of the Arabs in American enclaves, and were anti-Semites wearing not two faces, but none, with a handy-dandy Nixon mask and pink curlers.

I read in our local Gazette that the CETA was sponsoring a community project of music lessons. Classes in music theory and harmony would be held weekly for a fee of two dollars. I had had some basic theory, and I had a whole lot of music in my head. When I arrived at the local firehouse, where the classes were to be held, I had still another form to fill in: *What is a diatonic scale? Sketch the circle of 5ths.* I took my completed form upstairs, handed in my form to the teacher who glanced at it strangely. There were perhaps thirty people in the room, most of them young. After taking and passing a test for my knowledge of intervals, I was assigned to the intermediate class.

David Ancker was my CETA-sponsored teacher; we were all in the same boat! After several weeks of basic harmony, I became David's star pupil, nemesis, and close friend. I interrupted his classes irreverently. We were studying Walter Piston's book *Harmony.* When David asserted that music ended on the tonic, I asked, "What about the tango?" The Hindemith *Elementary Training for Musicians,* where we were supposed to tap on the table to one rhythm and ta-ta to the other, I could only do by using two hands. I became David's Peppermint Patty. If he asked if there were any questions, I would reply that I had a joke, and lay a be-bop joke on the class. I infuriated him by scorning the classical notation, and insisting that I needed to understand B-flat 7. The following year, I became his assistant teacher.

David encouraged me to learn orchestration, and I soon had a large book of arrangements I had written for a vocal group of six people.

They called themselves the "Deep Six." I found writing for six voices cumbersome, and they became "Quintessence." That year, my first arrangement of Keith Jarrett's "Quiet Place" was performed. I had arranged it for strings, voice, and guitar. (I didn't know shit about writing for strings; someone must have guided my pencil.) Oh joy! A piano, and new friends to help me move it in. At Christmas, David bought me a new battery for my car. He said, "You can't concentrate on music if your car doesn't start."

It had taken me three years to realize that I was happy depending on myself, that I didn't need to depend on a man and didn't need to replace Phil. I had found my own creativity. Now, at last, I could make my own music. I had found my voice. I wondered if all those years had been wasted in a traditional female role. But I realized how much I had learned through osmosis and experience. And I had survived . . . I had been a lake, now I was a river. I became garrulous; I wanted to communicate. I didn't want the music to stop, the people to leave, the party to end. I wanted to talk about music, I wanted to hold music in my hands, my mouth, my ears. I wanted to taste, chew, and swallow music. I wanted to melt and blend myself into music.

One cold October day in 1977, I was listening to Bird's "Yardbird Suite" when the phone rang.

"This is Ray Lafaro calling from Los Angeles. I'm sitting in the sun by my pool. We're doing a film about Charlie Parker and we would like you to be involved. Would you like to come out here?"

"Who is playing Bird?" I had seen James Earl Jones on television. When he laughed, his nose wrinkled just like Bird's. The resemblance was remarkable and he was a fine actor. I had even written him a letter to say that if ever a film was made, he was the only one to play Bird. The letter, undelivered, was next to the phone.

"Richard Pryor."

"Who is doing the music?"

"My partner, Stewart Levine, who played with Les Elgart's band."

I was cynical after the way Billie Holiday's life had been portrayed by Hollywood in "Lady Sings the Blues," and I had no expectations that Hollywood would do better by Bird. Lafaro's answers to my questions confirmed this. I reasoned that if I had some small say, perhaps I could be a restraining influence. I must admit, the thought of sun, warmth, and being pampered after the past three difficult years was very appealing. I agreed to go and received first class air tickets. Ray promised he would meet me at the airport wearing a rose. In view of the cost of my flight, I wondered what they would pay for my services. I flew to L.A. in all the comfort and luxury first class provides. Whereas the night before, I had rice for dinner and a fried egg at bedtime to allay my hunger, I was 39,000 feet in the air drinking champagne and eating chateaubriand, my first in years. I had decided to go all the way, despite my vegetarian leanings. My food stamps had been taken away two days before I left. Maybe that was a good sign.

Ray Lafaro took me to the Beverly Hills Hotel to check in, and then we went to dinner at Stewart Levine's home. Stewart was living with Quincy Jones daughter Jolie, who had been Baird's first love on the "Free and Easy" tour. Stewart showed me his horns, one of each and all new. He was smashed, but nice. He was funny, except when he uncased his alto and puffed on it. My strong insistence that Bird should be the music on the soundtrack elicited grumbling about wives who interfered in music. I responded that I had been involved with music before I knew Bird. Stewart said he was supposed to go into the studio the next day to produce Flora Purim's next album, and he wanted to go to the Roxy where she was appearing. We had already ingested a lot of booze and other Hollywood amenities.

When we arrived, Ray went to the dressing room door and announced himself importantly. He was rebuffed, and told that Miss Purim was getting ready for her show, and couldn't see him. Monty Alexander was in the audience and Ray introduced me as Charlie Parker's widow. I asked him why he hadn't simply said, "This is Chan Parker." Even then, my name was not unknown. I sweetly said to Monty that we were having a consciousness-raising that night. During Flora's set, Stewart growled that her pitch was awful, and that he couldn't produce her. I said that her pitch didn't bother me at all. That first night established territorial rights. At least they realized that I was more than just a widow.

A few days later, we had lunch at the Warner Brothers commissary with John Calley, the studio head. He asked me intelligent, pertinent questions about Bird. People circled our table, but I was there to sell my wares, and didn't notice Steve McQueen at the next table. The only person that Calley stood up to greet was Louise Fletcher, but I was too engrossed in conversation to wonder why. Ray had written a dreadful script full of clichés. Warners had optioned Ross Russell's book, but they were having trouble with him, as he wanted to write the screenplay. I felt Bird's presence constantly, and knew he was in charge. There were enough coincidences to spook and convince Ray and Stewart also. I found a tough Hollywood agent. Ray offered me $500 as consultant and $1,000 to use my character in the film. My agent demanded $50,000. When they refused, the agent threatened that if they depicted me in the film, we would sue for a million dollars. That brought the film to a grinding halt. I was relieved. I'd had two weeks of fun, sun, and luxury. I had played their game, spooked them, planted seeds, dazzled, tangoed, and impressed them with my thousand-dollar hotel bill. I felt like a lion tamer.

I had turned down the $11,000 they had finally come up with, but I was completely broke, at the end of my credit and all my bills were overdue. I had lived on $6,000 all year. I had just paid $60 to rid my house of fleas, and $15 more to find out that Gar had swollen lymph glands from flea bites. Describing my situation, and another brutal experience at the local food stamp center, I told a psychiatrist friend that I had felt suicidal. She asked, "Why weren't you homicidal?" I had been in opposition to the establishment all my life. I had been impassioned and vocal. I never wished my children mute. I wanted them to holler, to care, to feel passion. Why did *flower children's* music whine for the most part? I longed for my house in France.

I played a game with myself: *if you were in France now, what would you be doing?* I'd be sitting by the fireplace thinking about dinner. It would be two hours before the kids came home from school. There would be a jazz show on the radio at 6:30, the *Herald Tribune* already read, some knitting to be done. There would be the rest of a loaf of French bread on the table, and it would be time for a pastis or a kir. I'd open a bottle of *Cuvée d'Amitié* for dinner, and close the shutters in the dusk.

Gertrude Stein said that the French live their own lives and those lives are secret and belong to themselves. That's what made French elegance and style. She liked living there because her life could belong to her. I wondered whether most Americans, who prided themselves on being open, candid, and friendly, realized that they had paid for those qualities with their dignity. Life in America seemed so slick that it was difficult to elucidate what was wrong there, and often a picayune detail seemed to sum it up. Between 6:00 and 6:30, during the American dinner hour, American network television interrupted the nightly news with three constipation remedy commercials and another one for athlete's foot. Do people still get athlete's foot? Vulgarity!

The street signs on 52d Street were changed to Swing Street. The jazz giants were being honored by having their names engraved on the sidewalk. Baird and I shared the podium with Klook, Nica, Mayor Koch, John Hammond, George Wein, Monk Jr., Mrs. Pres and Pres Jr., who was now Doctor Young (How proud Pres would have been!), Billy Taylor, John Lewis, and Tiny Grimes, who accepted the award for Art Tatum, saying, "It was an honor to work for him; wasn't no pleasure, though." Years later I walked down the street. So many feet had trod on them that the names were barely visible. Same ole shit.

Billy Joel won two Grammy awards for "Just the Way You Are": best record and best song. They really belonged to Phil, who wasn't even mentioned for his solo. It was another drop for his cup of bitterness. Ah, sweet hemlock!

Gar's first meeting with Phil after three years was easier for him than it was for Phil. Gar said he didn't hate Phil and only felt indifference. He asked me if that was normal. I told him that, after all, Phil was his father. "He's never been a father to me," Gar replied bitterly. Then Gar started to speak of his own fragile creativity. That was a good sign.

I began teaching music again. I had so much energy, optimism and enthusiasm that I was euphoric. I tingled. I felt tensile. I didn't even want a lover. I had become my own. I felt pregnant. I'd like to say it was immaculate conception, but it was really multiple insemination. Perhaps the aimlessness and sublimation in my life had allowed me to become a neutral sponge soaking up energy and musical force. Subconsciously, I had spent years in musical apprenticeship. Remembering the outrage that Phil used to feel at every musical opinion of mine, I shuddered. Had he realized how obsessed I'd always been with music? Had he understood that music was more natural to me than the needs of his tender ego? Now, I had no other need. I was self-contained and I felt so free. I tried to strip my life to the basics. I never again wanted the responsibility for another living soul, be it child or man, pet or guest. I would never again bake, cook, or submerge myself in the sensuality of food. My only exercise would be opening the cork! There is more to life than nurturing. Every animal has that instinct. The amount of energy wasted on a mating game makes clear why animals have a seasonal heat. Outside my windows the cardinals were making a jazz sound. The crickets had a sophisticated rhythm.

I had learned that the teacher must bend to the student. Method is death to creativity. No methods for me and no strictures to voice or instrument (aren't they the same thing?). I think I was a good teacher. I encouraged my students to follow their own intuition, and learn through experience. "Take a chance. Guess, try," I told them. "It can only be right or wrong, and it probably will be right." One of my students told me I should at least come up with a methodology for my approach to teaching music. My formula, which relied on individual initiative, had become programmed into his consciousness. I told him that he had to have a vision and believe in it enough to make it become reality. No one else could supply the methodology. When the "dream" became absolutely necessary, and he had understood that no one else could make it come true, he would discover how to make it reality. Besides teaching, I was writing lyrics, and Quintessence rehearsed weekly at my house. They even had a gig at a local club and recorded a demo.

Bill Heyer came back into my life. He was still as handsome as he had been when, as newlyweds, we lived with my mother on 52d Street. He wined and dined me. He bought me gifts. I had been his first love, and he told me that he still loved me. My feelings were ambiguous. Although Bill was fun to be with, generous and great in bed, he was using a lot of cocaine. Cocaine had increased his natural intensity and disturbed the calm I had found.

Bill was working as the librettist on the new "Hellzapoppin" show, starring Jerry Lewis. Although he was making a lot of money, he was spending more on his coke habit. He was heavily in debt to the pushers and the IRS, but he wasn't worried because the show was to be televised on opening night and he would receive $50,000 for that, even if the show was a flop. If it was a success, he would receive a large weekly amount during the run. But Jerry closed the show during the out-of-town tryouts and Bill was in big financial trouble.

I left for France soon after the show closed. In spite of everything, I yearned for my house in Champmotteux. I missed France. I had made a deal with CBS records for the Bird tapes I still had, and the advance money meant that I was financially able to leave America again. (I was lucky I got the advance, because Bird's estate eventually blocked the release of the records, claiming they belonged to the estate.) Gar and Aimée had settled into life in America and didn't want to leave. Gar was in college and Aimée was a senior in high school. They took Snoopy, and moved in with Phil, Jill and her daughter. I returned to France alone.

A few months later, I learned that Bill Heyer had committed suicide. He had gone to his office and jumped off the roof of the building. The note he left said that he had nowhere else to go.

My grief overflowed:

It was over. Finished. Ended.

There is no time. We hesitate, waiting for the right moment to come when that moment has already passed. Do we spend too much time regretting? Allot your time! A time for explosion, a time when the top of your head might burst open and all the hate and guilt and rancor could escape . . . bubbling and spilling out like hot lava. I had a vendetta that filled me with bile; the bitterness churning, never still, polluting those nearest me, the ones within striking distance. Would I ever escape from that putrid jungle, or would it reach me always, forever, anywhere? This is the undisciplined self that I must try to master.

I don't believe anybody has the power to accelerate or diminish anyone else's self-destructive urges. I know I've never been able to help anyone I loved who wanted to self-destruct. But I wish I knew why some people have a great capacity and zest for living, while others have only a tunnel vision of death.

16. REPRISE

When you live in Champmotteux, you'd better know who you are. I asked myself hourly, "Who are you, Chan, and what brings you here?" As I undressed one night, I shed Gar's jeans, Baird's shirt and my friend Carol's socks. I put on a thriftshop nightgown and Phil's bathrobe. It didn't change me a bit. The garret sustained and energized me. I had fallen victim to this haunted house. I didn't mind, although it did seem rather Faustian.

A literary agent in America was interested in the manuscript of my autobiography and I was supposed to be doing a rewrite. But I procrastinated. I excused myself by saying that summer was the time to store up sun and energy for the long, grey winter. Then I would light a fire and be disciplined, introspective, and productive. In the meantime, I listened to new music, ran to the piano, came up against an alteration, got out my Persichetti, came up against modes, and realized my ignorance. So I'd say, "Tomorrow," and play Billie Holiday. That was easy and I'd feel guilty with a smile. "Everyone has a book in him," an acquaintance told me. "Everyone doesn't put it down on paper," I replied. "But who are you, that people would buy your book?" he asked. Precisely. I was anonymous. It took me ten years to start again. I was often tempted, when the logs didn't ignite, to just let them smoulder and give off a faint heat. Sometimes I did. But I usually stoked them up, knowing they would turn to ash more quickly. But while they burned, they gave off a more profound heat. That's all anyone could wish for. I was enjoying my solitude.

My neighbor, Mr. Gilbert, would pop in for a glass of wine when he had finished working in my vegetable garden. As he drank a second glass of wine, he would talk to me in his rural accent, holding a hand-rolled cigarette between his teeth, which were loose. His conversation was subdued, unhurried: the weather, the crops, his family, a birth, a death, someone new in town. I thought of the red-faced lady who had been the first person in Champmotteux to make us feel welcome. She gave Aimée a cutting of the small, white, wild carnations that smell of spice. Planted in our garden, they had spread and now filled several flower beds. A definite rhythm exists in this town and the people live with the seasons. The sky dictates all.

I answered an ad in the *Herald Tribune* for a second-hand stereo system. Stuart Troup, a journalist, was selling it because he was returning to America, after many years in Europe, to work for *Newsday*. Good guy that he was, he had let Babs Gonzalez crash in his apartment. Babs was difficult and demanding, and Stuart asked me if I didn't want to take Babs off his hands. I flatly refused. A few months later, Babs called me from the American Hospital in Paris. He had had a hernia operation, and was going to be released the next day. Could I pick him up and bring him to my house to recuperate? I couldn't refuse.

On the way into Paris, I stopped at the marché and bought food for five days. I bought special things I thought he would like: baby artichokes, leeks for vichyssoise, tomatoes, hard-to-find mozzarella for my special pasta, and all the wonderful fresh fruit and vegetables of the season. Babs was waiting for me in a wheelchair in the hospital lobby. I don't think he weighed a hundred pounds. That night, I asked him if he would like vichyssoise. He didn't know what it was, but agreed soup was what he wanted. He tasted it and pushed it away after a few spoonfuls. The next night, I made pasta and got the same reaction. I protested that he wasn't eating anything, and he told me he didn't like my food. The next day he gave me a shopping list including hard-to-find peanut butter. Even though it was spring, he was constantly cold and wanted me to order oil and wood. I had to listen to tales of his sexual exploits and anti-feminist anecdotes. Women to him were meat.

I felt invaded. After five days, I was physically ill and spent as much time in bed as possible. I finally told him he was a ball-breaker; he would have to leave. After he left the house, I cleaned it of his presence. I washed the sink, the tub, the linens, my hair, and myself. He didn't know, nor did I, that he had terminal cancer. He died a few months later. I felt guilty and supposed I should have felt pity for such a scarred human being. But I had felt that I was under siege. His vicious gossip, hostility, repressed violence and hatred, boasting, bravura, and ruthless disrespect made him impossible. He was the first to use my house as a way stop, but not the last. This old house and this old lady were not meant for crowds.

Ever since I read *The Alice B. Toklas Cook Book,* I rued never having been able to have lunch with her and Gertrude Stein. One day, three friends and I packed some bread, cheese, and wine and went to the Père Lachaise

Cemetery to have a picnic lunch on their graves. Alice was buried next to Gertrude but the Stein family, scandalized by their relationship, had seen to it that Alice's stone faced in the opposite direction from Gertrude's. Someone had placed three plastic roses on Gertrude's grave, which I removed. Although I recognized the sentiment, I felt that plastic would have offended Gertrude. As we ate and drank our wine, a passerby wished us *bon appétit*. In America, we would have been arrested. We wondered if Alice and Gertrude, like other women we admired, would want us to refer to them as "heroes" or "heroines." Had they resented the feminine suffix as a sort of apartheid?

I felt sure that I could call them my heroes. I smiled as the association of words made me think of Bird who had as much trouble pronouncing "heroine" as Lyndon Johnson did with "Niggra" in the old Lenny Bruce routine. Lenny's widow, Honey Bruce, had become an Avon lady! America was the great leveler.

A year after my return to France, I received a phone call from Louis Schiavo in Corsica. He is a Bird fan and was organizing a jazz festival on the "Isle of Beauty." When he invited me there for a week, I said "Sure." ("Sure" is a word which had sneaked into my vocabulary. It seemed more definite and assertive than "okay," "uh huh," "yeah," or even "yes." "Why not" is wishy-washy. On the other hand, a definite "no" will suffice.) After notifying my friends that I was off on an adventure to an unknown island sponsored by an unknown man, I flew to Corsica. For the second time in four years, Bird had made it possible for me to fly to the sun. Thank you, Bird. On that first visit I made another friend, René Caumer. René and Louis have made it possible for me to return yearly to my favorite place in the world.

I was contacted by another stranger, Jan Horne, from Norwegian television. He asked if I would come to Oslo to discuss participating in a projected program about Bird. That word "sure" popped out again. My life was becoming filled with strangers who would become friends. When Jan asked how he would identify me at the airport, he wondered if I would be wearing a rose. I told him I was usually met by someone carrying a rose, but I would be wearing rose-colored glasses. We signed a contract. The fee came on April fifteenth, just when my finances were so tight that stamps at the post office were a luxury and I couldn't afford gas for my car. Jan came to Champmotteux with his crew to film my part in his documentary. He has produced four hours of the best Bird tribute ever made.

A phone call came one night from a man who worked with Radio Ivre, a private radio station. He had decided to change the name of the street where he lived, Rue Cail, named after a French industrialist, to Rue Charles Parker. I was invited to the inauguration. Sure enough, I found myself on Rue Charles Parker; the sign RUE CAIL had been replaced on all four corners. Two of the disc jockeys had simply donned workman's clothes that morning, and said they had orders to change the street signs. They had overheard a conversation between two of the residents, one explaining to the other that Charles Parker was a famous writer! I could envision the residents of the street sending out change of address cards. I wondered how long it would take for French bureaucracy to catch on to it. I would have loved to witness the confusion beginning, I'm sure, with the post office, leading to endless searching through records filed in shoe boxes for the authorization papers. (Despite the advent of typewriters and computers, the average French bureaucrat was still dependent on Bic pens, paper clips, pins ,and shoe boxes.) Individual anarchy was what I loved most about France.

Bird's tombstone was stolen and advertised for sale in a magazine. It had been engraved with the wrong date of Bird's death, which probably made it more of a collector's item.

I'd rather have a bird in a bush than a pig in a poke!

I read about a transcontinental humming experiment in America. (Where else?) The pitch was set for E-flat. Humming E-flat felt great. I used to be able to sing E-flat at will. That night I sang a note and went to the piano to check it. It was B-flat.

My friend Rob came to spend Christmas with me in 1983. During the hour train ride from Paris to Champmotteux, he had been musing on the ancient prophesy that Armageddon would come with someone bearing three names of six letters each: the devil sign. He asked if I knew Ronald Reagan's middle name. I didn't but even on Christmas day, I thought it shouldn't be too difficult to find out. After fruitless phone calls to the few American friends still in Paris over the holidays, Rob called the American embassy, but to no avail. Our next call was to the Associated Press. "Jesus!" exclaimed the staffer on hearing our question. Rob replied that he didn't think that it was that. The helpful staffer went off to make further inquiries, and returned to inform us that Ronald Reagan's middle name wasn't listed in "Who's Who" and nobody seemed to know what it was. I made the next call, and was surprised to hear, "Where does he work?" Smiling, I answered, "Hopefully in the White House." At the *Herald Tribune* office, we were finally connected with a reporter who finally said one of the editors thought it was Wilson. If the Americans didn't know our president's full name, perhaps the Russians would. Our last call was to the Russian Embassy. There was no one at the embassy who spoke English, and we were left with, "Nyet, Ruski."

It was no longer viable that a nation gets the government it deserves. The planet deserves better than the government it gets. The only way this could be corrected is for citizens to inform themselves and to take a hand in their future. I would like the American public to be better informed. A book called *A Nation of Sheep,* written in 1960 but still pertinent today, should be required reading by all Americans. The problem is that most Americans don't read.

Because of Reagan's politics and Poland's decision to boycott the Olympics in L.A., Kim was unable to perform at the Polish Jazz Vocal Festival in 1988. The American embassy would grant no subsidies for American artists to perform there. How could a singer undermine government policy? I can only imagine: by touching a human response which makes every person on this planet vulnerable to beauty. By reaching out to people of different cultures, artists in the past have undermined the barriers imposed by government manipulation. Art has always proven stronger than bigotry because artists the world over speak a common language. The threat to the existence of humanity lies heavy on all thinking people. Because of the stupidity of our world "leaders," we have all become an endangered species. There is a trickle-down effect which touches not only the athletes, but also the artists.

There will always be an underclass, be it white, black, or purple. We are not born equal and no wars, laws or demonstrations can make us so. Our intelligence, striving, and creativity make us all different. This is not to denigrate the equal rights laws, but rather to express surprise at the naiveté of those who are distressed by the millions who subsist in poverty, ignorance, and lethargy. It would truly be an ideal world if everyone had a dream. The sad truth is that most people, especially Americans, can't think past Saturday night. All people wish to be free to make a choice, but we must realize that all choices are not the same. This example should refute the premise that if we all had the same advantages, we would all be achievers: I have four grown children, all raised in the same environment. They all differ intellectually, as do their goals, achievements, and desires. Perhaps this sounds reactionary. I'm simply asking why we can't be liberal enough to accept people as they are, and not try to force our mores and unbending opinions on the whole world. So many millions have been killed throughout history by those who believed they had the true god. Don't we all have the right to decide our own morality?

In my youth, my only bigotry was towards rednecks, southerners, and the armed forces. Now, although I sympathize with their position as the niggers of the white world, I'm ashamed to say I don't understand the Arab fanaticism, violence, and aggression towards women. I have no sympathy for Israel and its other brand of racism. Who is capable of addressing the threat and terrorism from a people just finding their voice and demanding an equal share in world affairs? Israel tries to squash Lebanon, the Palestinians, and the burgeoning Arab world, and to exert influence over that area. Everyone wants to control the OPEC countries.

It is an exciting time in history. South Africa will soon have to retreat from its brutal racism. America tries to contain Central America and to influence South American politics. Russia finally realized it couldn't overpower Afghanistan or retain control over "greater Russia." China is stirring and the government represses the people. Even as I write this it becomes outdated. I hope governments will realize that people are surging and longing to be free, and to fuck up on their own.

The music-business convention in Cannes, the MIDEM, is all business and no music. At the MIDEM one year, I was asked by a hefty Russian woman to record an interview for Radio Liberty. Her aggressive manner and uninformed questions annoyed me. When she asked why Charlie Parker was so famous, I replied that he had revolutionized music. She turned off her tape recorder and angrily said, "I know you Americans love revolution, but you weren't in Prague, or a gulag." It was no use explaining that revolution in art was apolitical. The interview ended in hostility. I was sure it would never be aired.

I went to Belgium where Bill Evans was performing. I had known Bill through the years, but the first time we had a long conversation was there in Belgium, one night shortly before his death in 1980. He always offered encouragement to aspiring musicians and spent a lot of his precious time with me. I told him how arranging his music for my vocal group had opened new harmonics to me, and how much I had learned through him. I also told him that I had put lyrics to a few of his songs, but I had no ambition to be a lyricist. He told me that I must write everyday and said he had a new song that needed lyrics. The band called it the "Diddlya Song," but it was really more serious and the real title was "Your Story."

During the concert that night, he played it for me. At dinner after the concert, he ate my surplus hard-boiled eggs and told me many intimate things about his life. He touched my shoulder or my arm often, and it seemed he needed human contact. I didn't want the night to end, but he was leaving early in the morning and was exhausted from a long tour.

Three months later, when I learned he had died, I raced 70 miles an hour in my car to the supermarket to buy meat. I felt I, too, was dying. After that, I was no longer a vegetarian, and I still haven't been able to write lyrics to "Your Story." Fuck music. It's too painful. One tries to be brave, but when disaster strikes, all one can wish for is the comfort of a man's arms. A friend brought me a double Bill Evans album. When I took the records out of the sleeve, they were both Bird.

March is the month of renewal and the month of dying. March, 1985, we lost Kenny Clarke (Klook), who was seventy-one, and Zoot Sims, at a too-young fifty-nine. Paris mourned Klook and forty musicians, including Cedar Walton, Pepper Adams, and Max Roach, played a tribute to Klook, his wife Daisy and son Laurent. Max played a melodic drum solo with all the fire of eternal youth. That is the compensation that jazz gives to its faithful. A few days later, Art Blakey played in concert. His sixty-five-year-old spirit and fire are as young as his very young musicians. I was asked how he could play such breakneck tempos, and could only answer, "Chops." Soon after Zoot died, I heard Clark Terry, Frank Foster, and Charles Fox, who had played with Bird, and is, as they say in France, "of a certain age." Their drummer, a very young Terri Lyne Carrington, played with the authority of Elvin Jones. Jazz is ageless and keeps us all young.

But our giants are dying. They are international treasures and should be honored, subsidized, and recorded now. It is too easy to render homage after they have left us. We salute them after death with a week of tribute on the radio and a spate of reissues and bootleg recordings which benefit the record companies. A mass at St. Peter's means nothing if you can't get a gig while you're alive. The same thing holds true for a postage stamp honoring you, if our government ever got that hip; they did get around to Duke. The Swedish government has a postage stamp honoring Lars Gullin, but at least they considered him a national treasure and subsidized him while he was alive.

Now's the time to honor our living heroes. Let us pay tribute to Diz, C.T., Dexter, Buddy Tate, Benny Carter, Johnny Griffin, Max, Roy Haynes, Cleanhead (Eddie Vinson) . . . all heroes. Giants still walk the earth. We should say thank you, while we have the chance. Jazz has no age and it's easy to forget the years are passing. I'd like to personally say, "Thank you, guys, for half a century of the best memories and the very best of times. You still fill my life with joy." No dinosaurs are we, as long as we can shake our ass and cook.

When Bill Evans was cremated, I thought how hip that was. Why should the dead take up space on a crowded planet? Why should the survivors be burdened by a barbaric funeral and the upkeep of a grave? I would like my children to take my ashes up in a glider and strew them over the fields. They certainly would be better fertilizer than the chemicals now used.

I took Bill Evans's advice and began seriously writing lyrics. They came pouring out of me, often one tune a day. I began to collaborate with Per Husby, a Norwegian pianist, who was as prolific as I. He would send me a tune and I would send back the written lyrics. Or I would send lyrics and he would send back the tune by return mail. We soon had a score of songs.

I put lyrics to a Leonard Bernstein classical piece in ten minutes, and sent it to him. I received a letter saying he thought it was "quite charming," and gave me permission to use it, signing the French form for royalties from the SACEM. It was wonderful to receive royalties for something I had created. I was making my own music! I couldn't sleep. I lay in bed humming and rhyming. I was awake in the night working out patterns, feeling dumb and fettered by my limited tools.

Elliot Carter said, "Much of the music of the twentieth century has disturbed me because it's trying to avoid flexibility, developing a primitive, almost hypnotic effect which I find very dangerous, having lived through the time of Hitler." What would he think about rap music? Stravinsky said that music is incapable of expressing anything. Music expresses itself. People who don't read the papers need rock/pop hype to make them aware of famine, inequality, terrorists, and the plight of the whales. This is not to denigrate concerned souls, but I don't think it has anything to do with the world of jazz, which many of those musicians claim to represent.

Look where jazz came from. If you don't keep your sense of humor, you are lost. That is why I love old jazzers. Paul Winter has no humor, nor does Paul Horn or John Klemmer. They take themselves so fucking seriously, they become a bore. Now everyone seems to think they are unique in their suffering. It's not the music of Anthony Braxton that offends me, but rather his titles . . . and how long his tunes do go on and say so little: no dynamics, no tempo. For one and a half hours by the clock, he played *Composition Number 98*. He is prolific. If I had a lot of money, I would hire Kenny Drew for a fabulous sum and tell him, "No arpeggios!" I heard an uninspired Stan Getz concert. Someone wondered why he was playing so feebly. I answered, "Because he's 55, tired, bored and has been doing this shit for 40 years for twits like you." Listening to records of old junky boppers, I thought, "If those cats were any more laid back, they'd be dead." And then I realized, they *are* dead. That's what killed bebop . . . suicide.

When my mother was in France on vacation, we went to hear Johnny Griffin at a club in Paris, and were seated at a table with some people we didn't know. One of the men offered champagne. My mother coyly said, "I'm too well-bred to say no." We later learned that our host was Sempé, one of my favorite cartoonists. After the set, my mother complimented Johnny, saying, "As Duke Ellington would say, your music is exquisite ecstasy." Back home in New York, my mom hangs out at P. J. Clark's, the celebrity spot, and is always treated like a queen . . . everyone sends her a drink. She's been known to say it's her birthday, and receive a bottle of champagne on the house! She loves a party, and doesn't want it to end. For her ninetieth birthday, friends, family, and ex-Ziegfeld girls threw a grand fête. They took over the second floor of one of her favorite watering holes. As the party was ending, she, being blind, was led down the stairs. She asked plaintively, "Is the party over?" Then, hearing the voices from the few remaining guests, she turned around and marched back upstairs.

When I dozed on the couch in the afternoon, I was often transported to an unaccustomed place where I slept in my childhood. One memory recurred repeatedly and I had no explanation for it. We were driving to Florida for a vacation . . . my mother, Aunt Janet, Jimmy, and I. I don't remember the car. Surely it couldn't have been our snappy-blue Pontiac convertible with the yellow stripe. It was mid-winter, which made the rumble seat impractical. No matter. We spent the night in a tourist cabin in South Carolina. I awoke in the morning to snow, which I thought we had left behind in the north. I remember the pastel room and the cheap gauzy curtains vividly. I can find no reason why it should remain in my memory after so many years. But I can still summon up the early morning light and the breakfast table with my introduction to hominy grits. I also remember the smell of soiled underwear when I went to camp.

Years before, in first grade, I had dirtied my underpants on the way home from school, and I remembered the humiliation I felt. But at camp, I shunned the girls who smelled. I hated camp.

Where did these scents and thoughts come from in an overloaded sixty-three-year-old brain? Then there was me getting sick on daiquiris while trying to seduce the homosexual leading man in summer stock, getting sick on Pernod with Boyd Raeburn, drinking rye and ginger ale at the bar next to the Strand Theater with Oscar Pettiford and staggering home to the care of my roommates, trying to emulate Lady Day by drinking brandy alexanders at the White Rose Bar, my first tequila disaster with Phil and Quincy Jones in Madrid, throwing up in the bidet in Brussels, being bombed at Aimée's school festival in Los Angeles. Now I had chops.

17. FORTISSIMO

"I know you've heard this before, but we are going to make a film on Bird. Can I come to see you?" said a letter from Joel Oliansky, who was with Columbia Pictures. A director/screenwriter, Joel was coming to England for a command performance of his film "The Competition." He arrived in Paris with Bill Sackheim, who was to produce the film. Joel came to Champmotteux bringing a very good Bordeaux. Kim and her son Alek were here, and we made an onion tart for lunch. Joel, who is strictly a corned beef sandwich man, was impressed and spread the word about our great cuisine. He was easy to talk with, had a great sense of humor, and we felt immediately at ease.

Columbia flew me to Hollywood and checked me into the Beverly Wilshire Hotel. In my room, I found a huge basket of fruit from Joel and a big bouquet of flowers from Bill. The next day, I went to the Burbank Studios for a conference with Bill and Joel. After answering many questions, I suggested that they should read the manuscript. The following day, Bill stopped in Joel's office while we were talking. When Bill wondered why Joel wasn't taping our conversation, Joel replied, "I don't have to. It's all in the book." Joel has a photographic memory!

Because of the air controller's strike, I had to fly home on the Concorde. No one could understand that when I hit my bed in the garret, I could yell in delight, "It's so good to be home!" Kim called to tell me that Clint Eastwood was looking for me. I had heard rumors that he was planning to do the Bird film and I was apprehensive. Although I had seen and liked "Play Misty for Me," I knew him only through his reputation. I'd also heard he was politically right wing. A few days later, Joel called to tell me that Warner Brothers had bought the script for Clint to direct. It was his baby now. Joel was disappointed that he wouldn't be directing, but he was happy that the film would be made. Clint had asked him what I was like. One Hollywood wag had asked if Clint was going to play Bird in blackface. It seemed that while the script was still at Columbia, a typical Hollywood executive had remarked that it could be changed to a story of a singer, and Prince could play the lead; after all, who knew anything about saxophones!

A call from Clint woke me up at 2:30 A.M. He told me about the project and asked if I'd like to come to Hollywood. He was interested in my tapes. I didn't tell him that CBS had them tied up. But I did say that I didn't want them to go through the airport X-ray machine. Could he come here to listen to them? He said he'd love to, but he was busy on preproduction. They planned to start the shoot on October 12th. We could arrange the airport control of the tapes by sending them on the Warner Brothers' D.C.3. He would call back in a few days at a more reasonable hour. I replied that I would be more alert.

He asked, "Can I call you Chan?"

"Sure. Can I call you Clint?"

Three days later his secretary Judy called. Clint was out of state playing in a golf tournament and had asked her to call. He was coming to Paris for three days and was hoping to spend two of them with me. Was I free? I said I would arrange to be.

When Clint arrived in Paris, he called me to ask if he could come to visit me the next day. He asked what time I got up. "Early. I'm a farmer." He arrived with Sondra Locke. We were all a bit nervous, but Roma, our Persian cat, broke the ice. "Oh, look, Clint. Look at that sweet kitty." Clint is allergic to cats, although he loves them. Roma didn't leave him alone all day. Clint asked if he could take me to lunch. I had planned to make a toad-in-the-hole, a salad, and I had a lovely cheese platter. Clint said he didn't want to put me to work. He had blanched at the mention of the toad-in-the-hole. When he asked if I wouldn't like to go out to eat, I replied, "Sure, I'd love to."

Clint, who is a careful eater, ordered fish and a white wine. He needed bifocals to read, but put them back in the case as quickly as possible. When the waiter poured a taste in his glass, Clint, scorning tradition, impatiently said, "Fill it up." Over lunch, Clint spoke about his ideas for the film. They were close to mine. He had kept his desire to make the Bird film secret, because Columbia would have upped the ante. Another script had been traded for Joel's, and my contract had been included in the deal. If I would trust him with my tapes, he would have digital copies made for me. I was surprised that no one was ogling him or bothering him. However, in the lobby after lunch, he was surrounded by the staff, asking for his autograph.

We went to the bank to retrieve my tapes, and returned to my house. While Sondra, who was still suffering from jet-lag, took a nap upstairs, Clint and I chatted. He made himself right at home, and took over my rocking chair. He told me about how he had met Bertrand Tavernier at a dinner in Clint's honor given by the *Cinémathèque*. At the time, Bertrand was looking for backing for "'Round Midnight." He had been turned down by all the money men at Warner Brothers. Clint had personally tried to get them to reconsider Tavernier's "sweet film" to no avail. Clint has his own production company, Malpaso, and he can pretty much write his own ticket. Clint was finally responsible for "'Round Midnight" being produced. He was also responsible for the release of "The Last of the Blue Devils." He told me about "Play Misty for Me." One day, he had received a sixty-page treatment in the mail. The author, who has since died, was a woman who had been a close friend of Clint's when they were young. They both had a burn: he to act and she to write. When he read the treatment, it reminded him of a similar experience he had been through with a woman. He sent for Errol Garner to redo "Misty" with strings. That day, I learned about his great love for jazz. He even sat down at my piano and played a bit.

"I know it's corny, but it's not every day that Clint Eastwood comes to Champmotteux and I have some film in my movie camera. Can I take some home movies?"

"Sure, I love home movies."

We went out to the back field where I grew vegetables. I saw him bend over and pull out a carrot, as I filmed him in the dappled light of the orchard. I asked him if he had eaten that carrot without washing the mud off.

"Naw, I was just pretending for the camera."

At the time, Aimée had come back to France and was living with me. When she got home, I introduced her to Clint, who stood up to shake her hand. "This is the way we do it in France," said Aimée, and gave him kisses on both cheeks. When she remarked that she was hot and sticky, Clint allowed that this was the perfect time to meet her. Sondra came downstairs. Aimée asked her why Clint had let her get away with murder in "Sudden Impact." Sondra said, "That's the kind of guy he is." But in response to the same question, Clint said that she had already suffered enough.

We talked about animals. Clint told us about the time he was driving to Carmel and saw some people who had pulled off the road and were beating their dog. He stopped and asked why. They replied that the dog was ill behaved. Next, he inquired about where they were going. They answered, "Carmel." Clint replied, "We don't want any fascists in Carmel." He told us that he should have bought the dog. When he was filming in Mexico, he had spent over $40 on the iguanas for sale in the marketplace: they were tied up and their lips were sewn together. Clint would buy them, cut the stitches, and set them free.

We all went outside and took more films. Clint grabbed my camera and shot like the true professional he is. He had brought a bottle of Moët et Chandon which he had forgotten in the car. He made sure to put it in the garage out of the sun when they left. The next morning, a car and driver came to take Aimée and me to Paris for breakfast at the Plaza Athénée with Clint. He told us that Sondra couldn't come as she had gotten her period and was out looking for tampax. What a guy! He ordered orange juice, yogurt, and honey and asked if it was possible to get oatmeal. I thought, oatmeal in Paris? But the waiter said, "Of course." He later returned to the table and apologized: no oatmeal, but they had porridge. Clint laconically asked us, "Isn't that the same thing?" He washed down a handful of vitamins and ate two croissants with his honey. No wonder he looked so good at fifty-seven. On our way out, he introduced us to the Warner Brothers publicist, Joe Hyams, who said he was going to see Francis Paudras. He asked me if Francis had anything. (Francis still had my documents and photos which had been used in the Bird book.) I replied, "Yes, he has everything."

We went to a studio that Clint had hired to dub the tapes. It was inefficient and we wasted a lot of time while they were trying to get things together. Clint was obviously annoyed. He sent his driver out to get lunch for us. We ordered sandwiches. When he was asked if he wanted beer, Clint said no, and ordered white wine. The driver returned with a half bottle, and my heart sank. But Clint didn't drink any and poured it for me. We were both ear-washed seven hours later, when the studio had finished with the tapes.

Clint asked if I would sign the Bird book when I came to the coast. Clint Eastwood asking for my autograph! He asked if there was anything else he should know about. We still hadn't spoken about the legal hang-ups concerning the tapes. I did say that "they" would be coming out of the woodwork. I said I hoped he had a stout heart. He was concerned about getting in the middle of the project and having it stopped. I finally got up the courage to follow Kim's advice and level with Clint. Fortunately, Clint did have a stout heart because when he returned to the coast, he was bombarded by everyone who thought they had a handle on Bird or wanted a piece of the action.

I flew to L.A. with the tapes and Bird's horn. Everything had been expedited by Clint, and I was well taken care of. When the plane landed, I was met by an airport representative who had someone come into the cabin to assist me with the tapes and horn. I was whisked through customs and taken to my limo. Clint had reserved a bungalow at the Beverly Hills for me. I was overwhelmed by the luxury: a huge living room with a wet bar, an equally large bedroom, two bathrooms, a kitchen, and six telephones!

It was 6:30 A.M. when I opened the bungalow door, picked up the *New York Times* I found on the doormat, and went to the Polo Lounge for breakfast. Exhausted after a sleepless, twelve-hour flight, I had just settled my jet-lagged body at a comfortable table when the room began to shake: the walls going one way and the floor coming up to meet them. The head waitress shouted, "Everyone outside!" There is an enormous tree in the outer dining area that has probably withstood many earthquakes, but I felt safer standing under the doorframe. A few people did go out to the terrace, but most of the blasé patrons remained at their tables and continued their phone business deals while they finished their breakfasts. The *Los Angeles Times* even wrote an account about the powerbrokers breakfast in the Polo Lounge. This was my second L.A. quake and being surrounded by pros made me feel calmer than I should have been. The quake was 6.1 on the Richter scale, the biggest since 1971. I had a ten o'clock appointment with the studio driver, and felt I would be safer in my bungalow. At the Warner Brothers lot, I met everyone from the executive producer to the actors, the wardrobe lady to the musical director, the hairdresser to the legal woman who quizzed me for three hours about possible libel suits. Red Rodney was there and we had lunch at the commissary with the cast. No wine was served.

That evening, a studio car took me to the airport to pick up Kim. We celebrated our reunion by taking advantage of all the amenities offered by the Beverly Hills Hotel. During the night, we awoke to the rumbling sound of my third earthquake, but Kim's first. At the first freight-train–like roar, we both jumped out of bed and headed for the comparative safety of the nearest door. I can only compare the sensation to the turbulence one feels in a plane. On a flight, you hope someone is in charge. But when you are on terra firma and the terra is no longer firm, you feel helpless because there is no one to fly the planet earth! It's amazing how sensitized one becomes to the slightest movement. For the rest of our stay, we asked each other, "Did you feel that?" We learned later that there had indeed been a small aftershock, plus two more at 3.5 and 5.5, respectively.

Diane Venora, who was playing me, spent a day with us at our bungalow, picking our brains and asking all the right questions. She was highstrung, intense, and dedicated. We went through the entire script doing line readings with her.

Kim and I attended a day's recording session of the Bird tracks. Lennie Niehaus, who was in charge of the music, had augmented the strings, and modernized the chords while remaining faithful to the original arrangements. Barry Harris was at the piano. As I walked into the studio and saw how Bird was being honored, and his music treated so lovingly, I said aloud, "Isn't this what you always wanted, Bird?" During the afternoon, the source music was being recorded by all the top L.A. studio musicians. Kim and I returned from lunch and danced into the studio to the sound of a society band playing "Moonlight Becomes You." The musicians, some of the hottest "Tonight Show" players, were playing with a Guy Lombardo vibrato.

Kim and I consulted with the assistant directors about backgrounds and ambiance on 52d Street. Kim's memory was invaluable. Our six phones never stopped ringing. On the only day we got to the pool, we didn't get wet because, even poolside, the phone kept us busy. Forest Whitaker came to dinner one night and we had a Bird briefing. Kim sang for him and we turned him onto Calvados. He didn't want to leave. As Kim and I slumped deeper into the couch, he said goodnight and leaped over the hedge outside, looking like Gene Kelly in "Singing In the Rain."

When actual filming began, Kim and I were to move to the Sheraton Universal to be nearer the studio. Our suite was not ready and we spent the day trying to get situated. It was back to reality. My lawyer finally got us installed in another suite. We had profuse apologies from the manager, who sent up a bottle of Dom Perignon and a fruit and cheese tray. The hotel was on rollers to withstand earthquakes. When we had a 3.3 aftershock, we wondered if we would roll into the sea along with the rest of California.

We attended two days of shooting. One was the scene at the Reno Club where, thanks to Clint, I had the only real beer on the set. The other scene was at Belleview, where Diane/Chan confronted the psychiatrist.

During the lunch break, she said she had a horrible headache. When I offered a special aspirin, she demurred saying that I had probably had a headache that day and she wanted to play the scene that way.

Clint works sweet, low and fast. He kept Bird's horn in his film vault. When he returned it to me, he confessed that he had taken it out of the case and blown one note on it. Good guy! The film was shown at the Cannes Film Festival and Aimée, Kim, and I were invited. We also attended the Paris preview at the Cinémathèque and Clint's farewell dinner at the Pré Catelan. Clint really knows how to throw a party.

Because of the film, I became a hot item: travel, interviews over a three-star restaurant lunch, and champagne at the Ritz couldn't continue forever, but I enjoyed it all at the moment. The phone kept ringing, friends came, we had parties, and old beboppers needing a refuge came to my door. That year, for the first time, I had enough money to indulge myself. I got a new Alfa Romeo. The hoopla of the film and the ensuing publicity kept me busy for more than a year. The perks were great and I love to travel. But each time I returned to Champmotteux, as I was driven up the farm road, I breathed deeply, my muscles relaxed and I knew I could never live anywhere else.

Champmotteux is situated on a high plateau, surrounded by fields, so that one has a great feeling of space. All the other houses in which I have lived were in valleys and sheltered by trees and hills. Here I can see the horizon. One leaves Milly-la-Forêt and begins to climb a gentle rise through the fields where, in spring, the road is lined by blue cornflowers, grape hyacinth, Queen Anne's lace and poppies . . . a veritable tricolored border. A stone wall shields a magnificent villa for one full kilometer, and ushers the way into Gironville, where the road goes past a small river and the abandoned village washhouse.

Here the road takes a steeper turn, winding up and around *Allée Bélier* and a bird sanctuary until it breaks out among open fields again. There is a nearby glider field where, like giant birds alighting, the gliders come to land with a whoosh. On this stretch of road, one often sees them soaring silently overhead. The road winds like a ribbon in the distance and, as one reaches the crest, there is still another hill to mount. On top of the very last hill lies Champmotteux, a village different from all the others in France, solely because it is my village. There are no shops and the men of the town mainly work the fields.

Tractors rumble past my window. The men take the traditional two-hour lunch break at the watertower, which is on a grassy plot planted

with flowers and shaded by trees. All these men probably grew up knowing each other and it's strange to imagine these weather-beaten farmers
walking into the Ecole Maternelle, or grade school, in some distant past.
Did they single out the little girls then for future brides? Perhaps, but
many have remained bachelors. Tractors, not cars, are their means of
transportation. I'm sure most of them have no indoor plumbing or central
heating, and there are some who have never been as far as Paris. On the
coldest winter days, no one wears a coat. These farmers are among the
few Frenchmen who don't take an August vacation. I can tell the weather
forecast by their activity in the fields.

I seldom go to Paris anymore. So many things have changed. The
Champs Elysées, which was so thrilling in 1968, has become seedy and
tacky with fast food restaurants. The safety I felt walking the streets no
longer exists. The metro has become dangerous. People used to smile and
make pleasantries. Now they push and shove, growl and are unfeeling. It
is not only depressing, it is frightening. What happened to the civility, the
grace, the respect for others that I loved about life in France? I search for
a sign of intelligence, but am only met with resignation or despair. If this
is the present, what will the future be? Heedless, hopeless, uncaring, nihil-
istic clockwork orange!

Even the architecture has changed, beginning with the Montparnasse
Tower and ending with La Défense. The pyramids of Pei in the Louvre
distract from the former stunning view from the Petit Carrousel extend-
ing to the l'Arc de Triomphe. The tourist lines at the Eiffel Tower make it
inaccessible. The buildings, walls, and train seats are covered with graf-
fiti. Life has become vulgar. Paris is still a beautiful city if one is in a car. It
isn't a city for walking anymore. One day in Paris is enough! I return to
the palpable silence of my farm road, breathe deeply to cleanse my pol-
luted lungs, say to my car, "Get me home quickly." Back home, I washed
my hands and face, and took something for my throbbing head before
having a pastis.

This December we have had recordbreaking low temperatures and
high winds. Some rare nights in the garret when the wind dies and it is
particularly still, I know I will awake to find the courtyard blanketed with
snow. I can smell it before I look out the window and I can feel the silence
that snow brings. I can usually hear a few cars sloshing through the rain
and puddles as people go to work. But when it snows, all is silent.

Like many small towns, Champmotteux had its share of colorful and
eccentric people. A short man with a gimpy leg is employed by the village

to cut the weeds along the roads. All day, summer and winter, he swings his scythe along any of the four roads leading out of town. He is the "Grim Reaper" of Champmotteux. He wears a beret in the winter, but never seems to be properly protected from the cold. He looks neither strong nor healthy, but my mother has assured me that a scythe is a heavy tool to swing. Baird always used to salute him as we would drive past, and got a nod in return. All I get is a blank stare. Maybe is isn't proper for a country woman to be so forward. In the evening, on his way to the café, the Grim Reaper passes my windows, scythe on his shoulder. Except for his red face, he does indeed look grim.

The Champmotteux post office is in Madame Malechère's kitchen. To transact postal business, I have to pass through their only other room. There is a blue sateen bedspread on which reposes a doll from the 1920s. Madame Malechère, a birdlike old lady, is badly crippled by arthritis but still spry on her gimpy legs. She is concerned with everyone's problems. Monsieur Malechère, the postman, is also the town electrician and handyman. Their house is always full of old irons and radios waiting to be repaired. The kids used to liken him to Einstein and said he could hold onto live wires. His hairstyle lends credence to this, cut only in the back, the front jutting out over his forehead. Madame Malechère is always handing him a comb, which he disdains. She is always fussing over him, trying to make him more presentable. As he yells at her in annoyance, she beams with tolerance and love. He rides a bicycle which has no brakes. To stop, he leaps off it and runs along side until he has it under control. He is our Jacques Tati. Monsieur Malechère is the height of Champmotteux fashion with an ancient worn tweed jacket, well patched at the elbows. His rubber boots provide the final touch. He has a dry sense of humor, delivered in a gruff voice. Often, when he comes to our house to repair something, he keeps me standing by the oil burner for hours as he explains the pros and cons to every question. By carefully scrutinizing the mail which passes through his kitchen, he knows everything about everyone. He was born in Champmotteux, expects to die here, and says the quality of life is better now.

Monsieur Blondeau, they tell me, is a hermit, a misanthrope, and never talks to anybody. On the other hand, he is also voluble, both with me and himself. He tends my vegetable garden and is fiercely possessive of it. I hear him out back talking to a stubborn tree or bothersome nettles. He sometimes brings me gifts from his garden: rhubarb, which he hates, or fine heads of lettuce. The former he throws in the courtyard, refusing to hand them to me. Once, in gratitude, I took him a dish of special rhubarb pie I make. When I asked if he liked it, his frank response was "Yetch!" Any gift to him is looked upon with suspicion. I offered him some unwanted chemicals to kill slugs and snails. He asked how old they were. I apologized that they had been left by a former tenant and might, in fact, be too old. Occasionally, he comes in through the back fields to plant potatoes and strawberries from his garden or to cut the overgrown fields for grasses to feed his animals. He, like the other farmers in my town, are the most honest people I have ever known. I shall sorely miss his grumpy help when he goes.

You won't find us on the map. Don't bother to look for Champmotteux. It is a village of no consequence. When we bought our house, Champmotteux had one road, called Rue Principale. Five years later, when prefab houses were built at the lower end of town, the name of our road was changed to Rue Michel de l'Hôpital, after the French Huguenot who lived here in the seventeenth century. Around that period, I learned that I had French Huguenot ancestors who had fled to the New World. I ask myself, "What is a nice girl like you from 52d Street doing in a place like this?" Perhaps it's racial memory or maybe I am the reincarnation of Michel. Champmotteux had thirty-eight inhabitants when we bought this house in 1971. Now, with the new housing development in the lower section, there are 139 people in town. I know none of the "newcomers." I live in what is called the "old section."

Champmotteux is indistinguishable from thousands of other small villages. A sign at the beginning of town proclaims its identity. One long road, lined by gray stone houses, ends with another sign, crossing out any further importance to a traveler. When asked how I found this out-of-the-way place, I answer that it is near the village of Jean Cocteau. I have called Champmotteux home now for so many years, and to me it has an identity different from any other place in the world. Here, I am still referred to as "l'Américaine" but I am on good terms with the local villagers and farmers. As branches are nourished by their roots, I find my strength in the sensual feast of Champmotteux.

18. FINALE

It is difficult to explain why I chose this small village and why I am content to spend the rest of my life in France. I love the bread, the cheese, the wine, the food, and, aside from Paris, the courtesy and the formality of French manners. I had never felt so completely at ease with myself until I moved to France.

In 1985, Aimée came back to live with me for a while, and I was apprehensive it might disturb the routine and balance I had found living alone. Her companionship added a new dimension to my life. She resented intrusion as much as I did, and we were both relieved when visitors left and we reclaimed our house. We made our peace with Phil, and Aimée travels with him when he tours Europe. Phil tries to control his demons. Kim and I have learned to be kind to each other and more thoughtful of each other's feelings. Kim has come to live in France. I travel with her when she tours Europe, and it's always a party. The three women of the family have bonded and our only chemical dependencies are cigarettes and alcohol. Aimée and Gar are close siblings and adore each other. When he comes for a visit, they make pilgrimages to all their childhood haunts. Baird lives happily with a great woman. The family continues and we are stronger than ever. Bird has continued to be a living presence who will never leave me. I suppose every story has a beginning and an ending. Mine hasn't.

I love this life, as I have loved and felt passion for life as far back as I can remember. I wouldn't change a thing. My one unfulfilled desire is to meet Archie Shepp (mano à mano) on a dance floor and have an ass-shaking contest. Does Archie still believe that "White people can't shake their ass?" If he loses, he must play "Lush Life" on my Yamaha piano!

I do have regrets: the death of my daughter Pree, the suicide of my first husband, Bill. I feel guilty. Perhaps I could have done more to prevent these deaths. I have shed so many tears that I have no more left. So I view life as a realist while remaining a naive optimist. The highs I have known overshadow the cautious person I might have become.

"Why," I am always asked, "do you live isolated in a village no one can find?" Everyone finds me.

Since this book was written Mildred and Aimée have died. Kim continues to sing, tour, and record. She also owns a gallery of handcrafted arts in Pennsylvania. Baird is married and has children. Gar owns two electronic stores and has married.

Many of my lyrics have been performed in concert and recorded. I travel to many jazz festivals in Europe and have participated in films, TV shows, and documentaries.

Champmotteux is changing with an influx of young married couples. My neighbors are British and German. My close friends are Andrée, a cosmopolitan woman with whom I share literature and world affairs, and Fusun, a Turkish woman who has a jazz festival in Turkey each year. I've attended the last three. We share jazz.

Mme Malechère died, but monsieur is still on the scene dressed in the same clothes and boots he wore when we first met twenty six years ago.

I love a day when I awake and say to myself, "I have nothing I have to do today!"

INDEX